Identity, Insecurity and Image:
France and Language

MULTILINGUAL MATTERS SERIES

Series Editor
Professor John Edwards, *St. Francis Xavier University, Antigonish, Nova Scotia, Canada*

Other Books in the Series
Beyond Bilingualism: Multilingualism and Multilingual Education
    JASONE CENOZ and FRED GENESEE (eds)
Language Attitudes in Sub-Saharan Africa
    EFUROSIBINA ADEGBIJA
Language, Ethnicity and Education
    PETER BROEDER and GUUS EXTRA
Language Planning: From Practice to Theory
    ROBERT B. KAPLAN and RICHARD, B. BALDAUF Jr.
Language Reclamation
    HUBISI NWENMELY
Linguistic Minorities in Central and Eastern Europe
    CHRISTINA BRATT PAULSTON and DONALD PECKHAM (eds)
Quebec's Aboriginal Languages
    JACQUES MAURAIS (ed.)
The Step-Tongue: Children's English in Singapore
    ANTHEA FRASER GUPTA
Three Generations – Two Languages – One Family
    LI WEI

Other Books of Interest
Chtimi: The Urban Vernaculars of Northern France
    TIMOTHY POOLEY
Encyclopedia of Bilingual Education and Bilingualism
    COLIN BAKER and SYLVIA PRYS JONES
'Francophonie' in the 1990s: Problems and Opportunities
    DENNIS AGER
Language, Culture and Communication in Contemporary Europe
    CHARLOTTE HOFFMANN (ed.)
Languages in Contact and Conflict
    SUE WRIGHT (ed.)
A Reader in French Sociolinguistics
    MALCOLM OFFORD (ed.)

Please contact us for the latest book information:
Multilingual Matters, Frankfurt Lodge, Clevedon Hall,
Victoria Road, Clevedon, BS21 7HH, England
http://www.multilingual-matters.com

MULTLINGUAL MATTERS 112
Series Editor: John Edwards

Identity, Insecurity and Image: France and Language

Dennis Ager

MULTILINGUAL MATTERS LTD
Clevedon • Philadelphia • Toronto • Sydney

Library of Congress Cataloging in Publication Data

Ager, D.E.
Identity, Insecurity and Image: France and Language/Dennis Ager
Multilingual Matters: 112
Includes bibliographical references and index
1. France–Civilization–20th century. 2. Language policy–France. 3. Language and
culture–France. 4. Civilization, Modern–French influences. 5. French language–
Political aspects–Foreign countries. 6. Symbolism. I. Title. II. Series: Multilingual
Matters (Series): 112.
DC33.7.A64   1999
306.44'944–dc21   98-31849

British Library Cataloguing in Publication Data

A CIP catalogue record for this book is available from the British Library.

ISBN 1-85359-443-1 (hbk)
ISBN 1-85359-442-3 (pbk)

Multilingual Matters Ltd

UK: Frankfurt Lodge, Clevedon Hall, Victoria Road, Clevedon BS21 7HH.
USA: 325 Chestnut Street, Philadelphia, PA 19106, USA.
Canada: 5201 Dufferin Street, North York, Ontario M3H 5T8, Canada.
Australia: P.O. Box 586, Artamon, NSW, Australia.

Printed and bound in Great Britain by WBC Book Manufacturers Ltd.

Contents

Figures

Tables and Maps

Acknowledgements

Acknowledgements are due to a number of people and organisations. Information, ideas and opinions necessarily come from reading, listening and talking to other people and from general observation. It is impossible to identify exactly the source of many of the opinions and ideas expressed here. Much of this book was developed in Aston University, and many generations of colleagues and students have contributed. Sabbatical periods in Monash and Macquarie Universities in Australia, visits and consultations in Paris, New Caledonia, Tahiti, London and Warwick have enabled the collection of material. The Délégation Générale à la Langue Française, and its documentalist Josseline Bruchet, have been particularly helpful. Anonymous readers have made useful suggestions. I am particularly indebted to Annis Ager for invaluable help in many ways, including the exchange of ideas, proof-reading and checking references and notes. Any errors or omissions remaining are the responsibility of the author. All translations have been made by the author except where indicated.

Preface

It is now nearly five hundred years since the French state and French governments made the first official pronouncements on the French language. Since then, government after government has declared the language a symbol of the state, insisted it alone be used as the means of education, fostered its development and controlled its use. But the 1994 Toubon Act on the use of French provoked much debate in France about the purpose of such language planning in a contemporary democracy. Did governments have the right to try to control language use? What was the real motive of its supporters: a purist attempt to keep French unsullied, or a simple fear of American imports? Was the very concept of protecting French a denial of the human rights of the Bretons, the Corsicans or the immigrants living in France? Was the law racist? Would it work? If this was an example of Right-wing xenophobia, how was it possible for a guide to the European institutions published by the Socialist government in 1998 to be equally protective? How could both Left and Right try to insist that French civil servants use French in international meetings at home or abroad, whether or not translation was provided, and whether or not the meeting was formal or informal? Are French governments supported by public opinion in such matters? Why do the French try so hard to protect their language, when it is in no danger of disappearance, is used in all the continents and, after English, is learnt by more people than any other European language? Why do they think that language is so important, and why do they agree that it is government's role to interfere in language matters?

This book aims to explore the reasons for the language policies of the French state. It looks for their origins and purposes, and their areas of application. It covers policies aimed at ensuring and maintaining the status and prestige of French, in France and abroad; policies towards other languages used in France, the regional and community languages;

and policies towards language learning. It aims throughout to seek the reasons and the motives for the policies. It concludes that French language policy is only apparently a matter of culture and cultural policy. It is not simply symbolic flag-waving. Language policy is also a matter of politics, economics and society. It is a matter of state and nation; of governments but also of individual members of civil society; of political and intellectual debate, but also of political history, tradition and self-interest. Language policy has long been a symbol of politicians' desire to change society, but there is a specifically French way of doing this which reflects the strength of two traditions of nationalism: pride in the universality of the Revolutionary and Republican view of democracy and the state, and the often conflicting pride in the French myth of the ethnic nation, in strong leadership and in regional loyalties. As a start, we posit three motives for French language policy: fear of the other; pride in the unique identity of the French nation-state; and a mission to spread the benefits of Frenchness world-wide. This book will examine each in turn.

Introduction

Language Planning and Language Policy

Language planning has been defined as 'deliberate efforts to influence the behaviour of others with respect to the acquisition, structure, or functional allocation of their language codes' (Cooper, 1989: 45). Language policy is a term generally applied to language planning carried out, not by individuals or interested groups like dictionary makers or campaigners, but by governments who have the capacity to propose legislation or ensure administrative action, with, possibly, fines or other punishments if lawbreakers do not comply.

An important distinction is that between status planning, corpus planning and acquisition planning (Kloss, 1969; Cooper, 1989; Chaudenson, 1991; Ager, 1996b). Status policy is concerned with the standing and prestige of a language and its acceptability to speakers of the political community (in the case of an official language) or the speech community (in the case of a standard language). The purpose of status policy is to raise the relative prestige of a language, which it does by ensuring that the language is used in official, public domains such as Parliament, the law and education, as opposed to private domains such as the home or local, non-official community relations. Status policy often specifies that it applies to a variety of a language like slang, or the elegant French of the educated Parisian, or a regional language like Breton, while dictionaries or official terminologies are often at pains to distinguish 'correct' varieties from popular or colloquial usage. Corpus policy, managing the language, is concerned with improving, modifying or adapting the fabric of the language, its terminology, its spelling, its vocabulary, its grammar, in order to standardise it, to make it usable in public domains, or to ensure it is capable of responding to change. Acquisition policies are concerned with teaching and learning language and languages. They deal with the teaching of the standard language and its relationship with dialects or non-standard forms. Acquisition policies also deal with the extent to which foreign and regional languages may be taught within the country: the mastery of which languages may be accepted within the formal educational system as certifying an acceptable educational standard. The aim of acquisition policy is to decide which citizens have access to the standard language and to the socialisation it implies, and which languages will be regarded as sufficiently prestigious for the country to invest in teaching them. These three types of language policy are implemented through macro and micro decisions (Tollefson, 1991). Macro decisions are taken by governments or by institutions they set up or fund, while micro decisions are those taken by individual speakers: a teacher in a classroom, a speech maker, a television presenter. Each in their own way, such individuals are invested with authority and both make and implement decisions on language.

Language and Society: the Policy Environment

'Society' is a loose concept, studied by a number of disciplines including political science and sociology. Its components are territory, human beings and the links between them. In discussing the relationship between language and society, we need to consider all three, but particularly the last. The main link we are concerned with is language. Language links (or divides) human beings because they all speak (or do not speak) the same language. But there are many other links which help human beings to decide which social group they form part of: kinship, skin colour, religion, a particular political or social organisation, a range of myths, taboos and beliefs which people share and which then collectively enable them to construct an imagined community (Anderson, 1991). We are particularly concerned with three types of social group or community: the speech community linked by language, the political community linked by political organisation, and the ethnic community linked by (the perception of) a common origin. As a political community, France is an independent state with certain supra-national obligations, particularly to the European Union. The French speech community is situated mainly in France, but is also world-wide since French is one of the major world languages of international communication. 'Ethnic' French people are somewhat more difficult to define, since France itself is made up of peoples with many different origins and has for centuries taken pride in being host to political, social and economic refugees from the whole world.

Similarly, 'language' has to be more closely defined, as does linguistics and the other disciplines involved. Linguistics is the science of language and in recent years 'core', 'autonomous' or 'pure' linguistics has resolutely refused to be involved with the use of language. We are more concerned here with those disciplines which do study language use. There is little clarity and less agreement over the use of terms such as official, standard, or regional language; dialect, variety or patois; and first, second and foreign language. 'French', in relation to society, has therefore to be defined in relation to 'geolinguistics': the use of language dependent on geography, politics and sociology; in relation to 'sociolinguistics': the social functions and domains of use of the language; and in relation to 'psycholinguistics': the chronology of its acquisition by those who use it, an important point if we are talking about a society which is increasingly multilingual and where French may not be the first language for everybody (Truchot, 1994).

Communities: the Structure of Society

The political community

The French political community is defined in France's written constitution, which is protected by a Constitutional Council and outlines the rights and duties of the political actors. The state is a republic which is administratively divided into regions, departments, communes and overseas territories. A president, elected every seven years, has some executive responsibilities, particularly in foreign affairs. The prime minister leads the government, which is responsible to the National Assembly directly elected every five years, although the president can dissolve the Assembly before then. The senate, one third of which is elected by the regional councils every three years, is the second deliberative chamber. Over the last quarter of the twentieth century, which is the time frame we shall mainly be concerned with, political power has regularly changed hands at elections, as Table Intro.1 shows. The Right has governed in the Assembly in a coalition mainly comprising the Rassemblement Pour la République (RPR) and the Union Démocratique Française (UDF), while the Socialist Party has been in the ascendant on the Left, sometimes working, although uneasily, with the Communists. 'Cohabitation', a president working with a government of a different political persuasion, has occurred three times since 1981: from 1986 to 1988, when the socialist President Mitterrand worked with a right-wing Assembly majority and Jacques Chirac as Prime Minister; from 1993 to 1995 when Mitterrand worked with Edouard Balladur; and after 1997 when Jacques Chirac worked with a left-wing Assembly and Prime Minister Lionel Jospin. On the occasions when this occurs, the country could theoretically be in a stalemate, and both Chirac and Mitterrand have occasionally made plain their objections to particular policies. But generally it works.

Table Intro.1 Presidents and the National Assembly 1974-1997

Election Year	President	National Assembly
1974	Giscard d'Estaing (51%)	Right
1981	François Mitterrand (52%)	Left
1986		Right
1988	François Mitterrand (54%)	Left
1993		Right
1995	Jacques Chirac (53%)	
1997		Left

Note: the percentages show the proportion of the popular vote each President obtained in the final round. 'Right' and 'Left' in the National Assembly indicate the sympathies of the majority of members after the general elections in each year.

The twenty-two regions, each grouping a number of departments, are governed by elected regional councils which have considerable devolved powers. The departments, including the four overseas ones (the Départements d'Outre-Mer or DOM: Guyane, Guadeloupe, Martinique and Réunion) have similar elected councils, and each also has a local representative of the central government, the prefect, whose duties are nowadays mainly concerned with police matters. The communes, of varying sizes but mostly consisting of individual towns or villages, are headed by an elected mayor who has real responsibilities and power, particularly in the larger conurbations. The overseas territories, the Territoires d'Outre-Mer or TOM, are French Polynesia, Wallis and Futuna, New Caledonia, and the Austral and Antarctic Territories. They have a large degree of internal autonomy and an internal government. France also administers the two small Territorial Collectivities of St Pierre et Miquelon, off the Canadian coast, and Mayotte, in the Comoran archipelago.

Citizens of the French state are defined as such mainly through their physical presence as residents within French territory, although there is constant tension between this *jus soli* and the *jus sanguinis*, or the right to seek citizenship through birth. The tradition of citizenship and the rights it confers is linked both with the French nation-state, and with concepts of the universality of human rights. The original declaration of the French Revolution was entitled the 'Rights of Man and the Citizen', and the relationship between membership of the French political community and access to human rights within France is clearly shown by the belief, and practice, that those who do not adhere to the values of the French nation-state should be expelled from its territory (Silverman, 1992).

The speech community

The French speech community consists of all speakers of French: the majority of the population of France itself together with French speakers outside metropolitan France. We shall, in accordance with accepted usage, call this francophonie with a small 'f'. Francophonie (capital 'F') is the international political community whose heads of state assemble in summit meetings every two years to discuss matters of common interest. The organisation is similar to the Commonwealth in some respects. A third label, espace francophone, is sometimes used to designate a cultural sphere, uniting those interested in or allied to the French-speaking world. This rather vague label conveniently accounts for Creole speakers, those speaking Romance languages (Romania), countries with interests in Francophonie (Bulgaria), former protectorates (Syria, Lebanon), regions where no monolingual French speakers remain (Louisiana) and any others who might wish to join Francophonie at some stage (*Année Francophone Internationale*, 1998: 12). In recent years, attempts have been made to establish the total number of speakers of French in the world, and the current estimate is that they number approximately 110 million. Of these, there are 58 million in France, 6 million in Canada, mainly in Quebec, 4 million in Belgium, while the remainder are scattered throughout the continents. The norm of both written and spoken French is generally agreed throughout francophonie to be the educated French of Paris. This form responds to Garvin's (1993) five functions required of any standard language: that it permit the inclusion of all speakers in an identifiable speech community and the exclusion of speakers of other languages and dialects; that it provide a norm of correctness against which deviant forms can be regarded as incorrect; that it confer prestige on its speakers and allow them to participate both in a full range of social domains and functions and in the social, technological and scientific changes brought about by modernisation.

The ethnic community

It is difficult to establish an equally scientific basis for the existence of a French 'ethnic' community, although the myth of a common origin and a range of unifying characteristics, particularly religion, language and shared values are part of the myths and taboos which create the French 'imagined community' closely associated with the sense of nationality. There are in fact two traditions of ethnicity which make the modern sense of Frenchness: one, derived from a supposed common ethnic background and based on a specific cultural history in which territory (i.e. Gaul), the regions, religion and the monarchy play a large part, and another which finds its origins in the French Revolution of 1789 and its beliefs, and in republicanism. This latter tradition is best understood as forming a cultural space in which values such as Liberty, Equality and Fraternity, the secular state, and human rights are regarded as both French and universal, and make Frenchness available to all people. The politics of identity and nationalism refer to either or both tradition, and so members of the French ethnic community can be closely defined or dispersed world-wide, for example in the DOM-TOM or in international Francophonie, even though many of the beliefs of the ethnic nationalists are centred around the sacredness of territory which they equate to metropolitan France.

Recent immigration has also resulted in a number of other ethnic communities living in France, although, because of the French tradition opposing 'particularisms', these are rarely officially identified and are certainly not recognised in political life as separate communities with rights or duties different from those applying to any citizen. Since their members are generally scattered throughout France, few of these communities are organised in any political or social sense, although some leaders, particularly of religious communities, occasionally speak on their behalf as though they were.

Language and Linguistics

The geolinguistic definition

French is the 'official' language of France: that is, it has been accepted by an overtly political act in the Constitution as the language of the political state. French is also the 'national' language: the language of the French nation. Within France, a number of indigenous or 'regional' languages are used (the dialects of German spoken in Alsace and Lorraine, Basque, Breton, Catalan, Corsican, Flemish, Occitan, together with the languages spoken in the DOM and the TOM). Non-indigenous languages, which are sometimes referred to, particularly in British or American discussion, as 'community' languages, while French specialists usually call them 'immigrant languages', are numerous, with the most widespread being (various forms of spoken) Arabic. Other terms used from the point of view of the geographical distribution or geolinguistic importance of languages include 'lingua franca', by which is meant a language used by (usually non-native) speakers as a means of general communication; 'vehicular': a language similarly used as a means of communication, but often in relation to a particular type of interaction, for example commercial transactions; and 'vernacular', usually used by contrast to vehicular to mean the language of a specific community. Insofar as France is concerned the distinction between 'majority' and 'minority' languages is clearly that of numerical dominance, but in relation to some areas (e.g. the DOM-TOM) it is well to recall that the term implies dominance which is not necessarily numerical but, rather, political or social. French in French Polynesia is thus the 'majority' language even though it is spoken exclusively by a minority of the population.

The sociolinguistic definition

A second group of terms describes language(s) or 'varieties' of a language seen from the point of view of sociolinguistic variation or function. Terms such as 'dialect' and 'patois' (the latter usually restricted to non-prestigious dialects) have traditionally been used to describe regional variants of a language, while 'sociolect' or 'code' are sometimes used to describe varieties distinguished by their use in social groups, categories or classes. Language varieties distinguished by their use in interaction include slang; popular; common, normal, or standard language; and formal language. Varieties distinguished according to domain of use, or function, include a major distinction between domestic/home/intimate/private language, which is contrasted with official/public/administrative varieties. In addition, there are many subject-dependent varieties like the language of science, commerce or the law. The distinctions in this group of terms are based on the function or purpose to which the language is put or on its domain of application; most terms are concerned with intra- rather than inter-language variation, and it is normal to expect that individual members of society will undertake 'code-switching' between (languages or) varieties according to factors like the communication situations they find themselves in, their interlocutors and their communicative purpose.

The psycholinguistic definition

The third group of terms and concepts applying to language includes those which imply a chronology of acquisition, of French and/or of other languages. Although France contains a majority of monolingual speakers whose only language is French, bi- and multi-linguals have always been numerous as in the case of speakers in Alsace who might use standard French, the regional French of Alsace, standard German and the Alsace dialect of German. Breton speakers in Brittany are bilingual in Breton and French. Today, with large-scale immigration, it is more and more difficult to conceive of France as a monolingual society. But the bi- or multi-lingualism which does exist is individual bilingualism, where individuals speak more than one language, rather than the societal bilingualism of a country like Belgium where the country contains two or more groups of monolinguals speaking different languages. In individual bilingualism it is normal for the child to acquire one language before learning the other. It is now usual in identifying the languages involved to use a simple sequence of numbers: L1, L2, L3, or first, second, third (etc.) language, to describe the order in which languages were acquired or learnt, although 'common-sense' words and expressions such as native language/mother tongue, foreign language, 'language of habitual/non-habitual use', are also in force.

Motives for Planning Language in France

Separate motives: insecurity, identity or image

Early in 1994, a law on the use of French, the Toubon Act, was discussed and approved in the French Parliament. This law made the use of French obligatory in five domains: education, employment, audio-visual media, commerce, and public meetings such as colloquia and congresses. The new law had, as its purpose, 'to guarantee to French people the right to use their language and to ensure that it is used in certain circumstances of their everyday and professional life'. In presenting the proposal to the Senate, the Minister for Culture and Francophonie, Jacques Toubon, declared that it was necessary for three reasons: firstly, that French, like Japanese, Italian, Spanish, German in their countries, should not be 'relegated to secondary uses' in the face of English. Secondly, that the best way of 'approaching universality and the highest level of dialogue was to give the best of oneself in the most authentic manner'; thirdly, that economic progress, social integration and the unity of Francophone countries outside France depended on defence of the symbolic role of French as 'language of democracy and freedom'. These three motives can be summarised as insecurity or fear of others, identity or pride in one's own community, and the creation and projection of an image, or the desire to ensure that others adopt or at least recognise the force of that identity. The motives explain much of the origins, the nature and the import of language policy anywhere in the world, and the political character of the discourse in which it is phrased. There are of course other factors which motivate policy actions, and one in particular - the correction or reinforcement of inequality - is powerful in some societies although possibly less so in France (cf. Tollefson, 1991; Ager, 1996b: 207-12).

Much French political discourse, from all political quarters, reveals a feeling that French society and particularly its cultural symbols such as language are threatened and menaced by change. Members of Parliament talk of attacks on the language, the culture it conveys and the civilisation it symbolises, and describe language change as a disease. In response, governments, groups and individuals use the military language of defence and stability. Defensive rhetoric like this seems to show widespread feelings of insecurity. But insecurity and lack of confidence is not the sole explanation for contemporary French political attitudes and policies. Insecurity originates in and leads to a sense of inferiority, and is centrally concerned with conflict and competition. Individuals, social categories or the whole nation may thus feel themselves to be under attack by external forces, by social, technical or cultural change within society itself, or by younger or less privileged members of society. But any self-confident society or section of the community, strong in numbers, power, and awareness of itself, will feel less concerned by these threats than a dominated one with poor self-image, few resources and little power. There is therefore a strong connection between the awareness of its own identity a society or social group has, and the degree of insecurity it feels.

Linguistic insecurity is a recognised phenomenon, usually found in speakers of a dialect or language used by a social group of low prestige. The speakers feel unsure whether the forms of language they are using are 'correct'. They have no confidence that their language can be used in certain circumstances, or that they have sufficient command of it to use it properly. In its extreme form, speakers of the dialect or language concerned may apologise for their use of the language, may say that their language is not a 'real' language, that the word or expression they use is 'patois' or not 'real' English, French or Dutch if they are a speaker of an undervalued dialect of these languages. They may deliberately set out to learn what they regard as a 'better' form of the language for use in public, a process that often leads to hyper-correction or excessively pedantic forms of the standard language (Gueunier, 1985). Linguistic insecurity may lead to language shift and the disappearance of the undervalued dialect, whether regional or social. On the other hand, if the (regional or social) community's self-image of its own identity is strong enough, the process can be halted or even reversed (Fishman, 1991). For many communities who wish to protect and preserve their identity, it is essential therefore to improve the community's self-image, the feeling people in the community have about themselves and their language.

French itself is in no danger of disappearance, certainly not from continental France. But English, or at least American English, is playing a greater role than before in some domains of French society, and linguistic insecurity accounts for some aspects of the defence of French in national language policy. The politics of identity account for others, and political speeches are full of pride in being French, in the history and traditions of France and in her cultural, artistic and intellectual heritage. But one amendment put forward in the 1992 Parliamentary debate on the constitutional changes required to implement the Maastricht Treaty underlined a third fundamental motive: the external image of France. Xavier Deniau proposed a new constitutional section on Francophonie, stating that 'France participates in the construction of a French-speaking area of solidarity and co-operation', defending his proposal by pointing out that 'France should become the advocate of French-speaking countries, presenting their difficulties and problems and attempting to find solutions'. Part of the defence of French, and many other aspects of French language policy are concerned with the image France projects of itself to other societies. This third motive is strong and is not confined to the defence of French within Francophonie. French is a symbol of a culture and way of life of which the French are proud and which they wish to defend, but which it is important also to disseminate. French is seen as belonging, not just to France, but to all mankind. The *rayonnement*, the influence and prestige, of French culture and the need to make it available to all is a theme to which governments regularly return.

All three motives, neatly expressed in three sentences, inspired the preamble to the Toubon Act:

> Article 1. Language of the Republic by virtue of the Constitution, French is a fundamental element of the personality and heritage of France. It is the language of teaching, work, (commercial) exchange and the public service. It is the privileged link between the states constituting the community of Francophonie. (Law 94-665, 4 August 1994 concerning the French language).[1]

Mixed motives: identity, insecurity, and image

The debates leading up to the 1992 constitutional change and to the 1994 Toubon Act showed very clearly the range of opinions politicians held about language at that time. These attitudes towards French reflect those which have long been held, and are still widely held in French society, and thus reflect the political environment within which the legislation was developed and presented. They also reveal underlying attitudes and the importance for us of situating particular items of policy in a historical context. The 1992 Maastricht debate was in the main a celebration of the status of French, together with a clear presentation of the fears most politicians had for its future. In the 1994 debate, two years later, these fears and concerns remained unchanged. In both debates, politicians from all parties showed that the threats they identified were political and economic as much as cultural and social, affecting all aspects of French society and its future. Behind these concerns one can identify two types of belief about the language, which seem at first sight to contradict each other. These two beliefs are firstly that 'French is France': the language is a fundamental component of French identity (or 'personality', the word used in the Toubon Law in order to avoid accusations of Fascism since the Front National used the word identity extensively). Secondly, that 'French is universal': the language belongs, not solely to France, but to everybody, and represents an underlying value and resource of humankind. These two attitudes recall the two forms of French nationalism, and are neatly symbolised by the two successive formulations of the 1992 Constitutional amendment itself. The first was discussed in the Senate: 'French is the language of the Republic' while the formulation was eventually changed to: 'The language of the Republic is French'. The relationship between the three motivators is close and language planning motives are often mixed, as the following brief summary of the points made during the 1992 Senate debate will show. We have arranged these as the political, social and economic fears each point of view expressed, but each also has its positive side.

'French is France'
Political fears
These were based on the potential loss of French identity, independence and importance. Different speakers noted the growing importance of North America and its imposition of its political will on the rest of the world. But the specific identity of France suffered also from the undeniable numerical lack of French speakers in the world by comparison with other languages, particularly English; and by the diversity of cultures to which French identity was exposed. French, itself, as a symbol of the Republic, was necessarily therefore also the language of all the individual collectivities making up the Republic; but the diversity of these, both in metropolitan France and abroad, represented a danger of fragmentation and disunity which should be guarded against. French political independence could also be in danger. In order to be and remain independent, France must not put herself in a

position of inferiority vis-à-vis other countries, and her defence and foreign policies must be both independent and strongly defended. Only an independent France had need of an independent French language, and the close relationship of foreign policy with cultural policy was a necessary part of this overall independence. France's importance on the world stage was necessarily declining as the strength of the superpower(s) increased. In this context, the importance of France would be reinforced by strengthening her image abroad, and particularly by working together with a group of supportive Francophone countries in all aspects of international diplomacy. A small, but important indicator of the importance of France and these Francophone countries in international diplomacy was the use of French as a working language in international organisations.

Social fears

Fear of social change, together with measures which might ensure that change was neither too radical nor too swift, was frequently expressed throughout the 1992 debate. It was feared that the power of established social elites was reducing; and that to protect against this all education should be in French of high quality, while diplomas and certificates of educational success should certify that young people had achieved success in language. French culture, too, depended on its expression through French, and any successful attack on French from English was liable to fundamentally alter the character, not merely of the language, but of the culture it conveyed.

Economic fears

Many speakers in the debate underlined the belief that French, and France, could not hope to survive if left to their own devices: intervention was essential to protect the French economy, the French way of life and the French language. Wealth, employment and personal incomes would drop if the French market was opened and if French producers were not in some way protected from aggressive competition, or indeed from any competition. French should hence be the language of commerce; it should be the required language of work, knowledge of it should be required of entrants to certain professions and particularly of anybody working for or with the state. Commerce should be better developed between French-speaking countries, who, after all, were present across the world.

'French is universal'

Political fears

The opposite belief, that French is not confined to the French nation-state but is available to all humanity and indeed represents a universal value, was underlined by repeated concerns about democracy. French, after all, is the language in which the Rights of Man were first formally expressed, and political democracy started in the modern era with the French Revolution. The French language, and indeed the French concept of the nation-state, in this view, transcends France and has the right, as well as the need, to be protected by humanity at large.

Social fears

Fears that high culture and the development of the intellect were under attack were frequently expressed. French, representing a humanist and universally applicable approach to the development of human capability, was subject to attack from degrading cultural uniformity   projected through the media and through the cultural industries, dominated by commercial values and by appeals to the lowest common instincts. Although popular culture was not to be condemned, imposition of the same low values throughout the world and particularly on cultural worlds of different traditions and on different levels of society would only produce a lowering of standards everywhere. Cultural diversity would be destroyed and cultural uniformity in the Disney model, expressed through Anglo-American, would prevail.

Economic fears

Potential domination by the United States would ensure the disappearance of any alternative mode of economic organisation, and world commerce and economic life would be dependent on the whims and preferences of the huge US internal market, on producers and their financial resources, and on their aims of world domination through globalisation. French and French interests however were not limited to France nor to Europe; as a world power, France, and Europe generally, had claims to influence far outside her own frontiers and the right to occupy a significant place in world commerce. For this to be effective, the international role of French must be seen as of universal value: French, and French views on such matters as protection, tariff barriers and the control of free trade and economic rationalism were symbols of commercial freedom for all peoples.

France and Language

In this book we shall be mainly concerned with macro policy and the ways in which the language behaviour of French citizens has been, and is influenced by the French state. We aim to look beyond the policies to motives and methods. Language policy takes place within a political, social, economic and cultural environment to whose priorities and concerns it conforms, but which it also attempts to shape. Language itself cannot sensibly be discussed without also discussing its users, and language is both shaped by and to a certain extent shapes society, since it is only through language that some ideas can even be formulated. Language change in any case happens by a mixture of choice and chance: here, we are concerned to distinguish the two and to investigate whether, and how, the choices the French political community has made and still makes bring about language change. Language policy derives, like any other form of policy, both from the social, political, economic and cultural environment, and also from the policy priorities of political groups in power. But language has a special role to play in society, and particularly in French society. It is a means of communication holding society together; it is the symbol of the community; it is a tool for shaping and for controlling society. But society also obtains its meaning from the concepts and meanings inherent in the language. It is not too much to say that the French language has long had an influence on how France sees itself and sees the world. Language policy has been the concern of the state for at least five hundred years, while the state reflects many of the myths, beliefs and attitudes incorporated in French.

Let us start by considering how the first motive, of insecurity or fear, has provoked specific policies, and whether there could be specific explanations for them. The three policies we shall examine are those responding to fear of the regional languages; policies to strengthen the boundaries within which French society could ensure cohesion and inclusion and thus counter social fragmentation; and policies to repel attacks from outside, particularly from the English language as symbol of American and global cultures.

Part 1: Insecurity

Chapter 1

Territorial Insecurity: Fear of the Regional Languages

The Linguistic Regions

Metropolitan France can be roughly divided into areas in which different languages have been spoken in the past and to a certain extent still are today. Latin, the lingua franca of the Roman Empire, here developed into Gallo-Romance from about the ninth century AD. Gallo-Romance itself was diverse: in the North, its dialects were collectively called the Langue d'Oïl, and in the South, the Langue d'Oc or Occitan. The third division is Franco-provençal, spoken in central eastern France. Non-Romance languages spoken in the North are Breton in the Armorican peninsula, Flemish around the Lille region, dialects of German spoken in the Alsace-Lorraine area, and Basque spoken in the south-west. Catalan, in the area around Perpignan, is a Romance language, while Corsican is a dialect of Italian. These indigenous languages, present on French territory for centuries, will form the subject of this chapter. In addition to them, recent immigrants have created a number of other linguistic communities of which the largest in metropolitan France is formed by Arabic. Overseas Départements and Territoires which lie outside metropolitan France have their own language(s). French Polynesia has a number of Polynesian languages, New Caledonia has more than thirty Melanesian languages, and in the multilingual overseas Departments (Réunion, Guyane, Guadeloupe and Martinique) different French-based Creoles are widely used as well as standard French and other languages.

Map 1.1
France: the linguistic regions
Source: Battye and Hintze, 1992: 357

The Langue d'Oïl and the Langue d'Oc split into a large number of dialects in which new words, grammatical structures and pronunciations differentiated the means of communication used in different villages and towns. For a number of reasons - poor communications, feudal systems preventing free movement, diet and consumer habits which meant that there was little need for the exchange of other than luxury goods, lack of political control needing large armies or bureaucracies, a religion which saw its social role as supporting feudalism and stability - these dialects were little used outside specific territories or regions. Where it had been possible for there to be mutual understanding throughout Gaul this was gradually lost between about 450 and until well after 1500 AD. For more than a thousand years therefore linguistic and social fragmentation was the norm. But as one dialect of the Langue d'Oïl, Francien, came to the fore it was used more and more as the common language for all the French, and has now developed into standard written and spoken French in a process which has been extensively studied (see, for example, Pope, 1934; Rickard, 1989; Posner, 1997).

The other languages of France were spoken around the periphery of what has become modern France. All apart from Breton and Occitan are also spoken outside France, although naturally the forms and dialects used differ to a great extent from those spoken within French territory. Breton, in the north-west, is a Celtic language similar to Welsh and Gaelic. Flemish is a dialect form of Dutch. The Germanic dialects of Alsace and Lorraine form part of the dialect continuum of German itself. Corsican is a dialect of Italian, while Catalan is spoken in the powerful Spanish province of Catalunya whose main town is Barcelona. Basque is also spoken in Spain, where the population of Basque speakers far outweighs that of France. Quite apart from the question of the survival and future role of these six regional languages, to which the Langue d'Oc or Occitan is usually added as the seventh, the linguistic dimension of the regional issue has two further aspects. Firstly, the question of dialects: each of the main divisions of Gallo-Romance can be further subdivided into dialects whose survival, use and present importance vary. For the Langue d'Oïl the following main internal divisions are usually recognised: Gallo, Normand, Picard, Wallon, Lorrain, Champenois, Bourguignon, Francien, Angevin, Poitevin. The Langue d'Oc has the following: Gascon, Béarnais, Auvergnat, Limousin, Provençal Alpin, Provençal Maritime, Rhodanien, Niçart. The second aspect is the issue of regional French: various regional varieties of spoken French have developed as French itself spread throughout France, particularly after about 1500. These are quite difficult to identify, describe and classify as different from each other and from the regional French of the Ile de France area, which has become the standard, since each shares many features with social and situational varieties of standard French. Some of them have retained or adopted pronunciations which remind dialecticians of the regional languages or of the substratum of linguistic habits which these have bequeathed. Among their principal characteristics is the use of words or expressions specific to each area, although their speakers seem rarely to employ grammatical structures which differ greatly from those of the spoken varieties of standard French.

In this chapter we shall explore the continuity of state policy towards regional languages and dialects. In chapter two, we shall investigate how far three explanations for the policies and attitudes involved can be justified. These three are the myth of the Hexagon; the nature of centre-periphery relations; and the nature of French regionalism.

State Policy Towards Regional Languages

The continuity of policy

In France, intervention by the state in language matters predates the very notion of the state, which appeared at the beginning of the fourteenth century. Intervention by the central power over regional languages dates from the reign of Saint-Louis (13th century) ... (who) recommended that Latin should be eliminated from diplomatic and legal documents. (Szjulmajster-Celnikier, 1996: 39)[2]

The linguistic unity of France is generally considered to have been, and to remain, a deliberate policy aim of successive governments, from the kings of the Ancien Régime to the presidents of contemporary France, and the longest-lasting objective of the French state. In different periods of French history the policy has adopted different forms and emphases. The imposition of French through military, social and political domination, as the language of the courts and of public life, was a major characteristic of royalty. A stress on education and on the creation of the unitary state in policies aimed at socialising the citizen in a lay, uniform, centralised society speaking and writing one standard language, French, was the policy priority of the nineteenth and early twentieth centuries. The contemporary period has been marked by a defensive, protectionist approach aimed at maintaining and defending the territorial, cultural and social integrity of France and French against internal fragmentation through a revival of regionalism and against external attack, particularly in recent years from Anglo-American. In all periods of history, the aim has been to reinforce the use of French and make the use of other languages as difficult as possible. In terms of language policy, the fight for territorial integrity is also the fight against symbols of fragmentation: the regional languages represent regionalism and regional particularisms, and defeating them and all they stand for reduces the major danger: that France may disintegrate.

The continuing importance of this policy to contemporary France can be gauged from official statements and actions from the last quarter of the twentieth century. President de Gaulle's departure in 1969 was caused by his losing the referendum in which he proposed a number of changes in regional organisation, which would have led in particular to elected regional councils and thus to a weakening of centralisation. In 1972 President Pompidou brought in non-elected advisory councils with a small budget, but was certain that regional languages, and hence recognition of regional power, had 'little to offer a France which was destined to have a significant effect on Europe'. President Mitterrand supported a degree of freedom for the regions in his 1981 electoral campaign, and went so far in the 56th of his '110 Proposals for France' as to declare that 'the promotion of regional identities will be encouraged, and minority languages and cultures respected and encouraged'. He added that 'Attacking a people's culture and language wounds them most deeply. We declare the right to be different'.

In power, however, and despite setting up a special committee to examine the problem (cf. Giordan, 1982), he was clear that he could not be a party to any sort of regionalism which might have a negative effect on the unity of France. Michel Debré, an opponent of Mitterrand, agreed with him even more forcefully at the same time, commenting that:

> (Proposals to recognise regional languages conflict) with the work of generations who have created France - the Nation; with the secular and republican idea of the creation of French citizenship; with the great work of public education. (These proposals) confuse the respect we owe to provincial traditions with deliberate attacks on Republican unity; they are in effect a desire to tear the Nation apart. (_Le Figaro_, 9.8.1985)[3]

President Mitterrand nonetheless brought in far-reaching decentralisation as we shall see below, and thus to an extent put the problem on another footing. By channelling regional pressures for a degree of independence first to cultural and linguistic matters he marginalised the political activists, and then, by establishing a structure of twenty-two new Regions but retaining the existing structure of Departments and Communes, he ensured that the power of the regions would always be limited, and would always work by negotiation and within structures acceptable to the centre.

Both in the Senate, which is elected from and by the regions and is thus inevitably concerned by centre-periphery tensions, and in the National Assembly, many speakers in the 1994 debates over the Toubon Law remained much concerned at the lack of freedom and rights accorded to the regional languages, despite the passage of the Deixonne Act in 1951 which allowed schools to teach them:

> What often causes a problem in the Ministry of Education...is the absence of any special status for regional languages...Since the Deixonne Act, which was a move forward but which does not define a special status, there has been nothing at all. Our ambition for French is accompanied by the need to avoid the disappearance of the richness our regional languages and cultures constitute. (*Journal Officiel*, 15.4.1994)[4]

One speaker at least would have none of this:

> I express my homage to the lay, Republican school system which often imposed the use of French against all the forces of social and even religious obscurantism...it is time for us all to be French through that language. If it is necessary to teach another language to our children, let us not make them waste time with dialects they will only ever use in their villages. (*Journal Officiel*, 15.4.1994)[5]

The Minister of Culture, M. Toubon himself, instead of merely insisting on France's traditional policy of centralisation and domination and rejecting regional languages, showed a new twist by accepting that some regional words had found their way into standard French, and accepted Gewurztraminer, kouign aman, far or pottok as part of French. By this one sentence, and in others where Toubon agreed that regional languages were 'clearly part of the heritage of France', the French state had achieved the rather strange position where the regional languages and the cultures they represented, far from opposing the state, now in fact formed part of it. Support for regional languages could thus now be interpreted as support for France, with three important provisos. Firstly, the regional languages had been reduced to individual words and expressions, examples of local colour helpful to tourism, local cuisine and folklore. Second, the regional languages had to accept their new status: they must, in return, avoid attacking French since in the process they would destroy themselves. Third, there could be no question of any real use for regional languages as means of expression, as a vehicle for debate in local councils or in the Press, for example. We should note however that despite these statements, amendments to the Act which spelt out the approach ('The regional languages are an integral part of this heritage') were lost both in the Senate and the Assembly. One must conclude that the fear remained, openly described as fear of dismemberment, of 'fragmentation' and 'balkanisation'. If such a fear of disunity is so widespread, and so much in the mind of political leaders, there must be something to it: there must have been, and must remain, considerable insecurity about a real possibility of fragmentation.

Language policies to 1789

Language was not a prime concern of the medieval kings. The dukedoms, counties and other dependencies of the king, as they were conquered or recognised royal authority through treaties or marriages, continued to conduct their own affairs in their own language or dialect. When and where linguistic legislation became necessary, it was aimed at ensuring that the local population understood the royal message, that the courts did not become too remote from the population, that Latin be no longer used. These dangers were eliminated by recommending or insisting that either French, whose exact nature was unspecified, or the local language be used instead. An edict of 1510, for example, 'prescribed that investigations, enquiries and criminal proceedings be conducted in the "common language or the language of the region" (_en vulgaire ou langage des Pays_)' (quoted in Grau, 1992: 94).

Such edicts appeared regularly, indicating perhaps that the legal profession preferred to operate in one common language than in a variety of dialects. They were extended to the ecclesiastical courts in 1629 and to areas newly conquered or becoming part of France (Roussillon in 1563, Béarn in 1621, Flanders in 1684, Alsace in 1685). But it is Articles 110 and 111 of the Edicts (_Ordonnances_) of Villers-Cotterêts, signed by François the First in 1539, which are the first piece of legislation formally requiring French to be used in legal language in the courts and in the administration of justice throughout the regions conquered by the Kings of France. The Edicts made it clear that Latin was aimed at: 'because such decisions have often been based on the meaning of Latin words...we wish that all acts and procedures...be pronounced, recorded and delivered in the French mother tongue and not otherwise'. Whether the insistence on using French rather than the language of the region was a deliberate change of policy or regarded merely as a strengthening of existing custom is a matter of conjecture, but most opinion tends to the belief that French was already being widely used as the language of record. Ten years later, indeed, in most regions of what would become France, and even in some which the

French King did not yet rule (Béarn and Savoy for example), French had completely replaced both Latin and the regional languages in court usage, and in much of the administration (Brun, 1923; Lodge, 1993).

The use of three languages - French, the regional language (particularly the languages of the South) and Latin - must have been proving more and more difficult as transport became easier and the management of the law affected larger areas. The increasing interference of Paris and the king's government in local matters must also have been an influence, so using French by itself was more efficient and more effective. But, since the sixteenth and seventeenth centuries did not see an instant disappearance of these local languages which continued to be the normal means of communication for the population at large, another consequence of the policy was the increasing power and standing it gave to those in local communities who mastered the Parisian norm (Blanchet, 1992: 60). This elite group could gain easier access to economic, social and political power through their control of the means of communication. Their role, as 'interpreters' between the judicial and political authorities and the mass of the population, conferred on them social leadership of a type which is reflected today in the role of major regional leaders such as the presidents of regional councils, and especially the mayors of Communes, who interpret the will of parliament for the local population. From the sixteenth century to the French Revolution at least, most of France operated in diglossia, with French occupying the higher, official, level and the local language the lower, private and domestic domains.

The 1539 law, which made French in all but name the official language of France, is still valid today. Its provisions extend to the whole of the contemporary Republic, including the overseas Territories and Departments, although interpreters are provided for those whose control of French is not adequate.

The second significant development in the fight against regionalism and regionalisms was in corpus policy and in the codification and defence of standard French. The French Academy was created in 1635, with the role of giving central direction and control to the language, and such linguistic centralisation followed and paralleled the centralisation of power in most other domains, from the courts to the taxation system and to the construction of roads. The systematic codification of French in the seventeenth and part of the eighteenth centuries was not carried out solely through the work of the Academy. Both Court grammarians and the writers whose work was produced and published for the courtiers who represented practically the sole audience for literature tried to ensure the creation of a standardised, widely accepted written and spoken form of the language. While technical and common words and expressions were increasingly banned from usage, the main target of such purification was the regional expressions of those courtiers who flocked to Paris as the centre of economic, social and political power. Lodge (1993: 165-87) sees codification as a two-stage process in which, from 1500 to 1660, the '"best" French was spoken by the "best" people', while the motivation changed in the eighteenth century to the 'best French' being so because it was the 'language of reason and clarity'. As examples of the process one may cite Malherbe's exclusion of regional items (and many others) from the language of Court poetry. His influence was followed by that of Vaugelas, whose equally miscellaneous comments were aimed at both popular and at regional French from south of the Loire valley. The *Grammaire Générale et Raisonnée* of 1660, and particularly later commentators like Voltaire and Rivarol, ascribed qualities to written French which made it almost a measure of perfection, and the ideology of language which was generated then has remained with many commentators today. At this time was born the belief in the universality of standard French, in its innate clarity, precision, logic and elegance, and in its superiority over any other language and certainly over any regional form of French or any regional language. The seventeenth century thus developed a linguistic culture in which there was a mixture of control and a preference for a regionally and socially defined 'central' form, generally that of the Paris area and that of the elite at Court. The 1694 Academy dictionary, and the comments of court poets, dramatists and salon experts are not policy in the strict sense; but since strictures on language use emanated from the highest social and political element of French society, it was incumbent on those who wished to make their way in society to observe and adopt the new norms. Indeed, the special role of the Loire valley, whose speech is still today regarded as at least as 'good' as that of Paris, derives from the fact that it was a favourite area for kings and courtiers from the sixteenth century. Standardisation around a regionally and socially prestigious form ensured its acceptance for official purposes, without significant legislation after 1539.

The Revolution

Paradoxically, the culmination of the royal legislation and practice in the centralisation and social control of language was to be the French Revolution. The Revolutionaries came to realise that the creation of France required a common means of communication in which laws could be promulgated and which would be understood by all the citizens of the new state. Liberty, Equality and Fraternity, if they were to be interpreted as applying to individual citizens, required also that particularisms, deviations from the norm, should be unacceptable. Religious differences could not be tolerated, one citizen could not be distinguished from another because he was a Jew or a non-Catholic; and neither could the habits, traditions, customs or languages of one group of citizens mark them as different from others. Freedom in effect was only available on the basis of individual Equality, while Fraternity came about as a by-product from the individual citizen voluntarily accepting the social contract. But this is not how things started.

Translation of the Revolutionary decrees and laws was decided on by January 1790 and a massive amount of work was carried out by 1792, with over 96 volumes of decrees and 18 of constitutional laws (Certeau *et al.*, 1975: 10). In August 1790 the Abbé Grégoire was charged with discovering the language situation throughout the country. The 49 replies he received to his questionnaires by early 1792 gave him an excellent insight into the overall situation. His report was presented in 1794 and showed that 6 million French, particularly the southern peasants, had no knowledge of French at all, 6 million more scarcely understood it, while only 3 million (one eighth) of the total population of 25 million used the spoken language. In the early stage of the Revolution, therefore, the legal approach to the complexity of the language situation in the country was to be as liberal and helpful as possible, and the policy was concerned with a de-facto recognition of language diversity and with providing means by which to ensure that practical solutions such as translation could enable the people nonetheless to participate in the new democracy. But policy change was on the way, and the title of Grégoire's report indicated the mixture of repression of local languages and support for standard French which was progressively to come about, and indeed to characterise state policy towards regional languages ever since. The report, presented on 28th May 1794, was subtitled 'On the need and ways to annihilate dialects and universalise the use of French' (*Sur la nécessité et les moyens d'anéantir les patois et d'universaliser l'usage de la langue française*).

The relationship between education in French and the desire that every citizen should use only this language had been foreshadowed in late October 1793, when it was decreed that

> Article 6. Public education is to be carried out everywhere so that one of its benefits should be that French quickly becomes the familiar language in all parts of the Republic.
> Article 7. Throughout the Republic instruction will take place solely in French. (quoted in Brunot, 1967, 9, 1: 148)[6]

The Barère Report of 27th January 1794 then made a link between regional languages and attacks on the Revolution. Regional languages were said to be used by opponents of the regime to mislead and misinform the population, and the proposal was made to banish such regional languages in addition to the much slower process of educating non-French speakers in French, and the more pragmatic one of translation from French. Barère's reasoning was clear:

> ...the finest language in Europe, which first freely consecrated the Rights of Man and Citizen, which has the duty of transmitting to the world the most sublime thoughts of liberty and the grandest speculations of policy.
> ...Free men resemble each other; and the vigorous accent of liberty and equality is the same, whether it comes from the mouths of inhabitants of the Vosges, the Pyrenees or the Cantal region ...
> ...The first laws of education must prepare citizenship; now, in order to become a citizen, one must obey the law, and in order to obey law, one must know the laws...We have revolutionised government, laws, customs and habits, costumes, commerce and even thought; so let us also revolutionise language, which is their daily instrument.
> ...Federalism and superstition speak Breton; emigration and hatred for the Republic speak German; counter-revolution speaks Italian, and fanaticism speaks Basque. Let us destroy these instruments of damage and error. (quoted in Certeau _et al._, 1975: 291-9)[7]

The decree which followed the same day required the appointment of a teacher of French, within ten days, in every commune of the departments where these languages were spoken: in Brittany, Alsace-Lorraine, Corsica, and in the departments of Nord, Alpes Maritimes, and Basses-Pyrénées. Some speakers in the following debate wanted to extend the provision, and their point of view was that standard French was insufficiently known and used in many parts of France. In the Grégoire Report of May 1794, the two branches of the Barère approach - insistence on the use of French allied to rejection of the regional languages - were strengthened, and the earlier liberal and helpful policy of translation was finally rejected. But much of the Grégoire report was devoted to corpus policy, to the attempt to 'revolutionise our language' through perfecting it. The reasoning Grégoire advanced for thus mixing the attempt to ban regional languages with inculcating pride in (a newly rationalised and improved) French underlined the extent to which the Jacobins had won the argument on the nature of France:

> ...One can at least make the language of a great nation uniform, in such a way that the citizens who make it up can communicate their

thoughts without any obstacle. This enterprise, which has not been fully implemented by any people, is worthy of the French people who are centralising all branches of social organisation and who must jealously consecrate, at the earliest moment, in a one and indivisible Republic, the unique and unvarying use of the language of liberty.

...Everything we have said leads to the conclusion that in order to remove all prejudices, develop all truths, all talents, all virtues, to melt all citizens into the national mass, to simplify the mechanism and ease the play of the political machine, one must have identity of language. (quoted in Certeau *et al.*, 1975: 300-17)[8]

Proposals were made that every municipality should use only French in its deliberations; that notices in poor French should be corrected by a 'wise police', even that married couples should have to prove that they could read, write and speak French. The rejection of regional languages now became a proof of patriotism:

Feudalism carefully conserved the disparity of idioms as a means of recognising, controlling, fugitive serfs and strengthening their chains...the unity of language is an integral part of the Revolution...from this moment on let the zeal of citizens proscribe for ever the jargons which are the last remnants of destroyed feudalism. (quoted in Certeau et al., 1975: 300-17)[9]

Regional languages and dialects were simply unable to communicate modern ideas:

If in our own language the political part (of the vocabulary) is scarcely yet created, what must it be like in idioms some of which, truly, have many sentimental expressions to describe the sweet effusions of the heart, but are absolutely denuded of terms relative to politics; others are heavy and gross jargons, without a definite syntax. (quoted in Certeau et al., 1975: 300-17)[10]

Arguments in favour of regional languages were simply brushed aside:

Do you think that southern Frenchmen would easily decide to leave a language they cherish by habit and feeling?...Let us not insult our brothers from the South by suggesting that they would reject an idea which is useful to the Fatherland.

Knowledge of dialects may shed light on Medieval monuments... one must seek pearls even in the manure of Ennius.

The fear of change for the worse in the moral habits of the countryside...Morals! Without them there will be no Republic, and without the Republic there will be no morals.

While accepting the necessity of the demolition of the patois, some contest its possibility...Even if one can only obtain half a success it would be better to do a little good than to do none at all. (quoted in Certeau et al., 1975: 300-17)[11]

Dialects no longer needed the terms that feudalism and customary law had required. French would be widely disseminated.

---

(1) Enrich it, simplify it, make its study easier for nationals and other peoples.
(2) Our language is full of ambiguities and uncertainties; it would be equally useful and easy to fix them.
(3) It would be useful to carry out a general review of words to give precision to definitions.
(4) The wealth of a language does not lie in the fact that it has synonyms.
(5) One could allow some happy acquisitions...(through diminutives, and similar forms)...energetic expressions which should be restored...borrowing from foreign idioms the terms we lack and adapting them to ours, without giving way to ridiculous and excessive neologism...get rid of all the anomalies resulting from defective verbs or from exceptions to the general rules.

Source: Rapport Grégoire, quoted in Certeau et al., 1975: 300-17[12]

Figure 1.1 Grégoire's proposals for improving French

Grégoire's plea for 'revolutionising the language' through corpus policy, like his and Barère's attacks on regional languages, appealed to reason and foresaw only success. He pointed out that improvements in technology (in agriculture, in meteorology, in physics, in politics and the arts) required the uniformisation and improvement of technical vocabulary. But the plea was for even more naive, even more radical improvements, as Figure 1.1 shows. The 1794 decree did not take up these interesting suggestions. But it did put into force the general point that French itself must become the normal language of formal actions, and declared:

Article 1. From the day of publication of this Act, no official act may be written except in French in any part of the French Republic.
Article 2. One month after the publication of the present Act, no act may be recorded which is not written in French, even if it is a private document. (quoted in Brunot, 1967, 9, 1: 186)[13]

   The transformation of policy from a royal wish simply to ensure that the royal message was understood and implemented, to a policy of openness and wider information for all and thence to a democratic policy based on an ideology which required both the imposition of one language, perfected as the instrument of that ideology, and the abolition of all others, culminated in the decree of 20th July 1794 (2 Thermidor Year II of the revolutionary calendar). The significant revolutionary linguistic legislation in fact involved five separate decrees or instructions (Grau, 1992: 95):

* the conversion of private schools into state schools in which the language of instruction was to be French (21.10.1793);
* a decree to enforce the use of French in education (26.10.1793);
* a separate decree banning the use of 'German' in Alsace (17.12.1793);
* a decree to ensure that the population would not be 'abused' through the use of regional languages (27.1.1794);
* and finally the decree enforcing the use of French for official purposes (20.7.1794).

Indeed, one more should perhaps be added as a rider to this impetuous collection: the modifying decree of 17 November 1794 which permitted use of the _idiome du pays_ as a supportive means in primary education. This modification, which was in fact a rejection of the absolute instruction concerning education in French, was forced, according to Blanchet (1992: 71) by the sheer impracticality of implementing the original instruction.

Regional languages were banned through hatred, fear and suspicion of what they symbolised and the message of political fragmentation they carried, while French alone was to be the language of freedom and of universal values, and act as the doorway to the future and to individual development within the Republic. It is at this point that language policies became openly political in the modern sense, aimed at ensuring political and social integration and the protection of territorial integrity (cf. Judge, 1993). It could be alleged - and this is the reason we have quoted at such length from the Revolutionary texts - that the reasoning for, and the practice of, much of French language policy since 1789 has changed little.

   In sum, the Revolution and its aftermath did not upset really and immediately the daily language behaviour of the French, and hence those of the inhabitants of Provence. But it did insert, deeply, into French society a whole centralist linguistico-cultural mentality, which was to produce its effect progressively during the 19th and, more brutally, in the 20th centuries. (Blanchet, 1992:72)[14]

Policies from 1800 to 1950

Since the Revolution the courts have consistently applied the policy of linguistic centralisation. Grau (1992) for example cites three decisions of the Appeal Court (*Cour de Cassation*) in 1830, 1859 and 1875, all reinforcing the use of French in legal documents, even in Corsica and in areas which had not formed part of France before the Revolution. But there was no new legislation of principle on this matter, and the nineteenth century concentrated on confirming the policy giving status and privilege to French and destroying regional languages. This it did mainly through education. The Revolutionary wish to see all French citizens both understanding Parisian French and using it as the normal means of communication could not be put into effect except through a common education in and through a common language. But in 1794 it was impossible to put into effect the decrees imposing French as the sole language of the country, and the wish that schoolteachers use only French and teach to a common curriculum was beyond the capacity of the embryonic educational system. Even by 1832, when primary education was made universal, there were insufficient teachers to attain this objective. By 1881 however, when primary education was made obligatory, secular and free, it was possible to bring into effect the Revolutionary wish that the language of education should be French so that all children, on the same basis, could have access to knowledge and to the social advance to which that knowledge led, provided access took place through the medium of French. Jules Ferry, as Minister of Education, made it his aim to see that French education was carried out in French.

At this point the duty of the Ministers of Education and all the teachers, particularly in the primary schools throughout the land, was not merely to teach in French but to ensure that regional languages and local dialects were systematically excluded from school, even from the school grounds. Methods used to ensure this included ridicule of children speaking local languages by forcing them to wear a dunce's cap or a placard around their necks, and systematically ensuring that local culture and customs were regarded as backward (see for example Hélias, 1975). French, as representative of Nation and Enlightenment, had to be prioritised: 'French, the national language, must come before the others. It was and is the vehicle for all ideas of liberty and must be spread as much as possible' (Georges Leygue, Minister of Education in 1902). Even as late as 1925, the then Education Minister, A de Monzie, openly declared that 'In order for France to achieve linguistic unity, Breton must disappear', and that 'Lay schools cannot shelter languages competing with French' (both quoted in Martel, 1992).

Following the model of the revolutionaries who insisted that Belgium, Alsace and any conquered territories speak and use only French, and despite Napoleon Bonaparte's dismissal of such a policy with the comment that he couldn't care less what language the troops spoke as long as they used their sabres in French, the colonial empire which was conquered in the 19th and 20th centuries had to adopt French as its only official means of communication. The theory was that although colonies might be situated thousands of miles from metropolitan France, there should be no barrier to their assimilation into the nation-state. In fact complete assimilation never happened: a special status was accorded to colonial populations which did not give their inhabitants the full rights of French citizens in France. The policy was nonetheless not solely one of brute force: other factors were at work and encouraged the wider use of standard French. Education for all was a main influence in metropolitan France, and new means of transport and increased commercial relations ensured greater mixing of populations. The French army, and conscription when it was introduced, led to the necessary use of a common means of communication. The increasing efficiency of the French administration was based on and required greater and more widespread knowledge of the standard language. The promotion and indeed recruitment system for the bureaucracy depended on the examination of candidates in formal written tests. The practice of moving civil servants, including teachers, across the country - both practices are still in operation today - brought about the greater use of the standard forms. The world wars and the occupation of France by German troops, together with the 'anti-French' actions of some autonomists from Alsace and Brittany among others, meant that after both wars there was a widespread policy of restoring prestige to French and strengthening the advantages of belonging to a unified state. Slogans such as _Il est chic de parler français_ were heard in Alsace, and the policy mixed such positive, pro-French propaganda with the negative refusal to teach German in Alsace schools for many years after World War Two.

There were, of course, practical and pragmatic exceptions to the general rule of imposing French. Church schools and services maintained regional languages to a certain extent, particularly in Brittany. Organisations such as Lou Félibrige, created in 1851, used language as a symbol of their regionalism. Romanticism idealised groups such as the Celts. Occasional publications, particularly in

Provençal, together with cultural associations and organisations, encouraged pride in local culture. The depressed economic situation of some regions brought working class and regional activists together, although the lower level of industrialisation in France rarely allowed regional solidarity movements to undertake effective action against Paris-based capitalists. During the nineteenth and early twentieth centuries as the modern state was formed French took over as the common language. Inevitably, the regional languages lived in slow decline, gradually losing economic power and status, losing touch with their cultural past, and only surviving as the language of the home and of local industry - fishing in Brittany, viticulture in the South, mining in the North.

Policies from 1951 to 1998

In 1951 a permissive Act (the *Loi* Deixonne) gave formal status in education to four regional languages: Basque, Breton, Catalan, and Occitan. The Act marked the return of Brittany to a degree of acceptance by the French state after the flirtation of some regionalists with the Nazis during the war. It also ended the century and a half of systematic attacks on the use of regional languages. The Deixonne legislation, however, in no sense represented active support for language maintenance. Only four languages could be taught in the public education system, on the basis of the expressed wish of both teacher and pupils, for one hour per week. These languages could be taught as part of the provisions for general education; but they could form part of the examination system only as optional extras, not counting towards the overall grade awarded for the baccalaureate, and could therefore count only in minor ways to certifying the child's education. The Act allowed, but did not insist that education was provided. Neither did it make additional resources available immediately. There was no teacher training, higher education or research support, or teaching materials. The law had to wait a further eighteen years before it was applied. The ministerial circular giving effect to its provisions is dated 1969, and it was not until 1970 that achievement in the regional languages was included as part of the overall score for the baccalaureate. The provisions of the Deixonne Act were extended to Corsican in 1974, and have been gradually applied to other regional languages in later years. A systematic review of the situation had to wait until 1982 and later.

A new impulse was given to French language policy after 1966, under de Gaulle and then Pompidou as President. New institutions were created (the Haut Comité de la Langue Française in 1966, terminology commissions from 1972), the creation of a new international

Francophone movement was debated, and cultural diplomacy was more closely connected to the political, economic and commercial interests of foreign policy. But major changes did not occur then in policy towards the regional languages. Throughout the period from 1958 to 1981, but particularly in the late 1970s and in the Presidential campaign of 1981, the regional language question was one of the issues which the political Left used in order to attack the 'stagnation' of the Right. The domination of Paris in cultural as well as economic matters became a leitmotif of opposition. The pressure intensified and, as one response, Giscard d'Estaing as President in the late 1970s started to set up 'cultural charters' or 'contracts' with the regions. The 'Cultural Charter for Brittany' for example, signed in 1977, promised state support for a number of cultural organisations and activities, including language pressure groups, although many considered it to be an attempt to put language on the same level as bagpipe playing and to turn the language into one more piece of local colour. During this period also, and in contrast to the use of the language question as a political symbol by pressure groups, a number of 'community' initiatives led to practical attempts to improve the position of the languages on the ground and to slow, if not to halt, their gradual disappearance. Schools were established in order to enable children to learn and use the regional languages as their first language and to reinforce home use in the family. The Diwan schools in Brittany originated in this way, as did similar movements in the Catalan- and Basque-speaking regions. The initiative to set up such schools came from outside France, in particular from the Catalan movement in northern Spain, and from Wales. But the problem in France remained one of finance as well as one of status: volunteer teachers needed to be paid if their work was to achieve credibility, and in the French system that meant official recognition, training and certification.

The Haby Committee, reporting in 1976, was a major attempt during this period to reform French education. It also considered the question of regional languages and made some suggestions for their increased use such as allowing an increase to three hours of teaching per week and the inclusion of elements of local culture and civilisation in the programmes. But there was general and widespread opposition at the official level within the Ministry of Education to increased access to regional languages or to any promotion of their teaching by making them part of official examinations. Indeed, Occitan was withdrawn from some examinations (Caldwell, 1994: 298) and there was very lukewarm support for experiments with bilingual classes in Brittany.

After Mitterrand's election and the publication of the Giordan report, a systematic Circular on the teaching of regional languages was published on 21st June 1982 by the Minister of Education, Alain Savary (82-261). This established three new principles:

- that the state should be responsible for their teaching;
- that the languages should be taught from the kindergarten to University, with the status of a separate discipline;
- that teaching should be based on the expressed wish (_volontariat_) of both teacher and pupils.

The circular, together with another of 1983 (83-547), resulted in making it possible to include, on an experimental basis, teaching of other subjects in regional languages. The Savary Circular was generally welcomed by regional activists for establishing these principles and for confirming the state's commitment towards support for regional languages. It outlined the detail of teaching at primary and secondary level and included provision for teacher training, following the normal lines of a CAPES (Certificat d'Aptitude au Professorat de l'Enseignement Secondaire), although the regional language had to be combined with another subject such as French. Higher education was also included: there was to be a programme of research in areas such as the sociolinguistics of regional languages, their teaching and in bilingualism and ethnology. Departments of Regional Studies, and programmes of study in the area, could be developed, and University institutions were encouraged to collaborate with both associations and local collectivities. These, the municipal, departmental and regional councils had resources available after the 1983 decentralisation reforms, which could assist in the costs.

Outside education, and in response to the recommendations of the Giordan Report, a Conseil National des Langues et Cultures Régionales was created and a number of minor adjustments were made in other areas: for example, bilingual road signs could now be erected with the agreement of, and at the request of, local government. The expected legislation on the formal status of regional languages was not however forthcoming. Reviewing the situation later, Giordan and those who thought that his 1982 report would be implemented in full acknowledged that the decade from 1981 to 1991 had been one of lost hopes :

The proposals contradicted the Socialists' political choices...the National Council for Regional Languages and Cultures has met three times in six years and its influence has been negligible...(but at least) regional cultures are no longer regarded as factors degrading the national identity. (Giordan, 1992: 138-9)[15]

The teaching of the regional languages was systematically redefined again in 1988, when syllabuses were published which have generally remained in force. The regional languages which were recognised at this point and which could hence be taught in the Lycées were, as named by the Ministry: Basque, Breton, Catalan, Corse, Auvergnat, Gascon, Languedocien, Limousin, Niçart, Provençal, Vivaro-Alpin, Tahitien, Gallo, Alsace regional languages (syllabuses for all these were approved on fifteenth April 1988), Moselle regional languages (approved later, on seventh September 1991), and four of the over thirty Melanesian regional languages (Aijé, Drehu, Mengone, Paici; approved on twentieth October 1992). All these languages could now be taken for the baccalaureate examination, as either the second or third language and as either an obligatory subject or as an option, depending on the particular type of baccalaureate. Gallo, and the Alsace and Moselle regional languages are examined orally, while examinations are conducted only in those Académies (i.e. education areas) where competent examiners could be provided, which in essence means the particular region plus Paris. In bilingual schools or classes using both French and regional languages, examinations in history and geography could be presented in the regional language for the baccalaureate. In private bilingual schools (Diwan for Breton, Ikastolak for Basque) an improved status was regulated by an agreement of 20.7.1994, which means the state pays teachers, who have been assimilated progressively from September 1994 as their qualifications were approved by the relevant Instituts Universitaires de Formation des Maîtres (IUFM)). These schools could also be supported financially by local communities after the beginning of 1995. It should be noted that the Ministry has held firm to the view that the languages of the South are many and varied, rather than one form of 'Occitan' or 'Provençal', and requires pupils to choose an examination in one or other of the 'languages of the South' it defined as such for this purpose: Auvergnat, Gascon, Languedocien, Limousin, Nissart, Provençal, Vivaro-alpin. Both spellings of Niçart/Nissart have been used in Ministerial documents!

In 1998, the provisions of the 1995 Circular (95-086) define both the principles and modalities of teaching regional languages. This reaffirmed the state's commitment and the Savary principles. The provision relies on the *volontariat* of pupils and staff; the state aims to preserve an essential element of the national heritage. Individual Académies were now requested to draw up academic plans jointly with regional authorities, and to appoint coordinators to ensure the provision of teaching materials and publicity for the provision. At primary level, all teachers were encouraged to make pupils aware of the cultural and linguistic wealth of the region. Regional languages could be taught for between one and three hours per week and used as the teaching medium for history, geography, sport, art or the sciences. Bilingual classes could also be organised on the basis of an equal amount of teaching in the regional language and in French, although the full allocation of hours to the teaching of French itself would be maintained. At secondary level, regional language streams would offer at least three weekly hours of teaching of language plus one or two other disciplines taught in the language. At lycée level and in the baccalaureate regional languages could be taken as a language option.

With the changes of governments between 1993 and 1998, the Ministry has prepared a number of possible scenarios and changes to policies for regional languages. These have mostly remained internal documents. The Poignant Report, presented to the prime minister and published in July 1998 proposes few major changes in education. This, together with the history of bureaucratic unwillingness to change means that it is most likely that any further developments will take place in slow, incremental steps. The only major development to be expected is that the European Charter for Regional and Minority Languages will be signed sometime during 1999, now that a legal opinion has set aside Constitutional problems .

How Successful has Regional Language Policy Been?

The intention of the policies of assimilation and oppression started in the Revolution was to make regional languages unusable in official domains. There is no doubt that the policy of assimilation has contributed to creating a unified, lay, centralised nation-state in which the use of a single standard language would symbolise the unity of the community. The political community, the speech community, and the cultural community would occupy the same geographical space. Much of the forced assimilation was the result of the adoption of the principles of assimilation by individual teachers, administrators and bureaucrats, willing and enthusiastic to see one nation created, and hence both macro and micro policy worked together to the same end. Some consider that this policy was not so much directed at destroying regional languages as at ensuring the creation of one indivisible nation through French. Others feel that the process was simply an inevitable product of economic change. Whether official or not, whether aimed at the promotion of French or the destruction of regional languages, has the process been successful?

Data on the inter-generational transfer of languages in contemporary France (Héran, 1993) shows that 16% of the nearly 10,000 people interviewed reported that their parents usually spoke to them in a language other than French, while 5% of people usually spoke to their own children in a language other than French. The overall picture we have then is of a strong 'power of absorption of French', with massive inter-generational language loss in one generation. Of the regional languages mentioned in the survey, Alsace dialects were 'by far the leaders: 0.6% of the national total, but between 20 and 25% of Alsace-Moselle families'. 'While 40% of the families in the region spoke Alsace dialects a generation ago, 25% do so today. It is used in a wide variety of situations, including at work, but not in the public service'. Breton is quoted widely as the language of childhood by primary school teachers; but since only 44 families were included in the sample and none still used it, Breton 'has practically disappeared among those under thirty'. Corsican, by contrast, was quoted by civil servants; but the sample was too small to venture other than a guess that fewer than 10% of children used Corsican in the family. Occitan had suffered abandonment 'nine times out of ten', and was not prized by interviewees, who usually called the language by a very local name (e.g. Corrézien) or labelled it as 'patois'. The families who best maintained the language were also the most socially deprived. For Alsace dialects, for example, the comparisons between those who do and those who do not maintain the dialect shown in Table 1.1 are instructive.

Table 1.1 Maintenance of dialects in Alsace

| | Percentage of dialect speaking parents who | |
	maintain the dialect	do not maintain the dialect
among those who:		
(1) married a speaker of the language	93	63
(2) practise a religion	45	24
(3) no educational qualification	32	18
(4) declares him/herself unable to help children with schoolwork	38	15
(5) unqualified worker	25	9
(6) child has repeated a year at school	38	22

Source: Héran, 1993: 3 (adapted)

Héran's general comment on this situation is that overall, there are no monolingual speakers of regional languages left in France. Regional languages have become 'the wealth of the poor':

the proportion of non-French-speakers in the parent-child relation increases as one descends the social scale...from 9% of executives to 36% of non-qualified workers (childhood language); or from 1% to 20% for the language transmitted to children.

Another indicator of the position is the situation in education (Figure 1.2).

	1986-7	1992-3	1995-6
Alsace (German)			
primary		82,432	87,821
secondary		66,826	80,000
Basque			
primary		4,563	2,950
secondary	1,867	2,193	927
Breton			
primary		7,343	9,689
secondary	3,756	4,000	730
Catalan			
primary		8,569	9,188
secondary	2,756	1,562	424
Corsican			
primary		11,749	18,874
secondary	2,982	5,183	840
Occitan			
primary		62,579	62,446
secondary	10,647	9,270	3,364

Source: Enrolments 1986-7 are taken from Quid, 1997:1444; 1992-3 from DGLF, 13.4.1994; for 1995-6 from DGLF, 1997, 1. VII, 1.

Figure 1.2 Regional languages in education

Education can be provided in three main ways: directly in the state schools, either as teaching of the language or, in bilingual classes, teaching through the medium of the language; in private schools contracted to the state system (mainly Catholic schools) or in private schools organised by 'associations' (for example Diwan for Breton,

Ikastolak for Basque or Calandreta for Catalan). These use the regional
language at first in total immersion classes and progressively introduce
French. In the whole of France however they account for a mere 5,000
children at all levels. Indeed, overall the provision for regional
languages in education applied to some 335,000 children of the twelve
million in schools in 1996-7. When one considers that children must
normally study two foreign languages, and some study three, and that
the total number of possibilities is over five million, the regional
languages account for a very small proportion.

The Poignant report (1998: 25) is fairly scathing in its assessment of
the actual, as opposed to the permitted, situation in education. Existing
texts are not fully applied, the plans required by the 1995 Circular are
not always complete, many schools have no regional language teaching
available. Overall, the policy aims of preserving the national heritage
and transmission of regional cultures and languages are far from being
achieved. How far, then, is there any likelihood that the regional
languages might reverse the trends towards language shift and regain a
significant position in France? The extent of the mistrust between
regional language supporters and the state has been great. The 52
proposals for legal action on regional languages submitted to the Senate
and the Assembly between 1977 and 1997, none of which was even
discussed, has left a belief that a game of cat and mouse was being
played (Poignant, 1998: 20). Nevertheless, official attitudes in France are
increasingly tolerant, noticeably so since the 1997 election of the Socialist
government which commissioned the report from Nicole Péry (*Le
Monde*, 4.2.1998) which was eventually finished by Bernard Poignant,
mayor of Quimper in Brittany, and presented in July 1998. This seems
aimed at calming regional pressures and at basing support for French
firmly on Republican principles. It suggests ten principles for policy
(Figure 1.3).

The report concluded that regional languages should be protected
and promoted by the state, not simply because they were part of
France's heritage, a cultural inheritance and an addition to the rich
diversity of life, but for a number of very political reasons. France had
made significant choices: for Europe, for Francophonie, for
multilingualism. Her choice for decentralisation should include the
'Girondin option' of supporting regional languages and cultures. One of
the report's main purposes seems thus to have been to accept regionalist
arguments for formal recognition, but at the same time to curb the
excesses of regional demand on the basis that the French language
represented a long history of freedom, democracy and insistence on
rights. Another telling point made was that the next century would see a

growth in regional sentiment, and if the Socialist government did not support regionalism, the option of regional nationalism was worse. This point had been made elsewhere, and in other European countries where the idea of a 'Europe of the Regions' had been hoped for, partly as a counter to the strong nation-states. Most French regional languages have extra-frontier support: Alsace and Moselle looks to standard German for the written form and to external TV broadcasts for use of the spoken; Basque and Catalan are strongly supported in Spain, where new regional governments have revitalised the local communities. Breton activists look longingly at Wales, where the 1993 Welsh Language Act renders Welsh co-official with English in a number of major public domains and central government money is available to support the introduction of language schemes in local authorities. Flemish looks to standard Dutch, which is its official written form, and to the strength of the Flemish language lobby in Belgium.

---

(1)   The rights of the child and pupil take priority.
(2)   French is the official language.
(3)   The French Republic should recognise regional languages and cultures on its territory.
(4)   Policy for these should correspond more with decentralisation.
(5)   School is based on integration.
(6)   Learning a regional language is a voluntary action which should be available for all.
(7)   Learning many languages is an advantage.
(8)   The same level of French should be achieved by all.
(9)   The state should ensure that regional language teaching is available in later stages, for example by correspondence.
(10) The state should recognise a diversity of methods: bilingual and immersion teaching.

Source: Poignant, 1998: 31-3[16]

Figure 1.3 The state and regional languages

The Prime Minister accepted the Poignant report with alacrity, and made positive comments in a communiqué on 7th October 1998, when the Carcassonne opinion was published. He expressed the government's firm intent to see the succesful signing of the European Charter. Significantly, the comments have been published by the Délégation Générale à la Langue Française, which thus may move into the position advocated by Poignant of acting as a government organ, not jut for French, but for all the French languages.

Regional languages are nonetheless generally moving 'down' Fishman's 8-point scale towards language loss, although some have apparently better chances of survival than others. In non-technical terms, this scale (Figure 1.4) ranges from a 'best' point where the regional language is used in government, media, education and the professions to a 'worst' position in which it is vestigial, a memory for old people. Caldwell's (1994) assessment of where the French Regional Languages (apart from Occitan) stood on Fishman's scale is as follows. Alsace, Basque, Catalan: 'reinforced by interactions with their extra-frontier population, and perhaps aided by European Union provisions, may sustain or renew itself through reformed conditions'. Breton was 'inexorably approaching Stage 7' (old people not passing the language on). Corsican was 'progressing through Stage 5 towards 4' (i.e. improving: from literacy and domestic use to being taught). Flemish, like Breton, would 'continue this rapid decline'.

Stage 1: some use of (the Regional Language (henceforth RL)) in higher level educational, occupational, governmental and media efforts (but without the additional safety provided by political independence)

Stage 2: RL in lower governmental services and mass media but not in the higher spheres of either

Stage 3: use of RL in the lower work sphere (outside of the RL neighbourhood/community) involving interaction between (RL and non-RL speakers)

Stage 4: RL in lower education that meets the requirements of compulsory education laws

Stage 5: RL literacy in the home, school and community, but without taking on extra-communal reinforcement of such literacy

Stage 6: the attainment of intergenerational informal oracy and its demographic concentration and institutional reinforcement

Stage 7: most users of RL are a socially integrated and ethnolinguistically active population but they are beyond child-bearing age

Stage 8: most vestigial users of RL are socially isolated old folks and RL needs to be re-assembled from their mouths and memories and taught to demographically unconcentrated adults

---

Source: Fishman, 1991: 88-109

Figure 1.4 Fishman's scale of Graded Intergenerational Disruption

There is some evidence that regional French, as a 'standard' to which local speakers are prepared to give prestige, is taking over from the regional languages as the preferred marker of difference (Taylor, 1996). These language varieties are of course French, and the main difference with the standard is in pronunciation. But many regionalisms in regional French derive from the original regional language: _wassingue_ (floorcloth) from Flemish, _pottok_ (pony) from Basque. Some of them have found their way to standard French and thus serve less as a distinctive marker of regional origin: _abeille_ (bee), _bouillabaisse, chalet_.

French policy towards regional languages has been largely successful in its aim of destroying regional identities and separate cultural traditions because of its fear of them. But it is time to seek for more detailed explanations. We propose to investigate the counter-identity that political authorities have invented for the central state. Relations between the centre and periphery, and the role of the regional representatives also merit investigation.

Chapter 2
Fear mixed with pride: the myth of the hexagon

Three explanations for policies towards regional languages have been advanced at various times and from various perspectives. All seem valid, and we shall explore each of them in this chapter. It is likely that each goes part way towards accounting for the traditional centralisation of the French state and the fear of disintegration that inspires so much regional and language policy, and that they work together. The three explanations are the power of the central state's imagined community; the historical nature of centre-periphery relations and the approach of the state administrative machine towards the regions; and the nature of French regionalism itself.

Explanation one: the Imagined Community

The two words 'France' and 'Hexagon' are commonly used in French as though they were synonyms. Geographically, France is bordered by the sea on three sides facing the Channel, the Atlantic and the Mediterranean, and on the three others by Belgium, by Germany, Switzerland and Italy, and by Spain, and thus is roughly a six-sided figure. The word hexagon and the adjective hexagonal are used in contemporary French to mean France or anything French: ideas, policies, writing, culture. Many historians believe that a myth associated with what might be called hexagonal centralisation developed, or was created, as a way of ensuring that the idea of France was attractive enough to act as a counterweight to regional identities. The almost mythical understanding of the French history and spirit which political leaders and their followers have created, whatever the historical facts may have been, associated with and based on a fear of disintegration through regional pressures, has been strong enough to act as a motive to support centralisation policies. Such a myth, with components like those of Figure 2.1, seems deliberately designed to entice regionalists away from their cultural identity. It is the basis of French identity, which we shall consider further in Chapter 6 below.

---

(1)   France has always existed in her present shape
(2)   France forms a natural unit, predestined to form one social group and one political nation
(3)   no-one has ever become French against their will
(4)   the myth of an anti-French conspiracy (attested historical examples include 'conspiracies' by Jews, by Freemasons, by Jesuits) and the idea of domination by external forces
(5)   the idea of the strong man as the saviour, associated in France with the concept of the legitimacy of the state
(6)   the belief in a past golden age
(7)   belief in unity.

Components 1 to 7, identified by both Mordrel and Girardet through analysis of the history of France, recur almost monotonously in the ideologies and beliefs of every contemporary political party in France. But they are not the only components of the myth. They are commonly associated with the Republican values (Liberty, Equality and Fraternity) to form a unifying set of beliefs which lie at the heart of 'Frenchness', and which include:

(8)   the sovereignty of the people, individually and not through membership of any group, class or category
(9)   the social contract, made as a free choice by individuals with the state
(10)   the idea of fraternity, or the expression of a general will to act together
(11)   the indivisibility of the state
(12)   the universality of the Rights of Man, of the ideas of liberty and equality and the belief that these are the inalienable rights of all humanity.

Sources: Points 1, 2 and 3 are taken from Mordrel, 1981: 23-30; points 4, 5, 6 and 7 from Girardet, 1986; other relevant concepts derive from Flood & Bell, 1997.

Figure 2.1 The myth of the hexagon

It is commonly said that since the Revolution France has experienced a struggle between two concepts of nationalism (Flood, 1997; see Chapter 6 below). In fact, there are probably three strands to be distinguished: the Jacobin, centralised nation-state in which all citizens voluntarily formed a united and indivisible whole and whose vocation was universal; its opposite, the ethnic state based on a federation of the regions and a common myth, in which membership of the body politic derived from blood not residence, and a third, a state in which power was given, by the people, to a charismatic leader - a king, a Napoleon, de Gaulle. For most of the two centuries since 1789 it has in fact been the monarchist or imperialist form of nationalism which has triumphed, while the 'democratic' struggle has opposed centralisation and regionalisation. To a certain extent, the monarchist or presidential fact - state power - has held the balance between universality and ethnicity. Put another way, the Republican values of universality and fraternity take on political meaning in France only if they are reinterpreted to show their specifically French origin, through the use of French in a French state. The myth of the hexagon derives from the three forms of nationalism, with the result that the myth of France contains all strands and encourages the revolutionary and the conservative, the republican and the monarchist, the national and the universal. Mordrel is of course not the only person to have shown that the view of their own country the French have has been created, nor is such a process of myth creation unique to the French.

> Imagination and power are two keys to our understanding of human history in general and that of France in particular. They have been misunderstood by early historians of the Republic, since their culture, their nationalism, their view of human nature could not see their import nor their motivation. Having secularised the conception of history, they thought they had eliminated the mystical element which they recreated, in their own way, through the cult of the Nation and the State. (Citron, 1987: 12)[17]

The myth has nearly always been described or externalised through a rhetoric of almost religious belief in the sacredness of France's mission, particularly in pursuance of the concept of human rights and despite the ample evidence that France herself, like most nations, has in practice pursued her own interests and been as guilty as most of ignoring those rights which did not meet her own interests:

> France's mission is to conduct humanity towards a brilliant dawn (Edgar Quinet, 1848)

for France, something additional is necessary...she cannot simply be a free country, she must be a great country, exercising the influence on Europe that she possesses, and she must spread this influence across the world, and carry wherever she can her language, her customs, her flag, her arms, her spirit (Jules Ferry, 1885)

France is only France when she takes on the burden of humanity (André Malraux, 1948). (both quoted in Mordrel, 1981: 206)[18]

The myth itself has been modified as circumstances require. During Revolutionary times external circumstances dictated the need for unity and the pragmatic necessities of centralised control, military force and a people's militia. In the Napoleonic period, the need was to impose the French view on the world. Later theorists included Renan, who in his 1882 lecture underlined that the French conception of the nation involved consensus and a 'daily plebiscite', but whose definition was strongly affected by the political circumstances of a time when France had rebuilt her self-confidence after defeat by Prussia and the scramble for Africa was about to start (Girardet, 1983: 65-7; Hargreaves, 1997: 188).

The myth of the hexagon is of course a myth: not merely has the present shape of geographical France only existed since 1945 and for short periods before, in 1866-71 and 1919-1940 (Mordrel, 1981: 183), but France itself is as diverse as any country and contains as many groups, communities and social categories as any other in Europe. In 1990, 40% of French people felt they belonged firstly to their immediate locality of *canton*; a further 14% to their region or province. 27% 'belonged' to France, 8% to Europe, 10% to the world (statistics from Riffault, 1994: 30). The creation of the state, far from being a natural development of pre-existing unity, represents chance, the play of power politics and is bathed in blood:

> France, having been constructed blindly and by chance, became a hexagon but could equally well have become a trapezoid or a sort of star - in which case the symbol might have called forth a direct celestial intervention. France is not a Republic like Athens, a Swiss canton or a State in the USA. It is a collective dictatorship exercised by the state apparatus, disguised as a democracy. A democracy limited to a number of concessions to the isolated citizen, but never to the group he belongs to...its political system is a magnificent war machine, designed by regimes which needed obedience to wage war. (Mordrel, 1981: 183 and 323)[19]

The myth has considerable power of attraction and strength. Girardet (1986: 64) quotes the example of the changed public attitude towards M. Pinay once he had been elected in 1951: his election transformed him from a mediocre politician into a symbol of the legitimate state, with all the associated dignity of authority and of the values he incarnated. Letters to *Le Monde* showed how offended readers were at any flippancy by commentators, even if they were the distinguished François Mauriac. Despite the figures we have quoted above, 32% of French people were 'proud', a further 48% 'fairly proud' of being French. The Poignant report of 1998 (p. 15) stresses that the Republican values are the point of reference for the French, who regard them as unbreakable when departures from the underlying principles are remarked. The Republican values and indeed all aspects of the myth have become part of the French political spectrum, the basis for the ideologies of particular parties and the accepted discourse domain within which French political, social and economic life takes place. The Republic is a common possession in the same way that French is a common possession. The Giordan report of 1982 was unsuccessful because regionalists of the time had not understood this; by contrast, the Poignant report of 1998 showed that destruction of this consensus, or the threat of it, would be an unthinkable disaster, and activists should accept the collective belief in the unity and cohesion of France. The effectiveness of the myth of the hexagon could not be better illustrated.

Explanation Two: Centre-Periphery Relations

The French administrative and political regions

The Revolution decreed a new organisation of French territory in 1790. This 'logical' approach to administration has generally remained, as have, to a large extent, the associated political structures. These included elected representatives to central government (députés), local representatives of the state (préfets), although centralisation of power was the key. Current administrative divisions of metropolitan France do not quite match the pre-Revolutionary cultural and linguistic regions. More than twenty administrative Regions, over a hundred Departments and nearly forty thousand Communes sit in sometimes uneasy relationships with seven regional languages and innumerable dialects, and with over thirty identifiable, main cultural areas. Comparison between these administrative divisions and the cultural/linguistic ones, as in Table 2.1 and Maps 1.1 and 2.1 shows how awkward the 'fit' sometimes is.

Metropolitan France has been formally divided since 1982 into twenty-two administrative regions. The regions are administered through an elected council, re-elected every six years after the first set of elections in 1986. The councils have an elected president, who has executive responsibility for implementing decisions. There is in addition an Economic and Social Council, unelected but representing the social partners (industrialists, trade unionists and experts). Regions set their own budgets, deriving resources both from some areas transferred from central government and from local taxation. Regions have responsibilities for economic development, for which they can raise additional funds from collaboration with the state, by borrowing, or from European Union sources. They have investment responsibilities, too, in other areas like higher education, research and the lycées - of which 'they built 220 between 1986 and 1992, compared with 60 built by the state in the preceding five years' (Stevens, 1996: 167). Overall, the Regions make high profile investments in order to promote their region and to plan its development, work with central authorities and mainly concentrate on support for particular projects. On the European scene, their separate existence makes them formidable participants in promotion of the idea of a Europe of the Regions.

The smaller units of local government are the Départements and the Communes, each with a long history and specified powers, and each with elected councils and headed by a leader who combines chairmanship and executive functions. The departmental structure was set up by the French Revolution, with the purpose of ensuring efficient and effective government on the basis of equality for all citizens. Departments were then ruled by representatives of the central power (the Préfet). It was not until 1871 (and 1884 for the communes) that elections to local councils started. It is for this historical reason that there remains at all levels of local government in France a mix of administrative and representative functions. The department remains the focus of much local administration and the locus for implementing government decisions. Electorally, departments are subdivided into arrondissements, each of which is also an administrative sub-unit managed by a sous-préfet. The arrondissements are themselves subdivided into cantons, each electing a councillor for six years, and communes. Elections for half the departmental councillors take place every three years.

Table 2.1 Administrative and cultural regions

Administrative regions (regional capitals)	Main cultural regions and (LANGUAGES) or (_dialects_)
Bretagne (Rennes)	Bretagne (BRETON)
Basse-Normandie (Caen)	Normandie (_Gallo_)
Haute Normandie (Rouen)	"
Nord-Pas de Calais (Lille)	Flandre (FLAMAND)
Picardie (Amiens)	Picardie (_Picard_), Artois
Ile de France (Paris)	Ile de France (_Francien_)
Champagne Ardenne (Reims)	Champagne (_Champenois_)
Lorraine (Metz)	Lorraine (_Lorrain_)
Alsace (Strasbourg)	Alsace (ALSACIEN)
Franche Comté (Besançon)	Franche Comté (_Franco-provençal_)
Bourgogne (Dijon)	Bourgogne (_Bourguignon_)
Centre (Orléans)	Beauce, Gatinais, Maine
Pays de la Loire (Nantes)	Vendée, Anjou (_Angevin_)
Poitou Charentes (Poitiers)	Poitou (_Poitevin_), Saintonge (_Saintongeais_)
Limousin (Limoges)	Limousin (_Limousin_)
Auvergne (Clermont Ferrand)	Auvergne (_Auvergnat_)
Rhone-Alpes (Lyon)	Dauphiné (_Provençal alpin_), Savoie (_Rhodanien_)
Provence Alpes Côte d'Azur (Marseilles)	Provence (_Provençal_, _Provençal maritime_, _Niçart_)
Languedoc-Roussillon (Montpelier)	Languedoc (OCCITAN), Catalogne (CATALAN), Roussillon
Midi Pyrénées (Toulouse)	Occitanie (OCCITAN), Pays Basque (BASQUE), Navarre, Béarn, Armagnac
Aquitaine (Bordeaux)	Aquitaine, Guyenne, Gascogne (_Gascon_)
Corse (Ajaccio)	Corse (CORSE)

Map 2.1
Administrative and cultural regions
Source: Stevens, 1996: xvi

- ●   Regional prefecture

- ——   Regional boundaries

The Regions of France

The president of the departmental council acts as departmental executive, while the local préfet retains considerable power and deploys some state resources. Departments' formal responsibilities now lie in areas like social work (homes for children and the old, disabled), infrastructure (roads and bridges), in the provision of support for education from eleven to sixteen, and, often in conjunction with communes, cultural and recreational provision including the promotion of the department.

The 36,750 communes, based on pre-Revolutionary parishes, vary in size and importance, and are responsible for many of the day-to-day concerns of life. Many participate in consortia to enable them to run expensive activities like water or energy provision or school building, although most prize their independence and the many attempts to reform the system by forced mergers have mostly failed. Specifically, communes (through their chief executive, the mayor) are responsible for:

- buildings, equipping and maintenance of primary schools
- cultural activities (museums, theatres etc.)
- town and country planning (land use, planning permission)
- public morality and order (holding processions, film censorship) In larger communes this may include administrative policing (Police Municipale), and such services as refuse disposal, pollution control, water supply and sewage, car parking, oversight of slaughterhouses and undertakers
- some infrastructure (local roads, public transport)
- promotion of the commune (tourism, development and restoration, low cost housing - many of these in conjunction with developers).

Their structure is the same everywhere despite the enormous disparity in size - from a population of under a hundred to over two million, which is the case of central Paris, both a commune and a department. The mayor has an important role as executive and as local notable: although elected by the commune, the mayor's responsibilities include acting as executive for the implementation of state policy including public order, and they are not accountable to the council (i.e. cannot be removed by vote between elections). In this role, the mayor is responsible to the ministry of the interior, and the mairie, the mayor's office, acts as (often the only) official building for citizens to interact with government.

In parallel with the structure of régions, départements and communes, the central government traditionally implemented its decisions through local officials, the préfets, (one per département), who were the executives in most areas (but excluding education, finance, defence and justice). As such, they took precedence over local officials and had oversight (tutelle) of decisions, budgets and procedures within local assemblies. The préfet is still an important figure, acting as symbol of the national president and parliament and now reporting to the prime minister's office (and hence is often seen as a political appointment), having responsibility for law and order and formal control of central government services within the département, although these now work more and more directly with Paris. They retain oversight, although this is now limited to a right to refer (some) financial decisions of the regions, departments and communes to the regional branch of the Cour des Comptes (the auditing body) and (some) political decisions to the administrative courts.

A tradition of conflict and opposition

Neither the cultural provinces, nor the linguistic regions, coincide with the regional and departmental administrative structures. Indeed it has been said that the purpose of dividing the country in this way was to prevent local management of affairs (Allum, 1995: 417). Only the communes, themselves based on pre-Revolutionary parishes, have retained the tradition of cultural identity. The provinces, or areas which have an awareness of themselves as culturally distinct from the centre, retain some memory of the historical process by which they came to form part of the French nation-state. Some (Brittany, Savoy) are formerly independent self-governing entities. One (Alsace) has a particularly chequered history as part of France or of Germany, with mixed political allegiances within living memory. Two (the Basque country and the Catalan-speaking area) have close connections with a nearby state, Spain. In the former case some of the attitudes and history of the tormented relations between the Basque provinces and the central Spanish power are reflected in continuing political connections with Basque independence movements. In the latter case, the fierce independence of Catalonia has effects on the self-perception of the region in France, while the strength of Barcelona as a regional capital and economic centre outweighs that of Paris. The other regions have different self-perceptions, but all as internal parts of the French State: the South, despite its long history of opposition to Paris, is diverse and itself fragmented in local rivalries and very different perceptions of the past. The mountainous area of the northern Alps was traditionally, as in Switzerland, made up of individual valleys cut off from each other in long periods of winter, isolated and remote.

Local government operates, in any society, in two directions: from the bottom upwards (in representing local communities to the central power, and ensuring that local concerns are brought to the attention of both the administration and the policy-makers), and top-down (in ensuring fulfilment of the central power's administrative and policy functions and requirements). In France, the second of these historically took precedence over the first, representing the fear central government had of local independence. The creation and deployment of the préfets, following the Intendants of the royalist regime, had the purpose of implementing central government's policies, and the status of the préfets gave them precedence over any local dignitaries. Relations between the centre and the periphery changed somewhat after 1871, and greatly after 1982, with the decentralisation reforms, and the full impact of the changes has not yet been fully felt. But there has been a tradition of conflict and opposition which has taken many forms, and the French system has generated a number of characteristics to cope with this and which in general show that decentralisation has been devised, like cultural and linguistic policy, in order to weaken regional political and administrative opposition to the centre.

The first of these characteristics is the role and position of the préfet. Originally, the duties of this group of professional civil servants were to implement the decisions of central government. In doing this, individual administrators had to take account of local conditions, people and opinion, but their responsibilities meant that they were distinctly in charge. After 1871 they had to conduct some negotiation with local notables, particularly with the mayors who were often also members of parliament or even ministers, and became more and more political figures, often colluding in the clientelism we shall refer to below. With the growth of decentralisation, most of the préfet's responsibilities are now shared, still with the mayors but also notably with the présidents of the regional councils. The change has meant that préfets are more and more 'co-ordinators and monitors, rather than executives' (Stevens, 1996: 178).

The second characteristic is the 'cumul des mandats' - the fact that individuals may hold a number of elected regional and national offices at the same time, although the number of these that could be held simultaneously was reduced in 1985 and the 1997 government proposed to reduce it still further. Politicians can thus act as mayor, as elected members of the regional assemblies (including as président) but also as members of the National Assembly, and indeed as ministers in government. In the 1988 Assembly elections for example, members included 262 mayors, 63 adjoints (deputies), 279 departmental councillors and 141 regional councillors (Knapp, 1991: 20). This mixing of the roles, even though it has been much reduced from what it was, means that individuals can play on their positions and represent themselves as power brokers, taking credit for obtaining resources for local actions and acting as though their patronage was a prerequisite for obtaining favours. Such clientelism, in which the préfets often colluded with local notables in each bolstering the influence of the other, has been widespread. To some extent the European Union is now also involved, in that membership of the European Parliament represents a further possibility for obtaining resources for programmes of benefit to the regions.

A third characteristic derives from the nature of the French legal system. Most laws are passed by the National Assembly in the form of general policy directives, and their implementation is decreed by ministerial orders which traditionally are then interpreted by responsible local authorities or individuals. Again, the consequence is the growth of possible clientelism. On the other hand, local conditions which vary widely within France can thus be taken into account, for example in questions of agricultural pollution or the application of measures designed to aid the homeless.

Both the second and third characteristics, particularly when added to the increasing financial resources available to local authorities, contribute to the power of local political leaders, some of whom have become almost legendary figures in their regions: Jacques Chaban-Delmas in Bordeaux between 1945 and 1995, Gaston Defferre in Marseille from 1953 to 1986, Cathérine Trautmann as Mayor of Strasbourg and Member of the European Parliament from 1989, Minister in 1988 and Minister of Culture and Communication in 1997. Overall, the nature of French local government has been designed in full awareness of the potential strength of the regions. The structure is aimed at weakening local opposition by sucking away the leaders, by balancing the influence of local notables through that of the Préfet, by bribes and favouritism for local notables through making them the channel for largesse from the centre.

How far does the strength of the administrative regions still represent a danger for the centralised French state? Mitterrand's decentralisation reorganisation of 1982 gave them a greater degree of independence, particularly in finance where local authorities now set their own taxes on rents, houses, land, businesses including hotels. This has proved to have two types of consequence: the capacity for independent action has enabled regional structures to concentrate on the improvement of their own region in economic and social terms, and to do so by using their own resources for purposes which may conflict to a certain extent with national priorities. The outstanding example of this is the Nord region, whose development plan, systematic allocation of resources, and self-perception has given it a leading role. In the areas with greater cultural awareness, there has been some reawakening of a cultural identity. Pressure from regional cultural activists has been deflected, to a certain extent, to these local assemblies, and there is little doubt that some councils at least are inclined to accede to requests for the local use of local languages and dialects. But necessarily the dilution of regional cultural identities in new, wider administrative units, has weakened the specific nature of the struggle.

The second consequence is the increasing independence of the regions from Paris, and their awareness of their own identity in the face of a new reorientation of power structures in Europe. Again, the Nord region sees itself as lying at the heart of Europe, as a cross-roads between France and Germany on the East-West axis, and between the Nordic and the Southern European countries - Spain, Portugal, Italy, Greece - on the North-South. It is on this argument that Lille has been advanced as the natural centre of Europe.

Indeed, the European argument is used more and more by regionalists to counter the strength of the French centre. The strengthening of regional identities is now a general feature of Europe, with autonomy for Scotland and Wales, for the Spanish Provinces, in Belgium and elsewhere generally having a linguistic as well as a political, social and economic dimension. A 'Europe of the Regions' would enable them to negotiate directly with Brussels, to develop their own identities and avoid the weight of the oppressive past. In France, there is little doubt that much of the struggle for recognition of the regions has been taken to the new international organisations. A significant example is the creation of the European Bureau for Lesser-Used Languages and the development of a Charter for Regional and Minority Languages. This latter was declared unconstitutional in 1996 since it recognised groups within the state. By 1998 the Poignant report proposed that a legal opinion be commissioned to see whether the Charter could nonetheless be acceptable. Such a favourable report was produced by a constitutional expert, Guy Carcassonne, in October 1998, and the Charter is likely to be signed in 1999, as we noted in Chapter 1 (*Libération*, 13.10.1998). If this were the case, it would indicate that the French government, having made deliberate decisions in favour of commitments to Europe, is prepared to accept the consequences.

Explanation Three: the Weakness of French Regionalism

French regionalism has taken different forms at different times. Although not unique to France, the connection is often made between protection of local cultures and political opposition to the centre based on rejection of its economic and political dominance. In some cases, and although the actions have never reached the degree of violence of the Northern Ireland situation or that of the events in the former Yugoslavia since 1990, the strength of feeling has taken the form of armed attacks - usually on tax offices or préfectures. Only in certain regions however - Alsace, Brittany, Corsica, the Basque country - has there been sufficient unity of feeling for the many different groups and associations to present a common front. It is more characteristic that there should be such diversity of feeling and aims that activists fight each other more than they fight together against the external 'enemy'.

In the South, this characteristic can be seen in the continuing battles between 'Occitanists' and 'Provençalists': in essence between those whose regional loyalties lie in Languedoc and farther west, but whose ambition is to unite the whole of the South, or in Provence (from the Alps to the left bank of the Rhone). Regionalism started with the creation of the Felibrige in 1854 (the oldest French regional association) with the Arles poet Mistral as its leader. He received the Nobel prize for literature in 1904, and partly for this reason, and partly because the Felibrige never instituted political action, Provençal regionalism until the mid-twentieth century was a cultural phenomenon. It was closely associated with the survival of literature and customs and with folklore, and had some significance in slowing down assimilation, making local identity acceptable and giving importance to regional languages. The Felibrige is considered by some to be a popular movement whose actions on the Provençal language reinforced spelling conventions and popular pronunciations and rejected elitism. Others consider it to be neo-Fascist, close to the populism of the Front National and so right-wing politically as to merit no place in contemporary thought. The word 'Occitan' was first used from about 1886, and developed into its present-day meaning from 1945 with the foundation of the Institute of Occitan Studies in Toulouse which saw itself as Left-wing, opposed to the backward-looking Felibrige. The movement got a particular boost from the spirit of 1968 and has been popular in intellectual circles. Contemporary 'Occitanists' give the word linguistic, cultural and political meaning and significance, described as follows by an enemy of the movement in terms which leave no doubt as to the strength of feeling on both sides.

(The ideology) postulates one language of which the Oc fashions of speech are dialects; there is an aim to normalise and an elitist normalisation of the 'one' language (creation of standard Occitan based on Languedoc archaic forms, development of complex and archaic spelling designed to include all speech varieties, within the same Occitan language); admiration for troubadour civilisation; vengeful Albigensianism and 'Occitan' anti-French nationalism; existence of an Occitan nation which could not exist politically because of French intervention in Languedoc; struggle against 'French colonialism'; admiration for the Catalan model. (Blanchet, 1992: 39)[20]

The same author describes the contemporary Provençal movement in the following terms:

Provençal regionalism, very active since 1950 (includes 5 groups in addition to the Felibrige:) lou Provençau à l'Escolo and lou Group d'Estùdi Provençau which are very effective centres for action, research and publication...L'Astrado Prouvençalo which is the largest publisher in Provençal, Parlaren whose action is much more political. L'Unioun Provençalo...(which) with the aid of lawyers, has developed a Statute for Provence...Most Provençal regional movements act at the international level, through associations like the International Association for Endangered Languages and Cultures and on organisations like the Council of Europe...the European Commission...or UNESCO. (Blanchet, 1992: 87)[21]

For some, linguistic awareness is an essential part of regionalism. Effective regionalism requires linguistic codification, or at least that there be a recognisable standard form of the regional language to which allegiance can be given. The lack of unity in the South, and the continuing disputes over any standard demonstrates the lack of any overall political or social unity in community feeling, and hence the essential failure of modern regionalism in this area:

The fact is that after the failure of the Felibres it has not been possible to define a general norm accepted by the variants and we can watch the preparation of grammars and spelling conventions, which break up the sense of a compact, underlying cultural identity, which was there from the Middle Ages. (Ferrer, 1990: 11)[22]

As we have seen, it has been the policy of the Ministry of Education to agree, and indeed to reinforce its centralising role by constantly stressing the variety of languages and dialects: divide and rule. The linguistic and cultural aspect of regionalism was overtaken for thirty years (1960 to 1990) by the attempt to associate culture with politics and particularly economics, and hence to gain broader support. The principal theoretician of the Marxist analysis of 'internal colonisation' associating it with the class struggle was Robert Lafont, for whom the only answer was a regional revolution. The Poignant report of 1998 agrees to an extent, repeating   Agulhon's comment that economic modernisation has been more the cause of linguistic centralisation than political acts. Regionalists would have done better to direct their anger at capital, rather than at the Republic. According to Giordan (1992: 133), 'despite the success of many battles, despite an incontestable growth in regional feeling, such regionalist theses never succeeded in gathering sufficient forces to counterbalance the national political apparatus'. Hence the need to regard regionalism as part of a national political movement of the Left: for the regionalists to join the national Socialist or Communist parties. But the price was the inevitable marginalisation of the more general regionalist aims.

There had nonetheless been movement in the sociolinguistic facts towards more use and more recognition of regional languages, as decentralisation and the creation of the regions enabled resources to be directed towards such concerns as regional language teaching or installing bilingual road signs. Towards the mid-1980s the regionalist movements seem in general to have decided that since 'their' Socialist Party was not prepared to accept their proposals for   greater autonomy and self-determination, pressure would be best transferred towards the international domain and particularly towards Europe. Hence the creation of international organisations for endangered languages and pressures towards an overt statement of European policy, initially through the Council of Europe, then the Parliament.

Regionalism's love affair with the Left is of recent origin. During the Revolution itself it was the counterrevolutionaries who fostered rebellion against the centre. In the Vendée, in Alsace, in most of the regions of France parties of the political Right were the natural supporters of the Girondins, and attacks on the Republic from the regions were associated with such causes as the restoration of the monarchy, the power of the Church and the restoration of group privileges. During the nineteenth century, too, the Left generally favoured a strong, centralised state while regionalists and politicians of the Right were more ambiguous. Between the wars movements for local autonomy and independence came from the Right, associating regionalism with local nationalism in contradistinction to the type of voluntary acceptance of the social contract the revolutionary republicans had developed. It was perhaps the excesses of the second world war, when Breton independentists formed battalions in the German army of occupation, and many young men from Alsace joined the same Army - not usually voluntarily, it must be said - that regionalists began to reconsider their allegiances. It was perhaps also the increasing immigration from ex-colonial countries, which was bringing in identifiably different groups from north and central Africa, that triggered the interest of the Socialist party during the 1970s. Both regionalism and multiculturalism became left-wing causes, but in power after 1980 it regained belief in centralisation and in unity. As the right later regained power, it adopted the theses of the strong unified nation, the rejection of immigration and of regionalism, each of which might lead to fragmentation. In effect, both right and left came to reinforce the theses of the Revolution, reinforced even if modified by Renan in the 1880s and by the socialisation processes of the educational reforms of the same time (Hargreaves, 1997). Regionalism and multiculturalism were both seen, by left and right together, as attacks on the fabric of society. To summarise, one could list the reasons for the lack of success of French regionalism and regionalists as in Figure 2.2.

- the connection between language and political action
- the awareness of language as symbol, but the failure to act on the language corpus and create standard forms
- the failure to capitalise on cultural identity and to associate it adequately with national politics
- the failure to avoid trivialisation into folklore
- the failure to realise that 'real' regionalism requires control of political and economic decision-making
- the fissiparous nature of regionalist movements
- their attraction for intellectuals; less so for the mass
- the (recent) ideological basis in Left-wing opposition
- and the (even more recent) internationalisation of the issue of minority cultures and languages.

Figure 2.2 French regionalism

Explanation and Individual Regional Situations

How far do these explanations account for individual regional situations? The high point of Alsace autonomist movements came in 1926, with the publication of the manifesto of Heimatbund. In 1924, after the war and the various special constitutions which had affected Alsace and Lorraine inside and outside Germany, Prime Minister Herriot announced that 'the whole of Republican legislation will be introduced to Alsace and Lorraine'. The reaction led to opposition, on occasions violent, among which language and language rights played a large part. The Colmar trial of 'those opposing the Constitution' in 1928 did not altogether prevent the continuation of political opposition till the next war, particularly insofar as concerns the special religious status of Alsace and its support for bilingual education. In the last 50 years, although the special status of education has continued after the immediate post-war period during which German was banned, the strength of the autonomy and independence movements has gone and the younger generations are moving away from use of the dialect. Today, German is popular in education, but the dialect is not. The motivation now may be more economic than political:

> favourable attitudes about the dialect focus on its worth as a major element of Alsatian cultural patrimony. It is seen as useful for communicative and instrumental reasons. Sentimental reasons, such as the beauty of Alsatian or personal satisfaction in speaking it, were hardly ever mentioned. (Vassberg, 1993: 170)

Alsace has a special history, and even without this its geographical position makes its population aware of the importance of standard German and standard French as languages of economic and cultural advancement, whether for well-paid work in Germany or simply for watching television. The future of the dialect in this triglossic situation seems very dubious. The explanation could lie principally in the myth of the hexagon: according to _Libération_ (13.10.1998), a bilingual class means in effect 13 hours more German and thus 13 fewer hours of French. A good level of French is essential to career progress.

Three of the seven Basque provinces are located north of the Pyrenees, although they have been part of France since 1598 and retained their own laws and customs until 1789. In Spain, strong autonomy and independence movements have continued campaigns of disobedience, bombings and shootings. It could be this, and thus the excesses of regionalists themselves, which have added to the decline in support for Basque language in France. Use of the Basque language is dying out rapidly despite the institution of kindergarten schools and the somewhat tepid recent support for these from state funds.

Brittany was an independent Duchy from 938 AD until 1532, and only lost the economic and political privileges of its nobility in 1789. Its opposition to Paris has been notable at various periods since. It was not occupied by the conquerors of Napoleon in 1815, and from 1940 to 1944 a Breton battalion fought alongside German troops. Breton terrorism still occurs. Active kindergarten (Diwan) groups support the idea of monolingual Breton education, and a strong Breton independence movement actively fosters language rights and seeks common ground with other European minority cultures. In Brittany, the force of the activists seems to be maintained and there is still some use of the language and some support for cultural difference. But there are no monolingual Bretons; the situation is far removed from that of Wales; and Poignant, mayor of Quimper and hence potentially a Breton nationalist, took the view in his 1998 report that that the use of French was more significant for democracy than that of regional languages. The hexagonal myth has clearly worked.

Corsica has had a chequered history of control by the kings of Aragon, the Genoese, the French after 1768, and a short period of independence from 1793 to 1796 under the Corsican hero Paoli. The island's apparent poverty, together with political and administrative structures based on a close-knit, clan-based family structure like that of Sicily, has led to a continuing history of fraud, political violence, corruption and a struggle for the recognition of local identity, all seen as acceptable forms of opposition to control by the centre. Financial fraud was detailed in a report by the Financial Inspectorate in August 1997 (*Le Figaro*, 27.8.1997), which went so far as to declare the island a financial paradise. Some of the devices the report described included the fact that about 40% of those liable to pay avoided declaring commercial income (on which VAT might be payable); many simply paid no VAT at all (about 50% paid nothing, a loss of more than 700 million francs); 'the local practice of postmen not delivering tax mail'; the role of banks ('which advise their clients to change accounts') and court officers charged with collecting tax who are 'of the greatest timidity'. Overall, financial and tax receipts in Corsica were the lowest in France for 1993, despite special tax regimes which cost the French state nearly a billion francs. Defenders of the Corsican specialities have pointed to widespread fraud in meat or clothing supplies in other regions; the timidity of banks and others might be explained by the fact that banks have been bombed and court officers shot. France itself has negotiated payments of more than three billion francs from the European Commission over the ten years to 1999, although Corsican GDP exceeds the 75% of European Union averages which should trigger regional aid. It now receives some 896 francs per inhabitant against 841 for French Guyana and 497 for Guadeloupe, much poorer regions by any measure (*Dossiers*, 1996: 25-6).

The use of violence in Corsican politics seems endemic. Not all violence is directed at the state in pursuance of the desire for independence. In 1994 for example Jean-François Filippi, deemed responsible for the disaster at a football match in Furiani, was gunned down and a vendetta response murdered Frank Muzy two days later. But even this, one more in a series of vendetta killings among the clans, had political overtones since Filippi had been protected by his section of the Front de Libération Nationale Corse (FLNC-Canal historique). Overall, the clan wars and the complexities of both history and the scissions of nationalist groups have produced a situation where, in Corsica, violence seems the norm. The comparison with mainland France in Table 2.2 is instructive.

Table 2.2 Violence and explosions in Corsica and France

	Year	Murders	per 100,000	Explosions
Corsica	1992	47	18.57	166
France		1342	2.35	1519
Corsica	1993	46	18.18	161
France		1519	2.65	438

Source: *Le Figaro* 30.12.1994

The demands of the nationalists are for either complete independence from France or for a status different from that of other departments and regions, such as that of a Territoire d'Outre-Mer and recognition of a 'Corsican people' as a distinct entity - the latter, of course, would be much more advantageous financially for the island. In response, French governments have modified the absolutist stance of 1859, when the Appeal Court declared that 'no distinction is to be made between Corsica and other parts of French territory' (Grau, 1992: 96). Most recently, after the return of the Socialist party in 1988 a special status was accorded in 1991 and the regional council renamed an *Assemblée Corse*; in the 1992 elections 25% of seats went to nationalists. Nonetheless, the French government has traditionally been firm in refusing openly to accede to the separatists' demands: Juppé, Prime Minister in 1996, declared in May that 'the government does not intend to modify the status of the Corsican local parliament and there is no question of recognising the Corsican people' (*The Guardian*, 29.5.1996). The Socialist party, returned in 1997, has been much more supportive of regional demands, and in Jospin's inaugural speech in June declared it would encourage 'the affirmation of Corsican cultural identity and the teaching of its language'. (Jospin, 1997)[23]

What then is the explanation for French government policy towards Corsica and the Corsican language? It is most likely that the second of the explanations goes some way towards clarifying the relationship. The French administrative machine has clearly been uncomfortable with Corsican habits and traditions, while Corsican autonomists and even the less extreme political groups have seen interference from across the sea as being unwelcome. Most violence has been undertaken against tax collection offices or against representatives of France, the most recent and most important of whom has been the Prefect Claude Erignac shot dead on 6th February 1998. But a killing like this underlines the dilemma of the contemporary state. The time of oppression of regional identities and languages has long gone, but the perceptions of the past held by some regionalists have changed little. It may be for this reason that the Poignant report stresses so heavily the close relationship it sees between French language and democracy, and is so insistent that the values of the Republic are the ideal to which its citizens, all its citizens, aspire.

Chapter 3
Social insecurity: fear of the social outsider

Social Inclusion, Social Exclusion and Language Policies

The goal we examine in this and the following chapter has to do with the protection of society against the dangers which French governments have often considered to lie within French society itself. Because of the history of the Revolution and the rejection of the aristocracy, the main issue is that of how to maintain social coherence among the other classes and categories. The danger is that of social fragmentation and division, that a society will split into numerous groups warring against each other. This issue involves defining inclusion in society and exclusion from it, developing barriers or frontiers which mark the edges of the inclusive society, and the consequential attitude of insecurity as to whether these frontiers might be crossed. There is a certain similarity between the French policy on centralisation, on regional and territorial questions that we examined above, and French ideas on social inclusion and exclusion. In defining France as a geographical entity the main aim was to control the regions and ensure the integrity of the territory; here, defining civil society, politicians and citizens seem to be aware of another danger, equally serious, that the nation might be destroyed and that fraternity could be under threat. The answer is inclusion: making sure not merely that the physical boundaries are secure but that members of society voluntarily adhere to the affective nation.

Any government's policies to ensure social inclusion, in any country, aim at safeguarding the larger social unit by enabling social categories and groups, but sometimes only some of them, to feel themselves part of this greater whole. Any one of three methods of inclusion may be involved: assimilation, the complete absorption of a new member of society, an immigrant or a social deviant until he/she is indistinguishable in any way from other members of society;

integration, allowing individuals or groups to retain their cultural differences, but producing progressively closer interdependence, participation in the social whole and acceptance of common values; or insertion, allowing cultural difference but encouraging participation in society, particularly in economic life.

As we have seen, complete assimilation has been the aim of French regional language policy. Today, although French social policy has traditionally had the same aim, and the socialisation of young people through education has tried to ensure their complete assimilation to traditional values and concepts, one can occasionally detect integration or insertion as more achievable purposes in relation to some social categories and groups. Recent immigrants, in particular, have often proved reluctant to lose their cultural identity completely and assimilate fully. Traditional French concepts of nationalism are based on individual voluntarism. Exclusion of whole social groups and categories, as a deliberate act by government, is generally agreed to be a necessity, applying for example to groups such as criminals. In the recorded past though, in France as elsewhere, other groups such as gypsies have often been deliberately excluded as have illegal immigrants and indeed all foreigners. Women have been excluded from society by simply being ignored in social life. Exclusion implies having no rights: to protection, to social benefits, to employment, to political activity. In order to measure whether inclusion has been achieved in relation to any one group, the five tests given in Figure 3.1 have been suggested.

How far has the group obtained
- equality of treatment
- overt anti-discrimination policies
- specific social and educational policies
- access to nationality and citizenship
- voting rights and eligibility for public office?

Source: Costa-Lascoux, 1994: 69

Figure 3.1 Tests of inclusion

Language planning is about social change, and language policy is one type of social policy. As Cooper put it, 'to plan language is to plan society'. This being so, language policy reveals the views on inclusion a particular state and government hold. But language planning is complex, has many purposes and serves many different views on society:

> language planning is such a complex activity, influenced by numerous factors - economic, ideological, political, etc. ... it is a tool in the service of ... many different latent goals such as economic modernization, national integration, imperial hegemony, racial, sexual and economic equality, the maintenance of elites, and their replacement by new elites. (Cooper, 1989: 182)

We can nonetheless trace how far language policies help or hinder specific groups, so in this chapter, we shall examine whether, and how, inclusion or its opposite has characterised recent language policy applying to four social categories, large-scale but often thought of as marginalised and hence excluded from mainstream society, deliberately or by lack of care. The four categories are the young; women; the poor; immigrants and foreigners. In each case we shall consider the nature of state policy, how far it can be considered to be aimed at inclusion or at exclusion, and the balance between macro policy and micro policy. In each case we shall examine explanations for the policies. In the next chapter we shall explore how far such policies represent more general attitudes towards social exclusion, how they relate to the French cultural environment, and the nature of the fear that lies behind them.

Young People

The Toubon Act of 1994 was clear that 'the mastery of French ... is part of the fundamental aims of education'. In the same year François Bayrou, as Minister of Education, carried out a major review of the French educational system's goals and purposes, developing the _Contrat pour l'école_ which has been implemented gradually from 1995 on. The contract's social purpose was clear:

> it is the mastery of fundamental subjects, French, spoken and written, personal working methods in reading and writing, mathematics, guidance for personal and social life, which creates equality in education. The priority of priorities is the mastery of French, spoken and written. (Bayrou, F. quoted in DGLF, 1996, 2, IV, 3)[24]

The overall importance of education to the Republic, as the main pathway towards inclusion and social equality of access, has been a common theme of every political party since the Revolution. The teaching of French throughout the Republic was then both a principal objective and also unrealisable in practical terms. In very recent years governments have also prioritised education, and within that the fundamentals of French and mathematics, and policies have stayed remarkably similar since the late 1960s. The reasons given for these priorities by Balladur, Juppé and Bayrou between 1993 and 1997 are practically the same as those of the socialist government elected in 1997. Jospin's inaugural declaration of general policy aims then had this to say; he could have been speaking at any time during the last century:

> School is the cradle of the Republic. In addition to its task of instruction, it must ensure learning about civics. From childhood, we must initiate and ensure a deep attachment to the republican values at the leading edge of which is secularity, respect for public activity and property, active and responsible citizenship, which is a whole made up of rights and duties.
> ... To get young people to participate in democratic life, particularly the young of the inner cities, represents an issue of particular importance. Every citizen will be automatically included on electoral lists from the year of majority. (Jospin, 1997)[25]

Educational policies towards the language use of the young are most obvious in contemporary policies concerning accuracy, correctness and precision of language use in the teaching of French. This is not to say that the language use of the young is in fact characterised by the opposite, although the annual assessment of competence in reading carried out in 1996 showed that at the point of entry to the lycées, 13.6% did not master basic competence, 39.7% had just this, 33.2% had a higher level of competence, while 13.5% showed 'remarkable' competence (Note 97.24, Ministère de l'Education Nationale). The official assessment of these figures is that about one child in seven or eight has reading difficulties on entry to secondary education. These figures are often compared with those for children leaving compulsory education without qualifications: 27% in 1973, 16% in 1980, 11% in 1991 and 7.8% in 1994. Although lack of basic education is not necessarily the only or even the main cause of social exclusion, the accepted view is that there is a close correlation between lack of success in education and rejection of society at a more general level. The task of teaching French, its aim, precise syllabuses and suggested methods are given in the annually updated school programmes devised and published by the ministry for the whole of France. Methods are prescribed, too, to a certain extent, but variation in approaches and individualisation of learning now characterise educational approaches and more freedom is given to individual schools, both in determining methods and devising 'diversified pedagogical patterns' for individual needs.

The fact that mastery of French is a prime and a practical aim of the educational system has been shown by the precise improvements and changes which have taken place since the _Contrat pour l'école_. First, by increases in the number of hours (classes) devoted to this subject at the different levels of compulsory education. Thus of the 27 weekly hours in school, 10 are devoted to French in the first year, reducing to 9 in the second and 8 thereafter in elementary education. In the collèges, 5 hours weekly are required, while in the lycées at least 4 are devoted to French, with 5 in the arts streams. These increases date from 1994, but were again increased to six as a minimum for the collèges from 1996. Second, by increased investment in libraries, data bases, CDROMS and other new teaching instruments, teacher documentation centres and support units. The creation of posts for young people in the public service, announced by Martine Aubry in late 1997 and designed to counter increasing unemployment levels even for qualified graduates, has enabled the appointment of helpers particularly in reading and documentation centres based in schools. Third, by the establishment of a national centre for reading and literacy (Observatoire national de la lecture) and the publication of lists of suggested reading.

The purpose of the state's education policy is to give everybody the opportunity to be included. It is a policy founded in beliefs of access and the idea that progress is possible for all. The fact that command of French is at the heart of success in education underlies most public speeches, and these stress time and again that it is not merely the success of the individual that is sought, but the success of society at large through the development of the citizen as a member of the Republic. As the DGLF report put it in 1997, 'Major progress has been made in basic acquisition of language, helped by the understanding particularly from the beginning of the 1990s, of the importance of the fight against illiteracy which is one form of exclusion'.[26] The overall aim of socialisation of the young could hardly be clearer. What is new in recent years is the individualisation of learning and the awareness of difference. Where, in previous years and in the traditional approach, equality lay in the concept of indifference to individuals in the educational system, the changes are now taking cognisance of the harshness of such a system and of its failures.

Women

Sexism, discrimination according to gender, could marginalise women in a number of ways: in employment, in access to social welfare and benefits, and in a more general way by provoking or confirming the exclusion of women from mainstream society. In discussion of this subject in France two opinions seem to have emerged: that the French language as recorded in dictionaries and grammars is by its nature sexist, and/or that the use of particular terms or expressions by certain speakers or writers is sexist. The first view was expressed by Yaguello (1978: 150. See also Ager, 1990: 118-25): 'The denigration of women is present in the language at all levels and in all registers'. Her examples included the masculine and feminine forms of professional titles (*le directeur* and *la directrice* apply separately to each sex, but *le recteur* (a high-level post) has no feminine equivalent while *l'ambassadrice* is the Ambassador's wife), while words like *auteur* have no feminine form at all (although *auteure* is now used in contemporary French). The second type of gender discrimination lies behind such corrective instructions as these given to authors by *Nouvelles Questions Féministes*:

> ... the terms 'homme' or 'hommes' are not acceptable in the generic sense (thus the expressions 'droits humains' or 'droits de la personne' may not be rendered by 'droits de l'homme'). Names of occupations, titles or functions must be feminised according to Francophone usage (Swiss and Quebec norms are acceptable). (quoted in Wilks and Bricks, 1997: 299)

There has been one recent major attempt by the French Government to tackle both issues: a Terminology Commission set up in 1984 by the then Minister for Women's Rights, Mme. Yvette Roudy, shortly after the law of July 1983 outlawing sexual discrimination in job adverts (see Houdebine, 1987; Evans, 1987 and Ager, 1996b: 179-82). The commission's report led to a prime ministerial circular published on 16 March 1986. This invited all ministries to ensure that specified rules of feminisation of names for occupations, functions or titles were followed. The work of the commission which preceded this report covered considerable ground, with terms of reference requiring it to study 'vocabulary concerning women's activities' and to complete 'gaps in French vocabulary in this domain'. The setting up of the commission was generally condemned by much of the press and a special note was published by the French Academy declaring the attempt linguistically misguided since in French social gender and grammatical gender should not be confused: masculine forms were acceptable because they were generic and not sexist. This 'Dumézil and Lévi-Strauss decision', so called because these two eminent academicians wrote it, was repeated in a letter from the Academy's Secretary, Maurice Druon, to the Belgian equivalent in February 1994 as the Belgian state was about to set up a code of feminine forms. The Belgian reply pointed out that the

Academy's point was wrong since, for example, French presidents themselves did not use the generic, 'unmarked' masculine form as an inclusive one in addressing '_Françaises, Français_' in their New Year and other speeches (Druon, 1994). The French ministerial circular itself, when published in 1986, was much reduced from the text of the report, which had contained 'the objectives and motives for the work, the political and ideological motivations, and the linguistic developments which served as examples' (Houdebine, 1987: 32). Indeed Druon prided himself in 1994 that the Academy's note had had the effect of 'immediately ending the proposed decree on feminisation'. Since that time, the work of the ministerial terminology commissions has been brought under stricter control by the Délégation Générale à la langue française (DGLF) and the French Academy given a general oversight of the recommendations involved. The provisions and requirements of the circular published in 1986 had not been forgotten, though, and occasional comments have arisen in the press as female ministers insist on the use of the feminine article (Madame la Ministre). By no means all female public figures do. A member of the DGLF staff, when introducing a female minister at a conference in 1994, did so as 'Madame le Ministre', pointing out later that he had done so at her request (Eloy, 1995: 87).

Policy towards 'sexist' language use is also evident in the editorial practices of the Press, in book and journal publication. In France, by contrast to many societies, these have fairly close connections to the state. It is the role of copy-editors (_correcteurs_) to check on questions of 'language quality' in publications, and there has been considerable official pressure on them to ensure that French is accurate and 'good'. Pressure is exercised in two ways: by state control of the examination and qualification system, as in most branches of work in France, and by repeated pressure on trainers such as the Centre de Formation et de Perfectionnement des Journalistes and the organisations of copy-editors through state agencies like the DGLF, or through pressure groups such as Avenir de la Langue Française. To assess how far such pressures work, copy-editors for _Le Monde_ and _Libération_ were interviewed about their practice and views in relation to non-sexist language, and a quantitative survey of issues of these two newspapers for 1982, 1988 and 1995 was undertaken by researchers to see whether, and how far non-sexist language was actually used before and after the publication of the Circular mentioned above (Wilks and Bricks, 1997). The results indicate that in practice 'new' feminised occupational designations have increased in frequency in both newspapers since 1982, but that 'neither newspaper accepts the concept of non-sexist language in its wider meaning such as is found in _Nouvelles Questions Féministes_ or in Anglo-

Saxon countries'. Both newspapers have nonetheless included comments on the use of non-sexist language in their style manuals, so to this extent anti-discrimination policies exist on the micro level.

Can one seek an explanation for French language policies in relation to women by exploring the role and situation of women in French society, and assessing the success of the feminist movement(s)? There is no doubt that, in the last quarter of the twentieth century, women have gained much greater equality in French society than at any time previously. The 1946 and later constitutions give women the same rights as men, 'in all domains'. Women have the vote on the same basis as men (but only since 1946); can dispose of their own property and income (but only since 1983); anti-discrimination legislation outlaws discriminatory practices in employment, recruitment or the provision of goods and services, and similarly outlaws sexual harassment. Some specific social and educational policies apply specifically to women and recognise their situation or role as needing special support or treatment different from that accorded to men, for example in family matters (Emploi, 1993).

The political record of the Mitterrand years from 1981 to 1995 is nonetheless considered by some to be a missed opportunity for women (see Jenson and Sineau, 1995). These analysts called the years from 1965 to 1981 'the time of (socialist) promises', but are critical of the actual actions of the president in power up to 1993. They accept that the legislative record was impressive, particularly between 1981 and 1986. Legislation on sexism had been discarded on the argument it contravened the liberty of expression. The underlying reality for women had changed little:

> women are still shunted into the less qualified jobs, less well paid ones, and those with fewest chances of promotion. Wages are still lower, as is the pattern of unemployment....none of the Mitterrand laws considered abortion or birth control through the health system as an integral part of civil rights. (Jenson & Sineau, 1995: 342-7)[27]

They drew a number of lessons for the future from this experience. Only women themselves could alter their destiny, by taking matters into their own hands. Women should hence participate more in political life, take places as candidates, attend meetings. Women's issues, too, should not be sidelined or treated as incidental to mainstream policies. Macro-economics and employment policies had direct effects on women.

It may be for this reason that Jospin found it necessary to make specific reference to the role of women in his speech on general policy to be followed from 1997. In two particular respects Jospin hinted that women were not yet fully 'included' in society:

> In the first place we must allow women to be engaged without hindrance in public life. In this field, progress needs, firstly, a change in attitudes and in behaviour. The Socialists and the Parliamentary majority have shown the example, traced out the path to follow. Yet we must go farther. A revision of the Constitution will be proposed, to insert the aim of parity between men and women.
>
> As for the movement favouring equality at work between men and women, it will be renewed. (Jospin, 1997)[28]

A study of European values (Ashford and Timms, 1992; Riffault, 1994) nonetheless showed that women's role in society is now participative and accepted. Women in France participate much more, in their own right and throughout their working lives, in economic life than any other group of Europeans except the Danes. Their working pattern is similar to that of men, and women are perceived as individuals with socially recognised and job-related identities as much as for the family role they occupy (Riffault, 1994: 243-7). Women and men participate in society together, but accept that their roles are socially conditioned. But even these social conditions change, as can be seen by observing what has happened to the institution of marriage. In 1970 it was rare for men and women to live together without being married. By 1990, about two million people were cohabiting in France - 10% of couples, 30% of couples under 35 and more than half those under 25. 'Cohabitation has become the norm', since 81% of the population agreed that life together was important, although single motherhood was thought acceptable by 37%. In terms of women's freedom, abortion seemed 'sometimes' or 'often' justifiable for 60%, while 32% (mainly for religious reasons) thought it 'never' or 'rarely' justifiable; divorce is sometimes or often justified for 76%, never or rarely for 24%. We should note that in France 230,000 abortions are estimated to take place annually, as are 280,000 marriages and 100,000 divorces. In these family values, France is close to the European norm, although with less opposition to abortion than the average (Riffault, 1994: 35-84).

The general impression observers have is balanced between the advances that have been made and the road still to travel on the issue of the role of women in French society. France may not show overt misogyny in formal policies, but in practice 'forms of exploitation vary with evolving power structures, but genuine change is needed as much as ever' (Cross, 1997: 165). The ideology of feminism has however had much less practical effect in France than, say, in America. This is partly because of the nature of French feminism and its supporters, many of whom have turned their backs on direct action or the political struggle:

> Feminists such as psychoanalyst Antoinette Fouque (now a member of the European Parliament) and writers including Hélène Cixous, Monique Wittig, Julia Kristeva and Luce Irigaray have become household names in French feminism, but these few women who preferred to create alternative space in cultural and philosophical terms and turned their backs on mainstream political institutions have had little inclination to cultivate the broader movement of solidarity, which existed for a short while in the 1970s. (Cross, 1997: 173-4)

Feminism, however, has, ever since the French Revolution:

- never been far from the political or social agenda
- in France, more often than not been associated with another social movement
- a strong culture of emphasising sexual difference, although this expression has not automatically led to a strong demand for political equality
- tended to become introverted and remain marginalised.

Although not all women would regard themselves as feminists or subscribe to the views of the many schools of feminism in France, it may be in this introversion that one can find another explanation for the apparent lack of success of overt anti-discrimination language policies such as the anti-sexist language example of 1986, and the continuing opposition to 'political correctness' in language use. It may be that the topic is no longer keenly felt as an issue to be pursued, since there have undoubtedly been some small gains in wider public attitudes and the language topic seems comparatively minor. The insecurity felt by the French Academy and the Press in 1986 is now no longer experienced. Marginalisation of women as such may now be regarded as less of a problem than that of social or class discrimination. The issue of Islamic head-scarves worn by girls in French schools has been less a feminist issue than one of racism. Arlette Laguillier, leader of a small extreme left-wing party and the first female presidential candidate, considered the 'problem' in her case to be less one of her gender than one of the class struggle. But it may also be that French society is still fundamentally sexist, and that the fact that French feminists have generally remained aloof from popular open debate on the topic shows that they feel that there is little likelihood of this changing. Fear that women might take over the heights of society remains high and the insecurity of the policy-makers remains a factor.

The Poor

The definition of who is poor and who is rich changes according to the nature of society and what is regarded as wealth or poverty in relation to the majority: 'Every society gives itself the poor it wants by defining the threshold for allocating assistance' (Paugam, 1993: 24). By 'poor' here is meant those who occupy a non-prestigious social position and who lack economic, social or political power. In sociolinguistics, powerless individuals or groups are said to use language varieties which are determined by their social standing, and there has hence been much analysis of the language use of 'working-class' speakers, particularly in English-speaking countries (cf. Labov, 1966; Trudgill, 1974). The distinctions that are normally made in sociolinguistics between language varieties in one language include those based on the regional origin of the speaker, his or her social class, the purpose or function of the language, and a number of other social factors such as the communication situation, the number of participants, the channel of communication (cf. Ager, 1990: 2; Chambers, 1995; Sanders, 1993: 27-54). The distinction we are making here is however based on one factor only, the social status of the speaker, and although there is general agreement that French does show such a set of 'non-standard' language varieties, or at least that some features of language use correlate with this social dimension, the explanation is that the particular linguistic variables relate to a mix of social determinants, and that, more significantly, their use is situationally rather than socially conditioned (cf. Ager, 1990: 126-43; Baylon, 1996: 71-109; Boyer, 1996: 15-47; Calvet, 1996: 76-91; Gadet, 1992).

Language varieties in French have often been given generally understood names: _l'argot_ (slang), _le verlan_ (reverse slang), _l'hexagonal_ (a convoluted style typical of intellectual verbosity), _langue soutenue_ (careful language), _langue populaire_. These are sometimes more technically called varieties, registers, levels of language or socio-situational categories of language, and five are usually recognised: _populaire, familier, courant, soutenu, académique/littéraire_. Each can be exemplified by different forms of the interrogative (i.e. different variants of the sociolinguistic variable 'interrogation'): the use of the particle -_ti_, lack of inversion, use of _est-ce-que_ + subject + verb, inversion of subject and verb, and special formulae such as _puis-je_. (Sanders, 1993: 29). _Langue populaire_, as used in French, is a widely understood term describing the stigmatised, non-prestigious working-class 'register' of language we are concerned with here. By contrast, _langue familière_ is 'careless' speech while _langue courante_ is everyday language; neither is socially stigmatised. Legitimate, state- and society-approved language is, particularly in French, at least at the level of the everyday and more usually the careful (_soutenu_) register. _Argot,_ whether the traditional form or one of its more recent variants such as the language of inner-city youth, does tend to be socially stigmatised; perhaps it is best thought of as a type of _langue populaire_ .

Langue populaire, particularly in its definition as the language of the mass, has been a target for condemnation almost since dictionaries began. Dictionaries of 'errors' have been published even from Gallo-Roman times and have incidentally been found to be good sources from which linguists of today can recreate the popular forms of the time although then they were intended to help users rid their speech of 'defective forms' (Gadet, 1992: 14-18). It is particular forms of speech, words such as _zinzin_ or _cinoche_, grammatical usages such as _le livre à ma soeur_ or _quand que c'est qu'il le fera_, pronunciation like that of _alors_ with a vowel like that of _peur_, which are condemned as plebeian, although any one of these may also be widely used in other registers. Hence _langue populaire_ is recognised as such by the consistent use of a number of such characteristics. Interestingly, what is stigmatised has remained remarkably consistent over the years, and many of the 'errors' of today's _langue populaire_ were condemned as being non-legitimate usage even in the seventeenth century.

Because _langue populaire_ can be recognised in speech, but is not formally described, condemnation of it tends to be limited to individual linguistic items. In this sense, state language policy on socially conditioned varieties of language is not clearly identifiable in the way that condemnation of a regional language is. Despite the _Tolérances_ published by the Ministry of Education (1997: lists of acceptable forms which markers must allow in student scripts) or the programmes and annual guidance for education, which again list acceptable and non-acceptable forms, language policy in this area is more usually at the micro level, with individual teachers or members of the public noting and condemning examples of non-standard language use. There are comments in dictionaries and in published lists of errors; some of these are the work of the French Academy or of its individual members.

The danger that the French of the socially marginalised classes presents for standard French is twofold. It might corrupt the existing standard and thus make it worthless. A second danger, and this is sometimes seen as a worse outcome, is that the language of the mass might replace existing forms and thus take over the commanding heights of society: it could be 'advanced' French or the French of the future. Language policies as such hence take two forms: frequent condemnation of the 'incorrect' French of the working classes, stigmatised as non-prestigious; and, as a second line of attack, ensuring the preservation of, and access to, standard French for all. Both policies can be traced in education, in the definition of the syllabuses and methods to be used for teaching the standard language, and in the Inspectorate's reports on the effectiveness of these. They can also be seen in the classes and provision made to counter illiteracy, particularly among adults. Illiterate adults have generally suffered more than most from an accumulation of handicaps in their lives: government actions aimed at improving literacy have the consequence of helping inclusion (cf. Ager, 1996b: 78-80). Although until the late 1970s illiteracy was said not to exist in France, the 1989 count was 2,200,000, or 6.3% of the adult population with severe difficulties and some six million (10.6%) with difficulty in writing. For these, provision is made through a variety of public and private agencies, including adult education conducted mainly through the Centre National des Arts et Métiers and its regional centres. Again, the policy is to teach standard French and to make no allowance for non-standard varieties (Borkowski and Dumoulin, 1994; Charlot, 1994).

The relationship between such language policies and generally accepted attitudes towards the popular mass can be seen in a number of ways, particularly in the belief that socially marginalised classes themselves might destroy standards, and that the masses might themselves take over the reigns of power from the elite. Policies for social inclusion to prevent this can hence be traced back, certainly to the Revolution. Defining social responsibility for the poor was indeed a main concern of the Revolution, which tried to ensure that charity was no longer their only recourse: 'No state has yet considered the poor in its Constitution...It has often been a matter of giving charity to the poor, never showing the rights the poor have over society, or those society has over them' (quoted in Paugam, 1993: 89). The RMI (Revenu Minimum d'Insertion), created in 1988 as the first general French income support mechanism to act as a final safety-net, nonetheless had to wait until long after such systems had been put in place in other countries, although the minimum wage (the SMIG (Salaire Minimum Interprofessionnel Garanti) was created in 1950, changing its name and basis in 1970 to the index-linked Salaire Minimum de Croissance (SMIC)). The motive of the 1988 Socialist government was the same as that of the Assembly of 1790: 'The requirement for solidarity is imposed upon us: it is a political, moral and also an economic requirement' and one imposed on the whole nation, according to Minister Claude Evin, quoted in Paugam, 1993: 90. This policy of inclusion covered all residents in France (including foreigners), but excluded those under 25, who are also required to make themselves available for 'actions d'insertion', agreed with the recipient: both these requirements imitate the Revolutionary requirement for citizens to be aged 25 at least and to be worthy of citizenship. In 1994, nearly two million people (including dependants) benefited from RMI. Like the RMI, policies for correcting illiteracy also had the aim of helping inclusion and preventing exclusion, or at least minimising its effects for those said to be functionally illiterate. We have noted elsewhere the correlation distinctly and deliberately made in France between poverty and illiteracy, and the welcome given in the early 1980s to attempts made to tackle both (Ager, 1996b: 78-80; see also Borkowski and Dumoulin, 1994: 244).

But if the explanation for language and other social policies intended to help the poor and powerless in society to gain access to dignity is that the state knew this represented a political, moral and economic imperative, why had such policies not been set up earlier? If these policies reflect revolutionary and republican ideals, why did it take two centuries before they were effectively put in place? Why is the language of the poor, and why are the poor themselves, still excluded from mainstream society? The only credible explanation must be that the poor and the powerless represented and represent too much of a danger: the French Revolution was a revolution by the middle classes, not by those at the bottom of society who still represented a force for evil. The nineteenth century process of integration, through education, of the 'barbarians who threaten society from the outskirts of our industrial towns', as the poor were described in 1832 (quoted in Charlot, 1994: 345), came about through the operation of three guiding principles. The first requirement was 'political and ideological integration in the state'; the second, also necessary if society was not to be destroyed, was to foster order, work and discipline as a moral requirement; the third, more philanthropical even if inspired by basically economic motives, aimed at ensuring the lower social classes could acquire a minimum of dignity and the chance to escape from utter poverty through education. Educational policies, including language policies, for the mass have hence always been political and based on the concept of assimilation to the Republican and Revolutionary values defining the nation. Indeed, the aim of the educational policies of the nineteenth century was twofold: for the successful, it enabled assimilation no matter what the political and social standing of the child; but the system was designed in such a way that the definition of success itself ensured that only those with a certain cultural background and the ability to deploy it could succeed, so the bourgeoisie ensured reproduction of its leading role even within an apparently open and equal educational system (see Gerbod, 1981). One cannot even avoid political connotations in naming social classes in French: many names have direct political implications in French which the English translations do not possess. The *sous-prolétariat* is the lower working class, the *classe ouvrière* the working class, the *petite bourgeoisie* the lower middle-class and the *haute bourgeoisie* the upper middle class, but each of the French terms has a resonance of hatred or approval according to their use by one or another political grouping (Baylon, 1996: 82). This background, the central importance of the political state, colours all French discussion of assimilation and integration, and indeed of democracy itself, and goes some way to explaining the nature of language policies, as well as for example the often violent opposition to any notion of selection at the point of entry to schools or universities.

There may be a number of other explanations, each based on a different interpretation of the nature of society and possible responses to it. If one accepts that linguistic variation between the social categories exists, there is less agreement about what such variation means, with at least three possible interpretations. For those working in the Marxist tradition, dominant social classes are able to enunciate a legitimate vision of the world while dominated classes passively accept this hegemony. Linguistic variation differentiates groups of speakers and those who master standard language distinguish themselves thus from those who do not: it is linguistic variation and society's general awareness of it which is a factor of distinctiveness, and society must constantly face the class struggle between the 'linguistic capital' of those who master standard French, and the powerlessness of those who do not. While education may thus provide an opportunity for all to acquire such linguistic capital, there is an inbuilt advantage for those whose families already possess it, and immense difficulty for those families who do not already use standard French. Stratificational sociology sees things differently. Individuals, differentiated by a number of factors including education, income, profession, may show different characteristics such as language use. But social mobility enables individuals to move freely through a range of 'classes', not just two, and any struggle is a matter of individuals not classes. On this explanation, individuals from a lower social class show the openness of French society and its inherent stability when they succeed in examinations. They can only succeed in examinations by adopting the language (and culture) of the elite, but if they do so successfully there is no bar to their social mobility. A third interpretation is based on the idea of the social market: individuals will master the language varieties they need in order to improve their socio-economic status, and will deploy their ability in a range or repertoire of varieties according to personal advantage in different interactions. Again, a successful individual shows how the spur of his or her desire to make social progress has resulted in inclusion via a normal social mechanism. But the individual has not, in this interpretation, been absorbed by the new social identity; he or she retains the ability to speak differently in different social situations.

Linguistic determinism which says that 'powerless speakers' have only 'powerless language' available to them indeed seems, on the basis of experience, too restrictive an explanation. It is common experience that we all use a number of different language varieties in different circumstances, and there is no doubt that 'powerful' people are perfectly capable of using 'non-powerful' language in appropriate circumstances, and that the converse is often true. There are many examples of successful French people in language-dependent professions like politics, literature, journalism or education whose social background was not that of the elite. Nonetheless, there is no doubt that the use of power language by those without power in society is much more difficult than the converse, and this fact has led to numerous educational and language policies in Britain, the United States and elsewhere based on the concept of language deficit, or on policies for correcting such inequality (see Tollefson, 1991). No such policy aimed at giving increased prestige to a socially stigmatised variety has ever been adopted in France, as far as we know; instead, the policy has been one of overt and covert condemnation of the stigmatised varieties.

The contemporary education system is based on the principle of equality of opportunity. Theoretically at least, all children have the same right of access to education and all may progress through the ladder of annual examinations from age 5 to age 16 and beyond. All may gain access to standard French. But there is no longer one pathway: on conclusion of collège (notionally age 14), children may have to repeat a year's education, join the lycée for general education or join a lycée professionnel or technologique, and increasing possibilities of choice of options give access to different qualifications. Designed for economic outputs to the labour market (and with school places thus costed and provided through the government's five-year plans), this system provides less social integration than was the aim of the nineteenth century and since the 1960s has aimed more at economic integration. Since 1989 the aims of education have been to reduce failure and raise the numbers and proportions of young people qualified; but in a climate of unemployment the lack of economic integration has also ensured a lack of social integration. It is not just the academic failures of the educational system who constitute the excluded, but also those, with qualifications, who can find no way to gain entry to society. Those leaving education in the last quarter of the twentieth century were more or less successful in the formal education examinations as Table 3.1 shows.

Table 3.1 Success in formal examinations

Year	1973	1980	1993
Level I, II and III (*deug* +)	132,700	160,700	293,300
Level IV (baccalaureate)	145,400	144,700	216,400
Level V (CAP + BEP)	333,100	395,000	202,300
Level VI (no qualifications)	224,000	131,800	64,200
Total leavers	835,200	832,200	775,200

Source: Quid, 1997: 1443
Note: *DEUG: Diplome d'Etudes Universitaires Générales,* the minimum higher education qualification. Baccalaureate: obtained at age 18 (unless a year has been repeated). CAP and BEP: vocational qualifications obtained at the end of compulsory schooling (notionally age 16).

The fear of exclusion through not possessing adequate qualifications could hardly be shown more clearly than in Table 3.1: there has been a massive shift towards gaining qualifications and towards improving them. But the fact that this has not always led to economic integration is evident in the Aubry employment proposals of 1997, which made the emergency employments by state organisations available to those with any level of qualifications and were not directed solely towards unqualified young people.

Immigrants and Foreigners

Linguistic reaction to the 'menace' of immigrant speech has taken two forms: protection of standard French from whatever danger might be presented to it by immigrants, and some limited degree of support for immigrants and their language(s). Such support was intended, not to recognise immigrant languages and thus give them status, but to provide immigrants with a way of retaining links with their original languages and cultures, in the expectation that they might return 'home'. The linguistic threat to contemporary French takes a number of forms:

direct borrowing from immigrant languages; the use of calques and the imitation of the syntax, mode of expression or style of the immigrant language; and, more directly, forms of expression in French such as *verlan*, which have been so taken over by some young and immigrant groups as now to be regarded as almost characteristic of them. Protection against these falls into the general field of the teaching of standard French.

Official language policy towards immigrants and foreigners (no distinction is made) hence takes two approaches: the provision of means of access to French as a second language, for both adults and children; and a very limited language maintenance policy. The latter policy was based on an earlier understanding of immigration as temporary, economic and short-term. Its purposes were to enable citizens of sending countries to maintain their links with these, and particularly links with the education systems. Provision is made through a programme, mainly in primary schools (Enseignement des Langues et Cultures d'Origine (ELCO)), for the languages of the countries from which immigration came during the 1960s to the 1980s (Varro, 1992; Ager, 1995; DGLF, 1997, Annexes: 56). The programmes started in 1973 and are funded by the 'sending' countries themselves, who provide the teachers and materials. Classes, for 72,908 children in 1995-6, are given in Arabic (by Algeria, Morocco and Tunisia), Italian, Portuguese, Spanish, Turkish, and Serbo-Croat, although since this latter language was supported by the former Yugoslavia it has now disappeared from the official statistics. A limited number of bilingual classes also exists. The teaching in schools is carried out by teachers who come from the relevant countries, and the curriculum and its delivery are under their control. Necessarily, since the teachers are not part of the normal French system, the assessment of the children's ability in their own language is not taken into account, while the quality of teaching is subject to variation according to the resources and intentions of the sending countries. In some cases the teaching may be concerned less with language and more with religious or cultural aspects, particularly of Islam, and this makes teaching of Arabic popular with children from 'Black' Africa, who often gravitate to such classes since their own languages are rarely on offer. This may not be what French language policy wanted or wants, but since the French authorities have washed their hands of language maintenance as a state policy, may be inevitable. There is no policy or legislation on the status of these languages outside education, and they are in effect ignored by the State in terms of any provision in services (Post Office, road signs, material for health or social services), although their written forms can be widely seen in street markets, shops and elsewhere in daily life.

The current general policy for foreign and immigrant children aims at a global approach, involving other ministries more specifically concerned with 'integration'. The intention is said to be to ensure integration - 'knowledge and respect for French cultural values by young foreigners as well as knowledge and respect of foreign cultures by French youth; not assimilation aimed at denying the original culture' - as rapidly as possible, with academic success for children of diverse social and cultural backgrounds being one of the objectives of the 1989 Education Act. The process is one of deliberate 'inter-cultural education' whose aims are 'to make foreign cultural values known, to examine other civilisations, to use the notion of cultural support and to cause reflection on phenomena which present problems'.

Despite the creation of classes for reception (Classes d'initiation expérimentales) and adaptation (Classes d'adaptation dans l'enseignement du second degré) in the early 1970s, there remains a serious lack of appropriate material, teachers and training for teachers for French as a second language. French is taught to immigrant children mainly in special groups withdrawn from normal programmes, in addition to normal classes. The main problem is clearly that of segregation and of the fairly recent policy change from attempts at assimilation to inter-cultural education. Segregation is often reinforced by the provision made for ELCO teaching, when the children are again withdrawn from classes. The extensive provision made in France for parental involvement in school often confuses the parents of immigrant children, who may be inarticulate in French, be unaware of the system and hence unable to influence it. Conversely, parental pressure to change the French system, for example by encouraging daughters to leave school early, means that comparison with other children and their success rates is difficult. Generally speaking, immigrant children do not succeed well as a group: they are proportionally very likely to join specialised education provision for the educationally subnormal, to be proportionately more present in vocational education, and not to stay on at school in large numbers after compulsory education finishes at age 14. Overall, although there may not be a deliberate policy of exclusion, in practice immigrant children are likely to find themselves excluded from normal schooling unless they have been born in France and have early acquired 'native' competence.

Outside the education system, there is little provision to teach French to adult foreigners:

Few employers offer linguistic training. Adult literacy classes are organized by a number of voluntary agencies, but the availability of courses is patchy: women...have often found it difficult to attend. (Hargreaves, 1995: 99)

Indeed, surveys conducted in 1995 showed that the places available covered less than ten percent of the demand (DGLF, 1996, 2, VI, 3). As a result, competence in French is low among adults, with some 38% of Portuguese males who came to France in 1970 speaking little or no French twenty years later. 57% of Algerian females and 16% of Algerian males, but 100% of Turkish females, had little or no French in the same survey. The Social Affairs Ministry has set up as a response to such statistics a needs survey and has started training the trainers during 1996 and 1997, while the Fonds d'Action Sociale devoted 232 million francs to improving language teaching for immigrants in 1996. At the same time, schemes have been started aimed at providing language training for women and pre-school children. France is a late starter in these matters, but the issue is being followed, still with the aim of integration.

Fear of foreigners is thought by many to lie at the heart of French rejection of them, and hence explains the weakness of language policy aimed at maintaining the use of their languages. *La France raciste*, the title of an influential book of 1992 by Wievorka, amply demonstrates the nature of the fear felt by some and shows how the modern version of this fear had not been studied in detail before the mid-1980s. The fear consists of the belief that French identity is being swamped or destroyed, associated with the feeling that the only solution to the problem of immigration is to reject and exclude all foreigners: 'We must fight so that France stays France'. In particular the religious fear of Islam and its effect on the 'Judeo-Christian' nature of France is strong: 'Pierre Bernard (Mayor of Montfermeil) justifies his actions by his faithfulness towards Catholicism, constantly referred to by the municipal bulletin'. There is paradoxically a fear of the immigrants' power, in sexuality and reproductive capacity: 'the birth-rate of foreigners is four times greater than that of the French', in political domination and in 'their' ability to exploit 'our' networks of social aid: 'We are under siege, will soon be dominated...most immigrants do not try to integrate but to take advantage of us'. The extent to which racism forms a component part of the culture of the police force was extensively studied in an analysis of police discourse in the same volume. In general discourse, too, amply exemplified in the study, 'the strength with which statements come from below and concentrate on the other - the immigrant, the black, the gypsy - is impressive':

Racism combines two fundamental principles. On one hand it naturalises the Other in order to show his inferiority, constructing a racial hierarchy to more or less compensate for a social hierarchy, which is under threat, has disappeared or been overturned. On the other hand, it postulates an irreducible difference in order to demonstrate a supposed incompatibility between French national culture and that of immigrant or foreigner. (Wievorka, 1992: 341-2)[29]

Racism is generally agreed, by the French themselves, to be widespread (89% of those surveyed in 1992), with its principal victims the Maghrebins (rejected by 83%) or their offspring (les Beurs, rejected by 65%) (Policar, 1994: 23). The economic fear, too, a major component of Front National speeches and amply represented in _La France Raciste_, is now a commonplace of French thinking and appears even in the opinion of more left-wing thinkers:

> Such a reform (i.e. of the Pasqua laws against immigration) even though it might be sympathetically regarded, cannot be put into effect in the context of massive unemployment: one would run the risk among other things of destroying, through competition from many workers ready to concede anything, the social protection mechanisms which benefit resident wage earners, whether French or foreigners (Joffrin in _Libération_, 27.8.1997).[30]

All these themes form part of the ideology of the Front National, which presents itself as representing the true ethnic heart of the nation and thus contrasts with the Revolutionary/Republican concepts of identity through voluntary membership of the socio-legal nation-state (Flood, 1997: 103-39). Instead, the FN underlines the need to demonstrate ethnic belonging and an affective desire to be part of the national community. Inclusion and exclusion are fundamental to such concern with the politics of identity, and the FN is opposed to the 'collusion of the evil forces' which the establishment, the state and its bureaucracies have set up: 'the core of national identity and the true basis of citizenship are shared ethnicity and participation in a common culture'. There is a constant fear of social breakdown, and the incompatibility of Islam with European or French cultural models means that the only answer for France is the exclusion of Muslims:

> The presence of large concentrations of non-European immigrants in or around major cities is blamed for rising crime, civil unrest, urban decay, the swamping and deterioration of schools, alien religious and cultural practices (such as polygamy or female circumcision) plus the imposition of colossal burdens on the welfare system, hence on taxation...Islam is entirely incompatible with secular European culture...it is a threat to Europe. (Flood, 1997: 117)

The facts of the situation are less our concern here than the perceptions of them which are held by the French population, by politicians and by those responsible for policy-making. But in France, the question of immigration quickly absorbs a number of others, and 'immigrants' are equated with 'foreigners', with 'Maghrebins' and followers of Islam, and rapidly thence with 'terrorists' and eventually 'criminals'. So the immigration issue rapidly becomes a way of affirming French identity, is racialised, becomes a religious issue, an economic one, and is then criminalised. It should be remembered that although the four million registered foreigners theoretically form only eight percent or so of the population, those children born and living in France who have at least one parent born in France acquired French nationality at age 18. This was obtained automatically until 1993. In addition, many people born in former colonies have French nationality. There are still nonetheless at least a million children, regarded as foreigners, in French schools. Many foreigners in France come from other European countries, particularly Portugal (900,000) and Spain (300,000), although North Africans (Algeria, Morocco and Tunisia) account for about one million. Some 600,000 people, some with and some without French nationality, originate from the overseas DOM and TOM and are sometimes regarded as immigrants; people born in Algeria could choose double nationality on independence in 1962, so many of them are already classified as French citizens, and their children, if born in France become French citizens automatically. In addition, ad-hoc immigration (*l'immigration sauvage*), welcomed until 1975, has now become clandestine and illegal, affecting anywhere from 300,000 to a million unofficial and illegal residents according to the commentator. Overall, and depending how 'foreigners' and immigrants are counted, there are anything between two and eighteen million such people of different ages in France. Islam is far and away France's second religion; second and third generation immigrants are assimilated to different degrees. The debate on such questions as nationality, citizenship and race is central to political concerns today, as is shown by the speed with which the Pasqua laws were introduced on the victory of the Right in 1993 and the fact that the question of their abrogation was almost the first issue dealt with in the summer of 1997 after the return of the Socialist government.

Jospin's declaration of policy on obtaining power in 1997 again makes clear how immigration is viewed. Racism and xenophobia are firmly rejected. But there remains a need for an immigration policy accepted by all, and one which retains the ability to exclude:

Residence is part of the French definition of the Nation...Nothing is more foreign to France than xenophobic discourse. France must define a firm, worthy immigration policy, without denying our own values, without compromising our social equilibrium...Immigration is an economic, social and human reality, which must be organised, controlled and mastered as well as possible, while affirming the rights of the Nation and respecting human rights...A policy of Republican integration, definite and generous, such as will gain citizens' approval, will be implemented...Irregular immigration and clandestine work - which does not just apply to foreigners - will be strongly combated because they both compromise integration and are contrary to immigrants' dignity. (Jospin, 1997)[31]

In summary, French state policy towards the recognition of immigrant communities, their culture and their language(s) seems even harsher than that towards indigenous minorities. But its origin derives from a similar fear of social fragmentation and disruption. This is true whether the fear is of possible destruction of universalism or of ethnic Frenchness. Fear that the universalism associated with republicanism, individualism, the voluntary social contract and the rejection of particularisms might be destroyed is one motive. Equally strong is the fear that _jus solis_ might prevail over the _jus sanguinis_, and the myth of ethnic Frenchness might be destroyed:

it is feared that any official recognition or support for cultural diversity will inevitably threaten the political integrity of the one and indivisible republic. (Hargreaves, 1997: 197)

Language policy is, for Louis-Jean Calvet, (1993:105-16), not so much negative towards such minorities as completely absent. Policy authorities are so scared of the issue that they turn a blind eye to it: 'French legislation...remains completely silent on the question of minority languages' . His view of the future is that there will be:

a slow assimilation to the dominant language, French, with only marginal borrowings from other languages. A strong monolingual vision of the state, culture, and communication, a centralised administration and the standardisation of French, all militate against any sharing of languages. There is no socially valued model of bi- or multi-lingualism. (Calvet, 1993: 116)

Chapter 4
Fear mixed with Guilt: the Myth of Inclusion

There are also two rather more general explanations for these French language policies towards various social groups or categories, policies which aim to reject their specific linguistic codes. Both these explanations are based on insecurity, worry that the poor, women, immigrants and foreigners, and the young may simply not be prepared to assimilate to the French conception of the integrated nation-state based on individual voluntarism. Groups of people, 'communities' in the English and American sense of the term, may thus be rejecting the norms of French society and particularly its linguistic norm, standard French. A first explanation is based on the fear that such non-co-operating groups may simply not accept the definition of society that historical and political traditions have developed. A second one is a more contemporary fear: that some groups reject the set of shared values and beliefs French people (are expected to) currently hold. Either way, mainstream society is afraid of certain social groups, and of their language use, fears they will destroy its views on language standardisation or on language quality, and as a consequence, fears that society itself may break down and disintegrate. Such fears strengthen the myth of inclusion.

The myth of inclusion may itself be outdated in contemporary societies: the concept of the inclusive society is felt by many thinkers today to be a relic of the past. For many people, in France as elsewhere, the shared values of the past are less and less relevant to today's concerns. A feeling of guilt about this inclusiveness can thus occasionally be detected. The idea of the all-inclusive, cohesive society, cosily sharing a set of selfish values aimed at keeping distinctiveness inside and ignoring all who do not accept the guiding principles and are not prepared to lose their group or community culture in order to absorb that of the greater unit,   seems less and less to respond to the conditions of modern society: mass immigration, the new social role of women, earlier maturity of youth, the continuing presence of the unemployed, the homeless or the deprived. The myth of inclusion is today less supremely self-confident than it was, even in France. Nonetheless the supporters of the inclusive society and its myths are still vigorous, whether in political parties or in sociological discussion.

Defining Society: Language and Inclusion in Historical Perspective

The most obvious explanation for the language policies affecting minorities is that social minorities which do not share the language, language variety, culture, or values of the majority are, at least potentially, a danger to the majority itself and should hence either be forcibly assimilated or deliberately kept at bay. The danger is an exact parallel to that presented by regional language varieties: language symbolises a different social existence which could destroy that of the majority. The 'majority', in this sense, is the socially dominant group even if, like any elite, they may actually not be numerically preponderant. The socially dominant group is that which determines the nature of the society in which it resides, and is the group whose social practices are the norms of that society: these are then accepted by all in society as being (the only acceptable) French practices. Social practices which threaten these also threaten the existence of (that form of) the society. Just as 'non-French' regional identities threaten 'French' identity, so too do 'non-French' social identities; they are just as feared, and fought against as systematically, although not in quite the same way. Regional languages have been systematically excluded in the hope of destroying regional identities, but while a similar attempt at destroying social minorities could be made, the language varieties typical of such minorities are much less clearly identifiable and hence more difficult to attack openly. It is here that the notion of the 'quality' of language has been used. If the language to be rejected can be identified, not as the language of a social group, but as language of poor quality, then its rejection may be a more acceptable act. It may be for this reason that there exists a long tradition in French of linguistic condemnation of 'faults' and 'errors' in language use.

The process of marginalisation and exclusion relies firstly on identification of a particular language variety or type of discourse as being typical of a definable social group and different from that of the majority. This difference then becomes the symbol of exclusion: this language use is treated as outside society, the imagined community to which all (should) belong. The close association between language and the French Republic, the political community which is France, means that defending one means defending the other. Those who attack French, or use French of poor quality, are also attacking France; if French is not protected, then France will be destroyed. At this point, protection of the language is protection of the nation. The various forms of nationalism combine: cultural nationalism and ethnic nationalism become one with the Republican, Revolutionary and universalist form to equate the nation with society and with the state, and with its standard language use regarded as a sacrosanct symbol.

In historical terms, this attitude of condemnation and the establishment of linguistic barriers to social inclusion is by no means new. But the details, the actual definition of the linguistic barriers, necessarily change. Historically, this social attitude of exclusion predates the Revolution. In medieval times the notion of the language of the courtier, of the style of French suitable for polite society, included both the ideas of *pur* and of *bel*: both a pure French, or one which avoided regionally or socially marked terms and was hence appropriate for aristocratic ears, and a good style of language selection which made the discourse appropriate for elegant and delicate subjects and a literary style. Those who aspired to inclusion in Royal society had to adopt the language and the style which defined it: 'The world of the courtier was made up of people who recognised each other through their shared values, which everyone accepted and tried to put into practice, and among which figured qualities of expression...To be admitted as a member of the society of the courtier it was essential to use fine words' (Chaurand, 1995).[32] But by the same token, medieval society was limited and exclusive, uniform and restricted. Only in such circumstances could the insistence on *belle langue et courtoisie*, on fine language associated with the values of the royal court, be realised. There was at this time, too, a major need in linguistic terms to manage the inflow of new terms from Latin, from other languages like Italian, from dialects and regional languages, and from technical registers, as the changes in society demanded new forms of expression.

The main period during which the notion of quality was developed in France is the seventeenth and eighteenth centuries, the period when *le bon usage* was the criterion. There are many histories of French which detail the actions of the grammarians of the time, their preferences for the language choices of the 'sanest part of the Court' and their actions in support of the social elite (see the references in Lodge, 1993). It was at this point, of codification of the standard, that French was evaluated as precise, clear, elegant, beautiful, measured, the language of reason, pure, logical, perfect, universal, rich and having a biunique relationship to reality (i.e. containing few synonyms, and few words with multiple meanings).[33] It was at this point, too, that the association arose between standardisation and social condemnation of poor quality, so that standard French became not only the language of efficient communication, using as few words as possible, but also that of effective communication, being as clear as possible. Protection from the twin evils, which were thus lack of clarity and lack of social identification with the elite, followed.

The nineteenth century was the century of social mobility. Through such social upheavals as the Revolution and the Napoleonic Empire the social elite became less aristocratic, although more bourgeois and certainly not open to the mass until the twentieth century. Three levels of public instruction were created in 1793 (primary, secondary and higher); secondary and higher education was a state monopoly after 1808, although the Falloux Law of 1850 allowed Church secondary schools; the Guizot Law of 1833 created a primary school in every commune; in 1881 Jules Ferry as Education Minister made primary education free, compulsory and secular. Primary education was open to all, but secondary and higher levels were for smaller numbers and access to the elite was through the jealously guarded baccalaureate. The century was notable for its views on social exclusion and on the necessity for keeping the great unwashed away from the levers of power. It is this feeling of insecurity, of the dangers of social expansion, that can be identified in language attitudes of the time. The first need was to ensure stability, to prevent change in this most perfect of instruments: 'French is an inestimable jewel which must be preserved as one would preserve a fabulous treasure'. The second was to prevent the language from losing its inestimable qualities as one faces up to the necessity of coining new terms and uses. It is at this point that 'grammarians' became the arbiters and the judges, gatekeepers handing down decisions on which new words are acceptable and which forms can be tolerated, and on the linguistic means for accessing social roles which are new. The political nature of such judgements was well known. There had been a well-publicised attack on the 'excesses' of the Revolution's language policy in a pamphlet called *Le Fanatisme dans la langue révolutionnaire*; comments and criticisms of newspaper style often found it difficult to separate language from content, and 'it was never easy to distinguish the linguistic from the political or at least from polemics' (Glatigny, 1995).[34]

But the notion of language quality, of the appropriate way of registering one's membership of society, is also a modern concept. The

belief that society is held together by its common language, by its selection of a means of expression which consecrates unity, shared values and, through its historical development and traditions, gives access to the meaning of French society, is still evident in almost every part of the DGLF reports to Parliament on the implementation of the Toubon Law, in public pronouncements on language, and in such evidence of public attitudes as the correspondence to newspapers or the comments of contributors to Web sites on French language. In this respect, legislators and politicians are at one with the French public:

> If we give way over our language we shall purely and simply be swept away (President Pompidou, quoted in Legendre, 1994: 1).
> We have duties towards the whole of the nation: French is the language of the Republic; it is the language of national integration, that which guarantees equality for everybody, which ensures the social tie... French is a language of liberty, of democracy. It is the language which inspires many prisoners who have long dreamt of democracy, freedom, independence! The role of the government and the Parliament is to tell all such people that France will not fail in its duty (Culture Minister Toubon in *Journal Officiel*, 12.4.1994).
> Whatever the public authorities want, a policy of promoting French only succeeds if it obtains the support of civil society and everybody's agreement ...A better understanding, in France itself, of what is at stake in the use and the legal status of French, as well as in promoting of multilingualism, is indispensable (DGLF, 1996, 3, II).
> The analysis of letters received by the DGLF...shows an increase in interest in what is at stake in the national and international use of French (and no longer just its quality)...decrease in the number of letters on the media, which targeted essentially the quality of the language used by journalists...and which constituted practically half the letters received before 1994. (DGLF, 1996, 1, I, 1)[35]

This explanation for the motive of insecurity in relation to social groups and categories like women, the young, the poor or immigrants relies on a common sense of history and tradition, which together have produced French society. In this sense it is one of the basic myths of French society that French civil society forms a perfect whole, clear, precise and logical, stable and unified, moderate, elegant and reasonable, and that its language uniquely reflects the same attributes. The idea that France is bound together by its language, that its language forms an indissoluble part of French identity, is a major component of the belief in a uniquely French identity. But the myth is not merely affirmative; it is also defensive, a protection against the world outside.

The myth of inclusion implies also the myth of exclusion. In order for citizens to be inside the defensive wall, there must exist people, groups, organisations, communities which lie outside. And in the history of France the Revolution's abolition of aristocratic privileges, on 4th August 1794, is strongly associated with the removal of privileges or exceptional treatment for any group or community in society.

The diabolisation of these excluded groups lies at the heart of political and social philosophies like that of the Front National and other, often extremist, political groupings. The popularity of such Right-wing thinking among French voters, who have in recent times often given significant support to such views, and among intellectuals, reflects the history of belief in the necessity for socialisation and in condemnation of those who will not conform. The power of traditionalism and of the collective memory should not be underestimated. But it is about the potential extremism of such a view that the guilt we have referred to above is centred. The DGLF, and the public authorities, realised soon after the passage of the Toubon Law in 1994 that the objections to it by the Socialist party at the time, and the reflection of these objections in much of the Press and in the Constitutional Council, were not solely political games. They also meant there was an absolute necessity to ensure that the general public, in addition to convinced politicians, could accept a policy which placed traditional inclusiveness above everything. To do this, not merely would the policy have to be presented in such a way as to counter the guilt feeling associated with the myth of inclusion but also it would necessarily and paradoxically have to accept other languages.

Contemporary Values

A second general explanation for French attitudes towards questions of social inclusion and exclusion lies in the self-image French people have of themselves today. Here the past is less important. Attitudes towards language now rely on the values and beliefs individuals hold in their understanding of what it means to be French in the year 2000 and beyond. Pride in being French has a considerable effect on what people say about language, and hence on what governments do about it. More general values, too, how far people define and share attitudes about a range of anti-social actions, correlate with their feelings about the society in which they live, in all its manifestations. The two sets of values we shall discuss are the specifically linguistic ones associated with purism, and the specifically social ones connected with perceptions of the other.

Purism

Defensive reactions aimed at protecting the 'pure' version of the language, and at rejecting others as 'impure', are common in many countries. Thomas (1991) categorises purism as archaising, elitist, ethnographic, reformist or xenophobic, according to which aspect of language use is rejected. The archaising purist believes that the language of the past is always better and hence rejects modern usage as inferior. The language reformer tries to bring about developments in the language to strengthen its strong points. The elitist form of purism, with its belief that the language of the higher social classes represents the best in the language, most clearly reflects social purism. But the different belief, that the language of a particular rural group, 'undefiled' by urban corruption, is typified by respect for the Loire valley accent as the best French, much to be preferred to any other. Xenophobic purism is widespread, and is of course closely associated with racist views and more generally with hatred of the other.

The purism of the past, the love for language forms which represent the moment of perfection of French which is usually agreed to be the eighteenth century and the language of the major literary figures of the time, is one of the basic motives for the repeated beliefs that today's language use does not represent true France. But three of the other purist reactions, the elitist, the ethnographic and the xenophobic, seem particularly relevant in discussing the insecurity motive in relation to contemporary French society, its uniqueness and its inclusiveness. Each represents a different explanation for policies aimed at excluding those who are not of the elite, do not represent the 'real' heart of the nation, or who are simply foreigners.

An impression of the way in which such attitudes are expressed can be gleaned from *Le Figaro Littéraire* of 8 February 1996. Ten 'threats to French' were described by Claude Duneton. Some of these were concerned with the dangers posed by English which we shall examine in Chapter five, but numbers five to nine of Figure 4.1 have their origin in a particular view of society, of 'modern' educational methods and imply a particular set of values. The same supplement presented the views of fifteen 'personalities' from a number of fields, who were again asked to identify contemporary dangers to the French language. The answers illustrate practically all the varieties of purism and show how few of these significant representatives of the Paris elite were prepared to consider that French was not in extreme danger. Just two, both linguists (Rey and Hagège), made it clear that the question was not really appropriate, but both still gave areas where French could be better served (by more pride in language, and by less stress on what was 'wrong').

(1)	Dependence on English.
(2)	Borrowings from English.
(3)	Slippage in meaning and moves towards the adoption of English meanings.
(4)	Computer jargon.
(5)	Radio and TV broadcasts.
(6)	Poor or uninspired teaching of French language.
(7)	Poor education in the basics, and, at a later stage, of the vocabulary necessary to understand philosophy.
(8)	Fashion in education propagated by the 'educational sciences';
(9)	destruction of the former system ('before 1960') and lack of present-day linguistic policy.
(10)	No commitment by intellectuals to the protection of French.

Source: *Le Figaro Littéraire*, 8.2.1996[36]

Figure 4.1 Threats to French

Apart from numerous comments on Franglais and on dangers from America, from international commerce or from globalisation, the dangers came from social change and from attacks on social stability. Some of them had to do with inadequate modern methods for socialisation of young people, and there was condemnation of new linguistic theories and of child-centred educational methods. Political correctness and an attempt to adapt language to those who did not master it indicated, for one contributor, that society had lost its collective memory, its culture and its literature. Language had become too vague, lacked precision and vigour, because people were themselves too vague, too prone to seek words with general meanings and a limp syntax. Alternatively, language that was too pretentious, too technical, too full of circumlocution. Computers forced people to use abstract vocabulary, abbreviations and acronyms like *énarque* (from the initial letters of the Ecole Nationale d'Administration). Modern society itself came in for much condemnation. Pivot condemned the speed of communication and the consequential reduction of language to ever briefer forms and to the truncation of words like *p'tit déj* (*petit déjeuner*), *l'appart* (*l'appartement*), or *la perf* (*la performance*). Modern media took no care over the language it used. Several contributors mentioned the shame and masochism of the French attitude towards language, which forced them to attempt to atone for the past glory of the language and left them without pride. 'French is too complicated a language, elitist, undemocratic'; 'The French should stop being ashamed of their language...Schools should inculcate in children a love of French by showing them it is a beautiful language, full of nuances. It is in this way that they will rediscover pride in French and the desire to promote it'; '(French should) be linked again with its regional and popular bases'.[37]

Participation and the other

A programme of research started in 1981 in an attempt to discover the values of European societies (Ashford and Timms, 1992; Riffault, 1994. Statistics quoted in this paragraph are from Riffault, 1994: 222-3, 287-8 and 329). For our purposes, this survey is of considerable interest in clarifying French attitudes towards inclusion and exclusion, and, like discussion of purism, provides the background for the initiation, the success or failure of language policy (and indeed many other types of social policy). Many of the questions that were posed indicated whether the French sample, chosen to represent the population, felt part of society or not. Pride in one's country is the most obvious test: 32% of the sample was 'very proud' of being French, 48% fairly proud, 8% not very proud, 4% not at all proud (8% no reply). Surprisingly, particularly in view of the myth of the hexagon we examined earlier and the apparent strength of both the revolutionary heritage and the republican values, these figures are not the highest in Europe and are even below the European average. Percentages declaring themselves 'very proud' of belonging to their country were: Ireland 76%, Great Britain 52%, Spain 45%, Portugal 42%, Italy 41%, France 32%, Belgium 27%, Netherlands 22%, Germany 17%, with the European average being 36%.

A second question asked about the degree of confidence French people had in their social institutions, with the results shown in Table 4.1. The French thus have more confidence than other Europeans in those aspects of society which represent the formal state. Particularly interesting is the confidence awarded the civil service (L'Administration), the body of law and the educational system, all of which are the most obvious representatives of the state. Although the police is less respected than in other countries, its percentage approval at 65% is the highest of any of the institutions cited, and overall one must conclude in a population generally approving its society, and wishing to form part of it.

Table 4.1 Confidence in the social institutions

Institution	France	Europe
Police	65	67
Educational system	**64**	**56**
Large firms	**60**	**51**
Laws	**55**	**51**
Army	**54**	**52**
Church	47	48
Civil service	**47**	**39**
Parliament	43	43
Press	**37**	**34**
Trade unions	30	34

Note: Figures are percentages with 'considerable' or 'some' confidence. Institutions in bold are those in which the French have more confidence than other Europeans. Source: adapted from Riffault, 1994: 329.

This degree of public confidence in institutions does not mean that norms of public behaviour are always respected, as Table 4.2 indicates. Making an incorrect declaration for tax purposes, for example, is regarded as more justified than receiving a bribe, travelling without a ticket, or fighting the police. For the purposes of the values survey, such behavioural norms were divided into three categories: those which define public norms - which interest us here; those which define private norms (e.g. approval or condemnation of taking a car without permission, or lying to defend one's personal advantage); and those which define moral norms (e.g. approval or condemnation of abortion or divorce). Results were as in Table 4.2, and generally show that breaking public or private norms scored below 4, while rejecting moral norms often scored above 4. This means, in effect, that the French are more prepared to approve those rejecting moral norms than they are ready to support anti-social actions.

These general scores conceal the fact that older persons generally condemn the disregard of public norms more than younger ones - some 40% of the age group 55-64, as opposed to some 17% of the 18-24 age group. But perhaps the most significant item in the values survey for our purposes is the increasing reserve French people have about the nature of public morality, other people and hence the state, and the increasing dependence on self and the individual to construct a scale of values.

Table 4.2 Justifying anti-social actions

Public norms	Score
Receive unjustified allowances	3.47
Not pay for a train ticket	2.62
Not declare tax	3.08
Receive a bribe	2.11
Fight police	2.73
Private norms	
Taking a car	1.44
Lying for personal advantage	3.74
Moral norms	
Abortion	4.99
Divorce	5.65

Note: Scoring is on a basis of 1 = never justified; 10 = always justified. Hence, the lower the score, the more the behaviour is condemned. Source: adapted from Riffault, 1994: 329

To a certain extent, self-reliance is another aspect of the individualism characteristic of the French approach to the construction of the state. But the strength of external forces in supporting the individual and reinforcing traditional values, seems to be of decreasing importance in contemporary France:

> Until fairly recently, the family environment, school and the Church took on themselves to teach 'values'; the value system seeming to be a tradition. Henceforth young and old apparently no longer have these guides. For example, two people out of three think that "there can never be clear guidance on what is good and what is bad: it depends entirely on the circumstances"...the consequence is the creation of two moralities, one for oneself and one's inner circle, the other "for other people" who will be treated with caution if not distrust. (Riffault, 1994: 298-9)[38]

Such distrust or even fear of the other may lie behind some of the policies, including language policies, which have always tended to exclude groups and minorities from French society. But in recent times, the fear seems to be becoming greater, and policies of exclusion and rejection of the other becoming even more marked.

Boundary Markers

How far does the persistence of the myth of inclusion explain the language policies of rejection felt by the four groups we have examined? Both historically and in terms of the values contemporary French society holds dear, inclusion is very much sought after, and exclusion is regarded as a fundamental problem. Language use, like gender or skin colour, is one of the more obvious boundary markers in society showing where the lines of exclusion are. Since 'other' people mark their difference from 'us' by using a different language or language variety, their language codes could be accepted as different habits and customs could be accepted in order to encourage them to feel part of 'our' society. French society seems more and more ready to condone a number of anti-social habits, ways of living, and even the rejection of society by the homeless or by protesters like lorry drivers or strikers of any sort. But French tradition, and the current attitudes of the population, have strongly condemned any acceptance of linguistic difference. In the schools, in any official situation, in Post Offices, in supermarkets languages other than French, apart from English, are simply not visible. The main reason for this is little to do with official policy, but rather to do with general social attitudes as we have seen. Officially, the policy is that of the Toubon Act: that if other languages are used, they must number at least two. The motivation for this was to prevent English alone being used, and there was little acknowledgement of the existence of community languages in France, despite one comment by a député that over sixty languages could be heard in his constitutency. The Toubon Act now makes it very difficult for other community languages to be displayed, let alone used in such everyday domains as banking, shopping or the Post Office.

French language varieties other than standard French can be heard every day and in a multiplicity of situations, although they are rarely written except in novels like those of Céline or San Antonio. Officially, and this is true of sociolinguistics too, language varieties like slang and popular French are simply regarded as situational variants, available to all and hence simply another indicator of inclusiveness rather than the opposite. Officially, there are no linguistic boundaries to mark.

Chapter 5
Americanophobia: Fear of Franglais

Etiemble Chose His Time Well

'Franglais' is English words and expressions, used in French. The word was coined by René Etiemble in 1964 in the first of a series of books aimed at demonstrating the bad influence of American English on contemporary French, and on showing how eventually French would be destroyed as a language of culture, representing the uniqueness of France, and replaced by a pidgin (*un sabir*), a second-class language fit for those who would be colonised by American commerce and (lack of) intellectual value. Etiemble's examples were chosen for propaganda purposes - the work is not one of linguistic scholarship, but makes a case for greater public awareness of the situation. The examples were arranged in a series of scenarios, short stories and a 'grammar' of the new 'language', deliberately extremist in the selection of American and Americanised vocabulary and expressions said to be used in French. As an example, the following extract is the opening of the book:

> Je vais d'abord vous conter une manière de short story. Elle advint à l'un de mes pals, un de mes potes, quoi, tantôt chargé d'enquêtes full-time, tantôt chargé de recherches part-time dans une institution mondialement connue, le C.N.R.S. Comme ce n'est ni un businessman, ni le fils naturel d'un boss de la City et de la plus glamorous ballet-dancer in the world, il n'a point pâti du krach qui naguère inquiétait Wall Street; mais il n'a non plus aucune chance de bénéficier du boom dont le Stock Exchange espère qu'il fera bientôt monter en flèche la cote des valeurs. Vous réalisez que ce n'est pas un crack, mon copain. J'ajouterai qu'il n'a rien moralement du play boy, ni physiquement du pin up boy. (Underlining by this author).

Most French readers of the time would have had difficulty in understanding many of these words, most of which still do not appear in the annually updated _Petit Larousse_. From the above extract, for example, about half of the fifteen Anglicisms did not appear in 1997:

short story	No: _story_ appears only in _story board_ (noted as a not recommended Anglicism); _short_ only as the English word shorts, and in _shorthorn_, _short ton_, and _short track_
pals	No
full-time, part-time	No. _Time_ appears only in _Time sharing_ (not recommended Anglicism)
businessman	Yes
boss	Yes
glamorous	No, but _glamour_ does
ballet dancer	No, but _ballet_ obviously does
in the world	_in_ does (in the sense of up to date); _world_ only in the expression _world music_
Wall Street	No
boom	Yes
Stock Exchange	No, but _stock_ does as 'English word'
réaliser	Yes
crack	Yes
play boy	Yes
pin up boy	No, but _pin-up_ does. _Boy_ appears defined as 'Young native waiter in former colonies' and as 'Music hall dancer'.

Etiemble gave examples of Anglicisms affecting pronunciation, morphology, grammar and style. His analysis of why these forms were being used was divided into three sections, entitled 'Yankee imperialism and the Atlantic Pact'; 'Publicity'; and 'Atlantic Press, Radio and Tele'. His call to arms followed, again subdivided into 'Making opinion aware'; 'How should we treat foreign words'; and 'Liberalism or direction?' His final conclusion was to call for 'a spontaneous, but persevering, reaction by opinion; failing that, energetic and lasting action by public authorities'. He specified the required actions to be taken by the Public Authorities in detail, with recommendations for each Ministry as well as for publicly owned media, as in Figure 5.1.

Etiemble himself was very conscious of the connection between language and economics, culture and politics. He warned the French of the dangers of 'being led to the abattoir blindfolded', of 'being colonised', of the danger of 'free enterprise being able to ruin France', of the decadence of 'hamburgers, cheeseburgers and eggburgers - filthy

things that I didn't eat even when I was poor in Chicago'. The real
danger was the loss of the language as well as of political influence.

(1)	Radio and television authorities to be 'invited' ('I know what I mean') to speak French, with fines for those using banned words and expressions;
(2)	Ministers of Education and Culture to take steps to ensure that the French Press 'proscribe all Anglo-Saxon words and expressions';
(3)	the Minister for Industry to ensure that the names of French products and trade marks be henceforth labelled in French...why not tax all pidgin signs?
(4)	the Minister for War to insist that the Army use French;
(5)	the Foreign Affairs Minister to ensure that publicity from abroad is either in French or the original language, rather than in Franglais, and that packaging for all imported products be in French;
(6)	the Ministers of Culture, Education and Industry to act in concert to ensure translators are qualified and well recompensed.

Source: Etiemble, 1964: 339-43[39]

Figure 5.1 Etiemble's recommendations for action on language

Etiemble's work first appeared during a flurry of language and
political activity. The Haut Comité pour la Défense et l'Expansion de la
Langue Française was created in 1966 with the task both of defending
French from change at home, and of promoting its use abroad. De
Gaulle had resolved the Algerian conflict in 1962 and was elected
President by popular vote under the new Constitution in 1965. In
politics, France faced two issues: on one hand she was forced to accept
the independence of former colonies and overseas possessions. On the
other she forged new alliances in Europe, particularly with Germany,
rejected the dominance of the USA and created her own strategic nuclear
force. The independence of the colonial possessions came about over the
period from 1959 to 1962, starting with the creation of the 'Community'
in the 1958 Constitution and ending with the declarations of
independence by the African colonies, who each set up treaties ensuring
continuing economic, political and military dependence on France, while
other parts of the Empire became either Departments of France or
Overseas Territories (Ager, 1996a). The formal end of the Algerian war
of independence came about in 1962, following both a worsening of the

military situation and the revolt by members of the Army and political elite who considered themselves betrayed by de Gaulle, threatening civil war on French soil as a result. France's rejection of American military involvement in Europe, based on de Gaulle's increasing dislike of American global policy but also on a fear of lacking control over French military resources, culminated in French withdrawal from NATO's integrated command structure in 1966 and in eviction of military headquarters and NATO offices from Paris at that time. The creation of a new Europe after the Treaty of Rome of 1958 was viewed as a new possibility for France provided that its structure as a confederal association of independent powers was recognised, a solution which found less favour outside France than in it and which led to de Gaulle's rejection of the British application for entry in 1963.

These were world events of major importance, and de Gaulle's charismatic personality and power placed France at the forefront. For some, his actions showed France's reaffirmation of her own independence and glory, coupled with a new dominance and leadership in scientific and technological innovation. For others, de Gaulle represented a dying flicker as France refused to accept the secondary nature of her power and influence, and fought a despairing rearguard action against the inevitable. Etiemble's uncompromising defence of things French, of the culture and the language represented the same refusal to accept any further encroachment of American ideas, of any form of modernisation, or indeed of the world outside France, and responded to a widely shared mood, reflected in other books of the era such as _Le Défi Américain_ (Jean-Jacques Servan-Schreiber, 1967) or _L'Empire Américain_ (Claude Julien, 1968) (cf. Kuisel, 1993). The 1975 Bas-Lauriol Act on the status of French represents the culmination of this attitude of protectionism and of refusal to accept Americanisation. The Act was prepared under Pompidou, the successor to de Gaulle as President, his Prime Minister and himself probably the prime mover in language policy, and only deferred until Giscard d'Estaing's Presidency because of Pompidou's death in 1974.

Before Etiemble

Etiemble did not discover the baleful influence of foreign words on the purity of French, nor are Americanisms the first external linguistic influence to stir the patriotic soul. Histories of French are full of examples of the influence of German (in the fifteenth century), of Italian, Arabic and Provençal (in the sixteenth century), of Spanish (in the seventeenth), of English from England (in the eighteenth and nineteenth), and in each case and in each generation some Cassandra has called public opinion to notice how the very uniqueness of Frenchness was being destroyed. Henri Estienne published his *'Précellence du langage français'* in 1579, opposing borrowings from Italian; Fougeret de Monbron a *'Préservatif contre l'Anglomanie'* in 1757; Béranger a *'Les boxeurs ou l'anglomanie'* in 1859. In the twentieth century the first World War, the consequent influx of American troops and American ideas into France, and particularly the insistence on English and on American ideas of diplomacy at and after the Treaty of Versailles provoked an outburst of such works in the 1930s. Indeed, it was at this time that the Office National de la Langue Française was created to defend French, in the widespread belief that more powerful and more political bodies were needed than the venerable French Academy. Modern Cassandras are numerous and the tradition of concern over the 'decadence' of modern French, associated with its destruction through borrowing, has continued well into the present (see Bengtsson, 1968; Berrendonner, 1982).

A Real Problem for the Language?

The word 'Franglais' was picked up again later (for example in Trescases, 1982), and there have been innumerable analyses of the reality of the invasion and assessments of how serious it is, particularly in the ten years before the Toubon Act of 1994. Claude Hagège (1987: 27-74) was concerned to try and establish whether English was having any effect on the 'real heart' of French. For him, simple borrowings of individual words were a normal part of any language's development. In morphology, the suffixes and prefixes such as the *self* of *self-service*, the *-er* of *container*, *mixer*, the *-man* of *tennisman*, the *-ing* of *dancing*, which are sometimes considered as an indication that French has lost vitality in word creation, are in fact easily absorbed and transformed into real French. The word *dancing*, meaning dance-hall, and *tennis-man*, meaning tennis player, are French creations, not borrowings. Borrowings from English which affect the grammar of French include changes in the order of words, particularly in geographical names such as *Sud-Bretagne* or *Nord-Viêtnam*, where traditional French would have used *Bretagne du Sud* and *Viêt-nam du Nord*. The position of the adjective, normally following the noun in French, is nowadays often changed, in imitation of English usage: *l'actuel gouvernement, les possibles objections*. Adjectives are used as adverbs: *il est arrivé facile, vivons jeune*. More subtle indications of the influence of English are to be found in the overuse of *pouvoir* and *devoir*: *on peut voir Paris* for *on voit Paris*; of *tel*: *de tels individus devraient être surveillés* instead of *des individus de ce genre*; in the non-use of repeated prepositions (*pour votre sécurité et votre confort*).

Most of these developments are nonetheless considered by Hagège to be perfectly acceptable. They reflect French traditions of linguistic innovation, are to be expected in journalistic or advertising usage, or are restricted to special domains and do not affect everyday French. Even when considering the supposedly large number of words borrowed into the French vocabulary, Hagège (quoting a 1975 study by Gebhardt) is phlegmatic: 'From 1550 to 1950, French borrowed 600 words from English, while English had borrowed 1914 from French up to 1854'. Nonetheless there are many lexical borrowings which seem to have entered the language, of which Hagège gives a brief sample:

> _airbus, attaché-case, bacon, badge, boat-people, brain-trust, businessman, clone, clown, cocktail, copyright, cow-boy, drugstore, duplex, ECU, ferry-boat, gadget, gag, hold-up, kidnapping, music-hall, planning, pub, racket, reporter, sandwich, standing, starter, suspense, week-end, whisky._

Of this list, many are technical terms, words used by some social classes but not others, or words describing items themselves borrowed with their designation. More subtle borrowings are the 'faux-amis' whose English meaning is now being adopted in French (_actuel_ for _véritable, privé_ for _particulier_ (e.g. _avion particulier_) and the calques based on English sayings - _dites-le avec des fleurs_/say it with flowers. After pointing out that many so-called English borrowings in fact have Latin or Greek origins, and that many will be modified or drop out of use, Hagège recalled the statistics of frequency: borrowings from English represent a mere 2.5% of the total lexical stock and 0.6% in running speech, or one word in 166 in _Le Monde_ of 1977. His conclusion was that:

> the vocabulary of French does not give a picture of invasion. Since the objective situation does not justify the tumult, one must look for other factors which might have given the debate such a dramatic aspect. (Hagège, 1987: 74)[40]

Other experts have not been so sure. For Pergnier (1989), the threat was real and could have disastrous consequences. Pergnier considered that the predominance of American socio-ideological products had 'considerable' effects on the French language. The dissemination process came about through the media and intellectuals, who read and worked in English and unconsciously reproduced English words and meanings: _en charge (d'une affaire)_ for 'in charge of', _initier_ in the sense of 'to initiate'. In very rare cases only did borrowings enrich French, providing a pragmatic solution to a difficulty of expression. Many borrowings simply added mystery or an aura of glamour to speech. Examples include _leader_, which 'covers in the same misty veil the realities

corresponding to a range of functions'. *Cool, feeling, clean, shopping* all
represented vague, opaque and unanalysable ideas which could be
represented by more precise and comprehensible French terms. Even the
creation of terms by the Terminology Commissions, approved by the
Délégation Générale à la Langue Française, came in for Pergnier's
criticism. With *'mercatique'*, created to replace 'marketing', 'they get rid
of the English sound but not the conceptual ambiguity - or even
confusion - of the term. They have elevated a number of operational
concepts to the dignity of a unique - scientific - concept.' (Pergnier, 1989:
194).[41] The voluntary acceptance and even creation of 'franglais' within
French, creating a pidgin or jargon which is neither English nor French,
was an acceptance of linguistic colonialism by those who are 'colonised'.
The acceptance of language implied accepting its inbuilt beliefs:
'franglais satisfies the more or less conscious wish of part of the French
population to identify with a mythical and one-dimensional model of
modernity'. (Pergnier, 1989: 203)[42]

---

* French attitudes towards English were basically positive, with
  approval for British English slightly more evident than that for
  American;
* the French generally were fascinated by the United States, and the
  attitudes of the general public were 'more positive than those held
  by their more vociferous counterparts in government, academia,
  and journalists';
* the French generally make a strong link between language and the
  culture ('ideology') it is thought to represent;
* older, better educated and better-off respondents were more
  favourably inclined towards English and towards the USA, than
  older members of lower socio-economic classes which shared the
  negative views of the power elite;
* 'Subjects neither feared the impact of American culture on French
  culture nor believed that speaking English would result in the
  adoption of American values'.

Source: Flaitz, 1988: 191-7

Figure 5.2 The ideology of English

Flaitz (see Figure 5.2) looked at this question in 1988 in terms of
discovering whether the French generally accepted the idea that the
English language, particularly in its American form, carried a particular

ideological message, and if so whether this message was viewed positively or negatively. The small study (four ethnographic interviews and 145 respondents to a quantitative survey) arrived at the conclusions of Figure 5.2, which tend to modify somewhat the more extreme fears of the elite.

Are the French justified in seeing a world-wide conspiracy to promote English? There is no doubt that both Britain and America, and to a certain extent other English-speaking countries, have deliberately fostered the use of English world-wide. Phillipson (1992)   studied the organised provision of English language teaching by Britain and the USA, in the context of a theory of imperialism. The main British vehicle for the promotion of English language and culture overseas is the British Council, founded in 1934 and funded by government through the Foreign and Commonwealth Office (FCO) and the Overseas Development Administration (ODA). The 1989-90 budget of £321 million was obtained from specific sources for specific purposes: £110M (from the FCO, for cultural diplomacy), £157M (from the FCO and ODA for schemes such as scholarships and technical assistance) with the remainder, some £55M, obtained through earnings from teaching, publishing etc. British Council policy is dictated by government, and government priorities dictate its activities, although a large number of advisory bodies are intended to ensure it is responsive to the needs of industry and the views of professionals. Its formal status is that of a non-departmental body. Phillipson concluded that there was 'very clear evidence of the integration of the British Council into the government machine, and of the interdependence of cultural diplomacy with economic, political, and by implication, military diplomacy...ELT (English Language Teaching) is unquestionably neo-colonialist and operates within a framework of imperialism' (Phillipson, 1992: 151). However, 'the absence of any policy or plan, other than a general wish to promote English through ELT professionalism' which characterised the actual teaching of English abroad, although it was no serious impediment to expansion in the former British colonial empire, meant that there seems to have been no deliberate attempt to target French-speaking areas of the world, and certainly not France itself. To modify the picture somewhat it is obvious that the British Council is not the only body selling English language teaching abroad.

For the USA, 'language promotion forms part of the American global strategy', and the strategy itself unites military and economic aims, as in the doctrine of the conditionality of aid developed throughout the Reagan era. The United States Information Agency, mainly oriented towards short-term political diplomacy; the Peace Corps, and the

Agency for International Development are the main government vehicles for teaching. The funding of English-language teaching has not been all, or even mainly, from government sources however: the Ford, Rockefeller and Carnegie Foundations have all taken a major role in supporting it, and again there is a large number of private enterprises involved. Both Americans and British nonetheless worked together in the development of a global strategy for spreading English abroad, which Phillipson dates from about 1960. In both countries, while the policy aims were clear at macro, government level, their implementation in language at the micro level was left mainly to the initiative of the ELT profession.

Other 'Anglo-Saxon' countries have been comparatively slow in following this policy line. Australia, for instance, did not develop an overall Language Policy until 1987, but now has a very comprehensive National Policy, which includes long and short-term aims for language maintenance within the country, for the teaching of English as the national language, and for the promotion of Australian interests abroad (Lo Bianco, 1987; Ozolins, 1993). These latter include not only the teaching of English for economic purposes in foreign countries, but also, in Australia, that of languages of geo-political (and economic) import (Chinese, Indonesian/Malay, Japanese, French, German, Italian, Greek, Arabic and Spanish). But the 'export' of English language teaching, particularly to Pacific Rim countries, is a major activity of Higher Education. Some Universities, for example, actively promote English language services in former French Indochina and specifically to Vietnam, and have been very successful in arranging courses and providing teacher training.

A Problem for the Culture of the Elite?

French, and France, are said to be surrounded by Anglo-American influences from which both are under constant pressure. These affect mainly the cultural industries, the intelligentsia and journalism. Conferences and colloquia take place in English; computers use English; information sources are in English. Films and the cinema have long been popular in France, but the influence of American mass production means that even this area of French cultural production is using English more and more:

> international commercial communication is mainly in English - job advertisements for example...shops, magazines, radio stations adopt English or Anglicised names...young people prefer English-language music...many French people thus find themselves in contact, if not

with English, then with some English, at the meeting point of such interests. (Pergnier, 1989: 208)[43]

In addition to these general and diffuse pressures, foreign language education in France has resulted mainly in English being taught, rather than a variety of languages. In Pergnier's view, though, schools were often unsuccessful in teaching proper English, and instead familiarised youth with a superficial form of the language, and gave a gloss to changes in youth culture itself by allowing the young to acquire a smattering of words and phrases which they then applied to the music, food and films they experienced. The cultural, or socio-ideological message conveyed by this superficial form was equally superficial, and through its quantity, tended to 'drag the world's cultural level downwards'. Pergnier was convinced that the development of franglais, rather than a proper bilingualism, would have incalculable cultural consequences. Proper bilingualism, a real understanding of English and its associated culture, literature and history, could well benefit France. But the problem for those who oppose the cultural invasion is that what is being imported has little cultural value. What is being adopted is not a language but a jargon: :

> one has difficulty in identifying the advantage that can be obtained from turning language into a generalised jargon and alienating people from their own idiom. Neither can one see what the world can gain from the pauperisation of its linguistic heritage, through a reduction in the number of ways of apprehending reality which languages are - and particularly is this so in the cases of the great cultural languages - on the standardised model of one language alone, even if it had been demonstrated that the advantages of this language were superior to those of others. (Pergnier, 1989: 208)[44]

The French cultural elite has frequently adopted this view, that imported English is likely to have the effect of dragging standards down. In _Colonisation douce_ (Noguez, 1991), the author likens the American invasion to a form of colonisation, agreeable and friendly but highly destructive. Noguez is a success of the French educational system (Ecole Normale Supérieure, agrégé in philosophy), a novelist, writer on cinema and literature, and friend of the Quebec francophone movement, having lived for three years in North America. He is an activist in matters of French language policy, and chaired the pressure group Avenir de la Langue Française in 1993. The book's title described the arrival of a friend who gradually insinuates himself into the home, taking over and forcing his 'friend' to listen, to deny himself and to adopt willy-nilly the preferences, habits and ways of thinking of his visitor. So it is with American, imposing itself on French. American language and culture had colonised the French; French TV and the film industry were submerged by Americanisms. This linguistic neo-colonialism had forced the French to believe in their own inferiority. The French are not racist, nor xenophobic, and are opposed to colonialism, anywhere; but since they were being attacked by a people and a culture with which they have so much in common, and which is not inferior in itself, they found it difficult to resist. Furthermore, said Noguez, this type of colonisation most affected those who are socially and culturally least able to defend themselves: those in the lower social groups and the worst educated. The problem with Americanisation of the language was that it produced a uniformisation of culture, whereas the French are in favour of diversity and plurality.   English, as a language, has characteristics which cannot be adopted in French without fundamentally altering the genius of the language: Noguez exemplified the use of prepositions in French, which cannot be dropped without changing French drastically for the worst (e.g.: *votre vol vacances n'est pas couvert par l'assurance risque passagers* instead of *votre vol de vacances n'est pas couvert par l'assurance offerte aux passagers contre les risques*).

Maurice Druon, Permanent Secretary of the French Academy, is one of the more significant of the many writers who have tried to awaken the French to awareness of the Anglo-American cultural invasion and of the effects this could have on the French language and the French soul. His politics are of the Colonel Blimp variety, and his attitude is much less tolerant of American or English culture. It may be the association of backward-looking politics with the anti-Americanism of his views on language, the association of franglais with 'inferior' culture, and a belief that the mass should be protected from such a potential lowering of standards, that causes many people of less extreme views to be very cautious about supporting the Toubon Law or indeed the general approach towards linguistic protectionism. Druon is full of praise of the past, of glory, of pride in the literature and science of France, but of despair at present-day 'crime' against French, carried out by the two sets of 'criminals': those who *informent* in the Press and the media and those who *forment* or educate in the teaching profession. His brief open letter to the French is very clear in its opinions on language and on politics, as Figure 5.3 indicates.

How far the French public, as apart from such members of the intelligentsia, really support condemnations of American language and culture, or this type of politics, is difficult to tell. Some see no threat to the status of French, nor to the national identity, and conclude that 'linguistic angoisse in modern France seems to be a luxury reserved mainly for belles-lettristes' (Ball, 1988: 104). Baggioni (1997: 329-30), a professional linguist, while agreeing that Anglo-American culture is invading France, considers that even elitist culture is under no real threat. He takes a different view on the cultural problem, regarding the use of English as merely auxiliary and presenting no threat through a significant level of cultural imports likely to affect the elite. English could never be the new Latin, for three main reasons:

- Latin was the sole language of work and culture for small intellectual elites, while English, often superficially mastered by executives, technicians...is an auxiliary working language
- the intellectual training of medieval elites was in Latin...
- the legitimacy of Latin was based on a belief in 'classicism' born out of a 'cultural transmission'...(Latin was) the vehicle of a cultural capital common to all Europe...Anglo-American...also has its own body of culture...which nobody tries to access through this medium. (Baggioni, 1997: 329-30)[45]

- Lack of respect for language reveals a lack of respect for everything
- the vulgarity of words reveals the vulgarity of the spirit
- Since when has the language of kids become that of adults?
- When do we hear that France is the third naval power in the world? Yet any minute far-off group claiming the secession of one of our _Territoires d'Outre-Mer_ has the right to special envoys and double columns
- France cannot retain its rank as a great country, and carry out policies on the world level, unless she continues to have a military deterrent and mastery of a universal language
- It is the greatness of the country which enables social welfare, not the opposite.

Source: Druon, 1994: 23-39[46]

Figure 5.3 Druon and pride in French

An official survey conducted in 1988 on the image that the French have of their language concluded that they held a fairly utilitarian attitude towards it, were pessimistic about the way it was used but were evenly divided over whether the use of English or American words was bad (50%) or good (45%) (cf. Ager, 1990: 224). More recently, a SOFRES poll of representative citizens in March 1994 obtained the results shown in Table 5.1.

Table 5.1 The image of French

•	How strongly are you attached to French?	
	Strongly	60%
	fairly strongly	37%
	not very much or not at all	3%
•	Who/what is responsible for any poor use of French?	
	Poor teaching of French at school	38%
	lack of vigilance by the French	35%
	many Frenchmen must use English for work	22%
	excessive influence of American culture	21%
	poor use of French in the media	17%
	globalisation of the economy	12%
•	Who should defend French?	
	Schools	59%
	the French themselves	29%
	the Media	15%
	the government:	10%
	business	3%
•	Is the use of English or American words 'bad' or 'good'?	
	Bad	44%
	Good	42%
	(since a language must adopt foreign words in order to enrich and develop itself)	
•	Is the use of terms like 'Shuttle' or 'Euronews' by public utilities shocking or not shocking?	
	Shocking	49%
	not shocking	49%
•	Is the use of English terms and expressions in everyday life	
	modern:	41%
	useful	30%
	amusing	19%
	snobbish	16%
	annoying	14%
	stupid	6%

Note: totals may exceed 100% as respondents could give more than one answer.
Source: SOFRES, 1994[47]

These results show that the French general public does not feel particularly insecure in its language, and that perhaps those policy-makers intent on protecting the language were over-zealous. Almost as many felt that American and English words and expressions can be happily used as did not. As many felt that the use of American terms is shocking as held the opposite opinion. If anything, there was a positive attraction towards the use of English terms: 'positive' feelings (modern, useful, amusing) outweighed the 'negative'. Results such as these are interesting for a number of reasons. First, it is clear from the circumstances of the 1994 poll, sponsored by the Culture Ministry, that it had been designed to impress sceptical Parliamentarians of public opinion. Second, the fact still comes through from the poll results that the majority of French are not anywhere near as concerned by feelings of insecurity as is the elite. Third, the general attitude towards Americanisms is much more practical than the idealistic and generalised dislike felt by that same elite. In effect, the general populace seems prepared to adopt Americanisms if they are useful or seem positive, and has no specific dislike of the English language.

If one broadens the question to consider the Americanisation of both elitist and non-elite culture, including 'life-style' as well as language, and most French supporters of language policy in this area subscribe to this view, then the mixed attitude of the French to Americanisation becomes clear. The question could be regarded as a dilemma: 'how could France follow the American lead and yet preserve a French way of life?'. The pressure after 1945 was towards modernisation, consumerism and individual materialism:

> Post-war America represented prosperity, especially in its elevated standard of living, and technological prowess. Or as the model was commonly conceptualized, America represented the coming 'consumer society'. This term suggested not just the mass purchase of standardized products of American origin or design such as Kodak cameras or jeans; it also denoted a style of life that encompassed new patterns of spending, higher wage levels, and greater social mobility. It featured new forms of economic organization including different kinds of industrial relations, business management, and markets. And the new consumerism depended on different cultural values. Consumer society suggested a life oriented around acts of purchase and a materialistic philosophy. It valued the productive and the technical and was accompanied by the products of a new mass culture, from Hollywood films and comic strips to home appliances and fast food. (Kuisel, 1993: 3)

But this model, extremely attractive and desirable and in the final analysis unavoidable if France was to modernise, was accompanied by 'American sins such as social conformity, economic savagery, and cultural sterility'. The dilemma was 'to find a way to possess American prosperity and economic power and yet to avoid what appeared to be the accompanying economic and social costs.' In particular, how could the specific French identity and culture be preserved?

The French have constructed an America which they can both love and hate. Starting in the 1960s, the previous opposition to the USA, orchestrated as part of the Cold War, gave way to vastly increased popularity of all the outward signs of American culture: films, music, dance, literature and fast food. In concrete terms - purchases of cultural artefacts, numbers of cinema tickets sold - the attraction of modernisation, of globalisation and of homogenisation outweighed the fear of absorption and the desire to be different. The objections, particularly those of the intellectuals of the 1950s, 1960s and 1970s, now seem outdated. By the 1990s, modernisation had become a fact of life and was no longer regarded as particularly American. Indeed, the Americanisation previously regarded as so foreign to French identity has been adopted just as much as in other European countries. But it has also been adapted: Euro Disney has taken over from Disneyland Paris, and the modifications made to the American theme park in order to make it fit with French preconceptions, while not going so far as to completely change the basic concept, have made such changes that the charge that the Park had become the fifty-first American State is quite untrue.

The French (re)construction of America in their own image has gone farther: 'Americanization neither obliterated French independence nor smothered French identity. France did change, but it remained the same' (Kuisel, 1993: 233). France adapted modernisation, and 'Gallic accusations of materialism, social conformity, and status seeking were a caricature of America'. Today's debate is about mass culture, although economic issues recur. Humility, the recognition of France's secondary position in the world in the face of American super-power domination, is difficult. Kuisel's analysis of why the debate should continue at all is that the French invention of America as reeking 'of materialism and vulgarity, wallowing in conformity and naive optimism' enabled them to construct a self-assessment of a France demonstrating 'individualism, humanism, good taste, skepticism, and, above all, civilisation'. Such civilisation was the 'holy grail that had to be protected from Yankee barbarism'; protecting and disseminating it was the basis of anti-

Americanism: 'the core of resistance derives from a sense of French difference, superiority, and universal mission'.

Such anxiety and debate over the influence of America continues, even if, as we have seen, the 'danger' is visible mainly to the cultural elite and the intelligentsia. The general population seems more concerned to enjoy the benefits of Americanisation, and to adapt it.

Have Things Changed?

As we approach the millennium the picture seems, on the surface of published books, newspapers and journals, and in the media, to have changed little, and indeed Van Deth (1995), close to policy-making circles in the 1970s and 1980s, was of this opinion. If anything, the complaints about Franglais and about the use of Anglicisms are just as strenuous on the part of the literary world and the policy community whose existence fostered the Toubon Act. We noted above (Figure 4.1) the continued expression of fear of 'Anglo-Saxon' language and influence as expressed in *Le Figaro Littéraire* in 1996. Then, many representatives of Parisian intellectual life felt that the language was either being prevented from expanding except in and through borrowings from English, or that the French themselves had so far lost confidence in French that they were unable to do other than tamely accept borrowings and the imitation of English grammar and style. The elitist nature of both the comments and the language which was felt to be most affected - the media, intellectual discussion, the teaching of philosophy in the upper classes of schools - was clearly a reflection of the interests of the policy community or of the media personalities who have considerable effect on political acts of any type. The sharpest anti-American comments on the situation come, as they have always come and unsurprisingly, from those working on language and culture in government-related organisations or in associations devoted to the defence of French, which tend to see an Anglo-Saxon (i.e. American) plot for world domination associated with attempts to infiltrate a range of cultural domains from film production to scientific research and popular music. This Anglo-Saxon plot, aimed at France as much as at Francophonie, is also aimed at high culture and at intellectual advance. It is widespread, manifests itself in politics, finance and science as much as in the arts, and is vocal:

> Among the negative tendencies affecting Francophonie, in recent years one has particularly manifested itself, called by the great author Milan Kundera 'anti-Francophonie'. This is a current of thought, an attitude, a type of behaviour which consists of criticising or

condemning the creation of an international Francophone community and particularly deriding the desire of Francophones to provide themselves with linguistic legislation and defend their cultural identity, specifically (when they do so) by supporting the cultural exception thesis in the free exchange of goods. (Etat, 1994: 514)[48]

Since the 1975 Bas-Lauriol Act putting Etiemble's proposals into effect political events have moved on. After the strengthening of the Act in 1994, the Right-wing Parliamentary majority approving it disappeared in 1997 and the President again has to work with a Prime Minister of a different political persuasion. Modernisation, globalisation and homogeneity are now not so much actions to condemn as necessary to survival.

Acts of Policy

The two main actions undertaken by government in recent years in pursuance of this motive have been the Bas-Lauriol Act of 1975, prepared under Pompidou as Prime Minister and then President, and its successor, the Toubon Act of 1994, prepared and presented by Jacques Toubon as Minister of Culture under the Presidency of Jacques Chirac. The Acts are similar to each other, the second being seen as an updating of the former and as a reaction to perceived weaknesses in the implementation of the 1975 Act. On the face of it, the Toubon Act, dealt with in more detail in Chapter 6 below, is not anti-English and driven by insecurity but, rather, celebrates the positive, identity motivation. Nowhere does it specify the language it opposes, and is everywhere couched in terms of ensuring the rights of French speakers to use their own language. It combines this agenda of human rights with an approach based on consumer protection, again ensuring that French speakers are protected from non-use of French in matters such as the labelling of goods or work contracts.

The motives for the Bas-Lauriol and the Toubon Acts, and indeed many of its provisions, can be traced back directly to Etiemble's disaster scenario. The precise motives for the 1994 Act were specified in the introduction to the Legendre Report introducing it in the Senate:

In the scientific domain, our language is more and more absent, even being chased away from colloquia. Is it acceptable that high level scientific activities, held in France on the initiative or with the help of public institutions or organisations should banish the use of our language?

...certain French film-makers envisage without any hesitation making their films in English because this language is the key to gaining access to the American market?

What can one think about a people which could soon no longer use its own language for song?

...It is also a fundamental concern that we should be able to continue thinking in French, singing in French, seeing the world in French. (Legendre, 1994: 5-6)[49]

The fear of domination was associated with fear of modernisation and fear of economic savagery and cultural sterility. Fear of the economic and social costs that accompany modernisation, globalisation and homogenisation were linked to a fear of the conformity to a different social regime. Fear of absorption by the English-speaking world and eventual replacement by it was associated with a self-perception based on the idea that French identity, different, superior and universally applicable, represented individualism, humanism, good taste, scepticism, and, above all, civilisation. The example of Quebec, and the incitement one hundred intellectuals gave, in an open letter to the French published in *Le Monde* just before the Parliamentary discussions, to do something about the imminent disappearance of their language, was cited in the report to show that the French should be at least as protective as they are, and that France should not merit the accusation of laissez-faire (*laxisme*). The whole tone and the sole purpose of the preamble to the Report is to place the reason for the Act on a defence of the right to speak French in the face of attacks, and the careful selection of negative terms reinforces the idea that a military action is required to confront the problem so that the French remain free to bring their skills and intelligence to the construction of a new world.

Apart from the Parliamentary Acts there have been two significant administrative actions. The first was the creation from 1970 of the Terminology Commissions in each Ministry, aimed at ensuring that relevant technical vocabulary has a French origin and uses French native terms as far as possible. Indeed, the selection of the legally obligatory decisions on words that the industry should use is based on finding French alternatives to American terms. The second administrative action has been based on the increasing concern of senior politicians, whose formal circulars and ministerial decrees have reiterated the necessity for public servants to use French on all possible occasions. But these demonstrate mixed motives, and the identity motive is possibly here as strong as that of insecurity.

Part 2: Identity

Chapter 6
Identity and the Status of French: the Language of the Republic

As we have seen above in Chapter two, the myth of the hexagon has a long history in France as a device to prevent disintegration of the nation-state. But the concept of identity is not simply a mechanism cynically adopted by those who hold power in order to retain it. In France in particular, there has emerged a specific conception of the nature of society, of the role of individuals and groups within it, and of managing the natural diversity of mankind that has since marked many countries. Contemporary French language policy, as demonstrated by the two high status public statements, of 1992 in the Constitution, and of 1994 in the Toubon Law, declares the French language to be official and insists on its exclusive use in a number of precise domains. It is not just fear and insecurity that has motivated these actions, nor is this type of action a phenomenon of the modern world. France has felt the need to include the language among the other symbols of the state - the flag, the national anthem, the very name (République Française) and the three words which signify the underlying republican values (Liberté, Egalité, Fraternité). There is a specific relationship between the state and language. French is, and has long been, *une affaire d'Etat*. Our purpose in this second part of the book is to examine the relationship between France as political community and France as speech community. In this Chapter we shall explore the identity concept as understood by today's politicians and citizens: the connection between the nature of French society and language use. In Chapter Seven we shall examine the ways in which the French state deliberately attempts to influence language and language use.

The Identity Concept and the French Political Community

Diversity and unity

The diversity of France is obvious: the climate range in metropolitan France goes from Continental to Mediterranean to Temperate; the relief from the plains of the centre to the Massif Central and to the Alps; family structures from the nuclear families of the North to the extended families of the periphery. Authoritarian family types in Alsace and Brittany differ from patriarchal families in a sort of tribe or clan around their common ancestor, a common pattern in the South at least in earlier generations. Blood types vary; traditional legal systems based on common law in the North differed from codified systems in the South. Languages, as we have seen, remained obvious indicators of difference until this century. Regions, grouped around a settlement system based on a large town, several small towns and rural villages, structured the environment in such a way that local economies and local loyalties survived the centuries. Regions, ever since the days of feudalism, have been strong defenders of their individual personalities. The reality of diversity still lies behind the strength of regionalisms and the cautious, defensive approaches to France as nation, and to Europe as supra-nation, that many members of the political community adopt today. France's so-called 'natural' frontiers, underlined in the myth of the hexagon as her natural right and merely continuing those of ancient Gaul, are quite different from those of the tripartite division of Charlemagne's Empire in 843, which used the rivers Rhône, Saône, Meuse and Scheldt - all well inside the mythical hexagon - as the boundary for the 'French' part. France and Germany have fought over the border strip left to Lothair ever since, twice in the twentieth century, and the actual frontiers of France have only rarely coincided with this mythical pattern.

There are historical reasons for the political unity created from such diversity. We have already discussed the insecurity the central political authorities felt at the prospect of strong regional forces. For Braudel (1986), investigating the positive aspects of French identity construction, unity derived from three main historical forces. The power of Paris, its prestige and its attractiveness to local elites, has sucked regional and local leaders and aristocrats away from their local bases since the time of Versailles. The choice of Paris as capital, symbolically land-locked and hence looking inward, her riches based on the wealth of the Ile de France, led to the later view that all France depended on this rich, overpopulated area which contrasted so much with the 'French desert' of the rest of the country. The necessity for a large standing army to control a large and diverse territory open to invasion, backed up later by the creation of a centrally managed administration, led to moving teachers and other functionaries across the country and reliance on them to create the state by their physical presence while other European states were poorly organised and administered and relied on mercenary armies. It is, in Braudel's view, hardly surprising that the army should have counted nearly a million men as early as 1709: much of its effort was devoted to maintaining internal peace. By contrast, the navy was small. France's concerns were with the interior, and 'France's potential sea power was too often unemployed, under-employed or thwarted'. A third factor was the power, but at the same time the absolute necessity, of a common means of communication: the French language.

The myth of geographical and historical unity is powerful, long-lived as we have seen and is still carefully fostered by a range of forces in contemporary France. France itself has had to be invented as a unified state. First and foremost, the myth of the territorial origin had to be developed, although it was not until 1642 at the earliest (in Richelieu's will), and only seriously after the Revolution, that the idea of restoring to France the dimensions of ancient Gaul entered the public consciousness as being the point of origin. Traditionally in French history, the picture is given of the Francs and their kings, particularly the Capetians, following a deliberate policy of extending their territory to re-establish this Gaul, although most modern historians believe instead that the extension of territory was much more dependent on circumstance and chance. The Revolution was probably the point at which the territorial coincided most clearly with the intellectual perception of France, although even then the actual line of the frontiers to be considered 'natural' was by no means certain. From that point, and even though Nice and Savoy did not join France until 1860, while 1945 saw a further adjustment of the frontiers, the territory coincided fairly closely with both ancient Gaul and with the mythical perception of unity. But the myth of unity is not limited to a misunderstanding or misrepresentation of the geographical, historical or economic facts: a whole range of other factors played a role in fostering unity, and still continually modify and modernise the concept of identity. First among these is religion.

The secular state

The relationship between Catholicism and the French state is as strong today as it ever was, as anybody who has attended a visit by the Pope and seen the French President welcome him and the French Prime Minister accompany him on his departure can testify. Yet the Church is not established, the state is formally secular, religion is excluded from the schools. The origin of the policy of holding organised religion at arms length goes back to the Revolution and the role of the Church in opposing it. While the Revolutionaries wished to insist on approving priests and owning Church buildings, they much preferred the public veneration of Reason, and a civic religion to free the people from superstition, and indeed, the political control which was also part of the Church's practice. The first schism between church and state occurred in 1795 when the secular state was established. The Concordat of 1802, which lasted until 1905, confirmed secular control over the Church while still recognising the special position of Catholicism in France. Priests were paid, bishops were nominated by the state; this Concordat applied in Alsace-Lorraine after its return in 1918 and until 1939: it remains in force today in three départements there. In the latter part of the century, and particularly after the defeat of 1870, the struggle between Church and State was fierce as Gambetta, then Ferry, developed anticlericalism, and secularised education. The Dreyfus Affair of 1896, and the struggles between anti-Semitism, Catholicism, Freemasonry, the elitism of the Army, the political attitudes which would lead to Fascism, and lay Republicanism sharpened the mutual distrust of the Church and the State, of political right and left. The Separation of 1905 broke with the Church in most of France, and put priests and churches into unemployment and disuse; significantly, in these first years of the twentieth century state subsidies were removed from Catholic education also, and were not restored until 1959. A certain tacit understanding that the Church was still a strong force in French life has remained: the free day (Thursday) was made available for use by the Church as schools were secularised from 1881, religion is recognised by the state even though the formalities may be partly hidden under laws for 'cults' or 'associations'. Nonetheless, the formal separation of church and state is part of the fundamental beliefs of the political world, and Jospin's manifesto of June 1997, the _pacte républicain_, placed secularity as the first of the republican values.

Today the relationships between the French state and the Catholic Church in education seem fairly stable, as do the finances of the Church itself even though the bulk of these come from the denier de l'Eglise (previously the denier du culte: instituted in 1907: a donation requiring a payment from the faithful of a day's pay) and Sunday or annual collections. Indeed, the strange situation of a factual relationship between church and state, and a factually great influence by the church on daily life, including politics, countered by a formal separation between church and state and a secular state many of whose servants see this division as fundamental, is perhaps best acknowledged in the status of church buildings. Most of these are the property of the commune which pays for their upkeep and makes a payment to the local *curé* as caretaker of the building. This, of course, is not an official salary. The curé is merely the caretaker. But the position reflects the tensions between clericalism and secular republicanism, about which a number of other dichotomies float: free-thinking and Papal authority, humanism and theism, royalism and republicanism, regionalism and centralism, the ethnic and the universal. Over the years, such dichotomies have often been symbolised by the regional languages: by the closeness of the Church to its believers and its willingness to use their language in church and to support their cause, often against the impersonality of the distant state. The mass demonstrations of 1984, as a result of which subsidies for church schools were confirmed, showed how there remains a strong sense that France is a Catholic country and that the Church has every right to retain a social, educational and political role.

The other churches and beliefs apart from Catholicism have not made a significant impact on the identity issue. The Protestants were hounded out of France in 1685, when 260,000 left and had to wait for the Revolution and the declaration of the Rights of Man to receive full equality. There remains in the collective memory, certainly of Protestants, the 1572 St Bartholomew massacre at the start of the Wars of Religion, and 1997 saw the first official Catholic apology for the massacre. But the main contemporary issue over the relationship of the state and religion has to do with the fact that Islam is now the second religion of France. Approximately four million believers use the several thousand mosques of different tendencies. The nature of the French state's interference in the control of Islam in France has been documented, for example in Kepel, 1994: 215-325. It goes back at least to the establishment of the Paris Mosque in 1926 which was radically changed in 1958 by the arrival of those who left independent Algeria. The state has constantly and systematically attempted to ensure a forum for discussion which will accept the basic notions of Frenchness, including the importance of voluntary acceptance of citizenship which is felt by many Muslims to be in opposition to the beliefs of Islam. The state has 'interfered' in a number of ways: by setting up fora such as the Conseil de réflexion sur l'Islam en France, set up by the Ministry of the Interior in 1990 and which lasted till 1993; and the Haut Conseil de l'Islam en France, founded in 1995 and intended to be representative of all tendencies. The state interferes also through the allocation of subsidies:

In its allocation of funding to minority-based associations, the fundamental aim of the FAS (Fonds d'Action Sociale pour les travailleurs immigrés et leurs familles) has been to co-opt people of immigrant origin who, while retaining certain differences, basically respect the cultural and legal norms prevailing in France...National initiatives undertaken by the Interior Ministry since 1990 under governments of both Left and Right have had a similar objective: to encourage the establishment of representative institutions reflecting the aspirations of the broad mass of Muslims in France...an important element implicit in this strategy is the conviction that most Muslims understand and accept the norms governing religious practices within the French tradition of *laïcité*. (Hargreaves, 1995: 205 and 214)

The relationships between Islam and the secular state are subject to two pressures, from immigration and from the continuing relationships with Algeria. Many but by no means all immigrants come from Algeria where battles between fundamentalists and government are vicious, bloody and conducted by many groups including the militant Fédération Islamique du Salut founded in Algiers in 1989. Immigration is possibly the most sensitive issue in contemporary politics, and is a continuing problem for the nation-state and its defence against those who would adapt the notion to the realities of the contemporary situation. It is in the contrast between the absolutism of the secular state and its strength in France, and the all-embracing nature of Islam, that the issue of identity has arisen. How can the secular state accept that a particular community can exist within it, establish and follow its own laws and practices, and yet ensure that all members have access to all the freedoms and rights available to other citizens? One answer might simply be pragmatic: that since an accommodation has been arrived at with Catholicism, it should not be not impossible to develop a similar arrangement with Islam. Indeed, the funding arrangements for associations and educational priority zones tacitly accept the involvement of the state with religious groups, particularly in their educational role. So far, the state's reaction has been to attempt to support those who wish to integrate and assimilate, and to weaken any who support communitarianism. Relations with Islam remain nonetheless difficult. They have been particularly problematic in relation to education and to the secular nature of the schools. In recent times, Muslim girls have several times been prevented from wearing the hijab, headscarves required for religious reasons, at school. During the most heated moments of the debate about this issue, after the exclusion of some girls from a school in Creil in 1989, two main themes emerged: the issue of racism and that of assimilation. Was the definition of French nationalism which rejects communities and particularisms, essentially racist? The issue raised a number of other themes, as well: the rights of women, the power struggle of different tendencies in the Islamic community, the freedom of the individual, the rights of immigrants to emancipation and the benefits of the host nation. These were loosely addressed in the resultant Ministerial circular which reaffirmed the secular nature of French education, modified its more extreme consequences, but passed particular decisions down to individual schools. It reiterated the refusal by the state to change the idea of an all-embracing unity to be accepted by all:

> This French idea of the nation and the Republic is by its nature respectful of all convictions, particularly religious, political and cultural ones. But it excludes the disintegration of the nation into separate communities, indifferent to each other, considering only their own rules and their own laws. (Bayrou, quoted in Conrad, 1996: 216)[50]

Henceforth it is at least clear that a main component of French identity must contain within it an element of coexistence with Islam. So is the state a secular organisation? Openly, yes. But there remains a creative tension between state and the Catholic Church, symbolised particularly in the tacit acceptance of a compromise in education. The identity of France is based as much on the existence of the substratum of religious belief as on the secular understanding of the rights of man. Republicanism's two strands remain at the forefront of politics and at the forefront of identity: the religious nation, associated with the ethnic and the regional, still opposes yet works with the secular one, associated with the national and the universal.

La France profonde

Another significant factor in this issue of the identity of France and its unity is the strength of continuing conservatism and the essentially rural nature of France. La France profonde (essential France), and La France éternelle are constantly recurring terms. Defining exactly what the concept covers is much more difficult. How conservative are the French, and how far does this conservatism affect the state in its search for, and convictions about, French identity? How far does the political community really reflect semi-serious views of itself like those of Zeldin in _The French_ (1983), Schifres in _Les Parisiens_ (1990) or Fenby in _On the Brink_ (1998)? The themes of Figure 6.1 seem to recur among the innumerable journalists, politicians and historians who have dared to try defining la France profonde: Among them one might quote just two:

It's true that I liked the IVth (Republic). It corresponded to the essential spirit of France. Nonetheless I regret it could not reconcile two things: the divisions the French have over everything of secondary importance, and the deep national unity which is that of the people and which needs a strong State. (Charasse, quoted in Ferney, 1992: 69)[51]

to describe French society in 1990, there is nothing better than the vocabulary of the Ancien Régime...quarrels between barons, thinking only of increasing their lands...political parties thinking only of indulgences and excommunications...elected seigneurs of provinces and towns, through clientelism and local power, tear the state's prerogatives from it, vitiating rules of equity and threatening the principles of national solidarity...justice is like that of the King, magnanimous towards the powerful, hard on the weak...the medieval guilds, peasant revolts and inner-city riots show that in the heart of industrial society Luddite reactions have returned. (Joffrin, quoted in Ferney, 1992: 135)[52]

- The French are peasants with one foot always in the countryside.
- The French are sarcastic, flippant and superficial.
- The French are convinced individualists, liking argument.
- The French are intellectual, in the sense that they prefer the abstract to the concrete, the symbolic to the pragmatic, the grandiose to the simple.
- The French talk but rarely act.
- The French love nothing better than explaining and teaching.
- On the political level, power is centred in the state, so political life is about opposing the state or wresting favours from it.
- The state is, on the one hand an Administration which is unchanging and all-powerful, and on the other an enduring belief system while political parties and politicians simply pass through.
- To obtain anything, change anything or do anything, the state must be confronted by violence because it is so difficult to convince. So peasants throw manure at tax offices, any strike or demonstration leads to violence and confrontation.
- Clientelism is fundamental to power structures.

Figure 6.1 La France profonde

Such analyses need to be set against the background both of the existence of a powerful extremist right-wing nationalist force in the Front National, possibly the most supported such organisation in

Europe and certainly one which has made considerable efforts in developing its ideology, and, at the same time, the widespread acceptance of the ideas of the Enlightenment and the Revolution. Figure 6.2 outlines some of the basic notions which seem to recur in Front National thinking.

- A preoccupation with the decadence of the Establishment, which is associated with free-thinkers, Freemasons, Jews, parliamentarians and big business.
- The elements of French greatness have been contaminated and destroyed: the Revolution and the preceding Enlightenment ushered in a period when the individual's 'rights' have overshadowed those of society, of the sacred, of the schools, of the family, of security for the individual.
- A belief that the Party stands alone. The parties of the left are branded, along with those of the right, as lacking any credible ideology. Indeed, at one stage Le Pen lumped all the parties together as 'Socialism': '...break with socialism. Not merely the socialism of the Left, but also that used before 1981 by the governments of Barre, Chirac and Giscard' (Le Pen, 1985: 283).
- French identity and cultural homogeneity are rooted in the past, and are the epitome of the European cultural heritage.
- France must stand for her independence and a forceful stance on foreign policy in defence of her own interests.
- Internally, policies on law and order must stamp out crime and punish wrongdoing with the utmost severity and at any expense.
- The financial and employment problems of contemporary France are caused by massive immigration, which threatens to swamp 'real' France.

Figure 6.2 The ideology of the Front National

La France Profonde, and the belief in an ethnic origin for French identity, are still basically right-wing concepts:

> In France two nationalisms and two theories of the nation have traditionally confronted each other ever since the great revolution of 1789. For the revolutionaries, and the left-wing tradition which they inspired, any individual, no matter of what origin or race, could become a French citizen by accepting the ideals contained in the Declaration of Human Rights, making the nation the result of personal choice, a social pact between reasoning individuals. For the

right, the nation is an 'ethnic' entity, predating the individuals who compose it, the product of a long common history and shared memories, something subconscious and instinctive. (Fysh, 1997: 85)

The defence of this latter tradition by right-wing thinkers, associating it with pro-Catholic, anti-Semitic, capitalist economic views, and also with the third tradition supporting monarchism, the strong leader and counter-revolutionary opinions, continued until the 1940s. Indeed, de Gaulle himself continually referred to his 'certain idea of France' as being derived from the depths of time, and which could not develop until France took on a world role, was in the front rank and united in pursuance of national greatness.

The Front National, in its contemporary ideology, has taken more from the Maurras and anti-Dreyfus tradition than from that of de Gaulle, but contains within itself many of the populist traditions of France. The Front National breaks with the tradition of the French extreme right in supporting republicanism and opposing the particular view of authority and elitism which attached these to monarchy, although it still believes in strong leadership. It has more or less taken over the use of the word 'identity' to reflect its own perceptions of France: hence the concern in the Toubon debate to avoid the use of that word, and replace it by 'personality'. It has forced the Right generally to define itself in relation to its views. As a result, many of its basic beliefs have been adopted by others in modified form, as have specific acts of policy among which the Pasqua nationality laws are the most striking. But the Front National has consistently portrayed itself as 'persecuted for defending the people', in particular against the might of the state. How powerful is the state itself?

Roles of the state

The French Revolution made the state all-powerful, in the sense that the abolition of privileges and of corporations got rid of any intermediary between the state and the individual citizen, who himself - at that time only the men - made an individual and voluntary contract to support the state. The Revolution had the task of politicising and democratising the absolute power of the monarch, and at the same time changing the basis of society from one based on the rights of the feudal aristocracy and those of corporations and guilds, to the basis of law, representation and the exercise of individual rights. Since the break was so sudden, and changes had to be made in both the political and the social at the same time, France had and still has a fundamental difficulty in allocating any democratic power or rights of representation to groups, classes, social categories, communities or corporations of any type. The _spécificité française_ is thus that France still believes that such intermediate bodies could seek, or would represent, anti-democratic privileges.

> The principal characteristic of the French state after 1789...is primarily in the sociological and cultural task, never previously met, of producing the nation, filling the void left by the collapse of corporate structures and finding a substitute for the former 'concord' of the traditional political body. (Rosenvallon, 1990: 99)[53]

It is the state which is the founder and guarantor of democracy, of concepts of equality, nationality and citizenship, of welfare and of economic well-being. But it is this very centrality of the state which brings about a number of features of the French administrative machine which have had considerable and notable effects, not only directly on legislation including language legislation, but on the whole surrounding environment including the very question as to why such legislation should be thought necessary in the first place. The state is founded on the notion of legitimacy, and the need to demonstrate legitimacy openly thorough accepted written texts. Hence the Constitution, hence the Declaration of the Rights of Man and Citizen; hence indeed the very basis of French law which is normally the passage of a permissive Act in the Parliament which creates the founding text. This text leaves the operation of the law and the details of how it will be carried out to agents of the state ranging from ministers to mayors, and from police force and the military to teachers and workers in state-owned firms. Cynics would say there is an almost mythical belief in the power of the written word approved by the official bodies, the authority of the text. But it is at this point that the question arises of who exactly is the state, and whether or not the state has now developed to such a point as almost to be an independent actor in political life. The concept of the 'autonomous state', which could act as such a participant in the policy-making process has recently been developed to account for the ability of state actors, particularly bureaucrats, to interfere in policy formulation as they have in France (Cerny, 1990; Ager, 1996b: 104-7).

Administrators appointed to serve the state have a time frame which is not that of politicians. Functionaries are chosen in France through a system of competitive entry, which automatically confers on those successful both a mental approach and a practical aim of preserving the general interest, sometimes in conflict with the general will (cf. Rosenvallon, 1990: 82 and 91). The administrative aim is not just to execute the wishes of the political leaders, but also to ensure that policies last, that they are technically sound, that they are not merely responses to passing ideological desires. Not merely has this made the French administrative system effective and powerful, with a _statut_ of its own conferring rights on local as well as central civil servants, it has also ensured continuity, passivity and considerable inertia. A particular example of this is the Ministry of Education, a massive organisation very difficult to change, consisting of both centralised civil servants and also of every teacher in France. Teachers' careers are managed, as is the detail of the whole system from curriculum to methods, from Paris and the regional Académies which are its outposts. The Ministry has been called 'a culture, a service, a system' (see Durand-Prinborgne, 1994). At the extreme, functionaries or similar groups preserve their own corporate advantage under the pretence of serving the nation-state: 'Too often, high rhetoric about solidarity is a mask for corporatist selfishness' (Fenby, 1998: 427).

This autonomy has policy consequences usually leading to the least disturbance possible, to minimal, incremental change. It has also generated counter-measures, the most significant among which is the ministerial policy units (cabinets ministériels), whose aim and purpose is both to ensure that political will prevails and to ensure that politicians have available staff as well-trained, intellectually capable and aware as are those of the administration itself. The role of the Ecole Nationale d'Administration (ENA) in the formation and training of both bureaucrats and technocrats, and of ensuring their collective status, is important. Training through the ENA gives access to the Grands Corps, the senior parts of the bureaucracy, and thence to major career outlets in government, business or politics. One aspect of the network is interchangeability: senior administrative staff are available to cover a range of jobs in government and in the many aspects of state-managed industry, so Finance Inspectors are often detached to serve the public sector, running industries like Air France or the railways.

A main consequence is the existence of the Paris network, a well-informed, able and articulate elite with access to policy-making. Another is the fact that the populace at large expects the state to be involved in every matter of importance to France, and particularly with social disputes. Every part-time farmer with a small-holding in Brittany will expect to turn to the state when his income drops; every Air France employee or train driver will expect the state to guarantee his future. It is the position of the state as target, and its involvement with every aspect of life in France, despite moves by right-wing governments since 1993 to foster privatisation, decentralisation and casualisation, that gives a particular flavour to questions of contemporary French identity.

Inevitably the concept of identity which lies at the heart of the French political community is based on the particular perception of the state as it originated in the Revolution, and as it has developed since. It is undeniable, too, that factors of religion, of beliefs about the French ethnic community, of the autonomous state, modify the perception citizens have of French identity as well as the general understanding of the political community and indeed of civil society. What might be of special importance to French identity is the particular role the French language plays in bringing together the political community and the speech community. Indeed the reverse is also true: language, and the speech community, seem to play a special role as a founding element in the concept of the identity of the political community itself.

The Identity Concept and the Interface between the Political Community and the Speech Community

The development of language policies

That French is an affaire d'Etat has long been recognised. French linguistic legislation is usually said to go back to 1539, with the Edicts of Villers-Cotterêts, although the official list of language legislation starts with the Strasbourg oaths of 842. Certainly language policy was deliberately and consciously made in the time of the French Revolution as we have noted in Chapter two above. Even if at this time the main purpose of linguistic legislation seems to have been to ensure that the regions could understand the Parisian developments, and thus language policy was driven by insecurity and fear, much of the rhetoric surrounding the debates and proposals put a positive gloss on the actual proposals, suggesting them as confirming France's special position and unique character. Grégoire's report was aimed at persuading the Assembly that the rational philosophy and practice of the Revolutionaries needed an appropriate instrument which would be as clear and systematic as the Revolution and the new Republic. There are many histories of the relationship of language and the French state, although few look for causes (e.g. Brunot, 1967; Ager, 1996b; Schiffman, 1996; Szulmajster-Celnikier, 1996; Posner, 1997). In this section, we shall briefly review the purposes of language policy before 1992.

The idea that language policy should be directed at not merely reflecting but also managing and manipulating a nation's self-perception and its language usage seems to have been present at about the time the nation-state developed. In particular the requirement that all citizens should learn the national language was very clearly stated, although quite impossible to achieve. Its implementation had to wait a considerable time in France, mainly because the educational system was not present nor sufficiently widespread to enable any such policy to be implemented. It was not until some forty years after the Revolution that it became possible to pass a law on elementary education (the Guizot Act of 1833), which specified that standard French should be taught and also indicated approved texts (dictionaries and grammars) which could be used, adding that a knowledge of correct spelling was a requirement for employment in the public service. Full implementation for all indeed had to wait until the Ferry Act of 1881-6, which made primary education free and obligatory for all, and in doing so made the major step of declericalising the education system. Henceforth French identity, as learnt through its language, would be secular and state-oriented. It would also be deliberately spread outwards from the elitist salons of the Enlightenment and from the hot-house atmosphere of political debate in Paris to become a normal component of the intellectual and social resources available to everyone.

By the 1930s the policy had developed to the creation of the Office de la langue française whose aims were based on the defence of the status of the national language - but only in 1937, just before the second world war. After the war, little was done about language policy for French except in Alsace, where the necessity to reinsert French into the educational system took priority. The 1966 Gaullist policy of exclusion of the Americans from French soil following his rejection of membership of NATO Strategic Command; the earlier refusal to accept the British request to join the European Communities under the Treaty of Rome mainly because they were not really 'Europeans'; the necessity to ensure that French reflected the glory of France; and de Gaulle's perception of the universal importance of French; all these factors meant that the language should be recognised as the important edifice it was, and hence be itself better managed. The result, quite apart from insistence that all the European institutions should use French, was the creation of the Haut Comité pour la Défense et l'Expansion de la Langue Française. The positive aims of this organisation were underlined in the mention of expansion, and despite the early demise of this as the organisation became simply the Haut Comité de la langue française, the purpose was clearly to promote French as central to French identity. The Committee got splendid offices in the rue Babylone, was directly attached to the Prime Minister, and was headed by civil servants rather than being left to the literati and the pressure groups.

The Bas-Lauriol Act of 31st December 1975 widened the domains in which French was to be used, directing that French be used in commerce and the workplace, and ensuring the use of French in advertising, external signs on commercial premises, and workplace agreements such as employment contracts. Any notice appearing on a publicly owned building had to be in French. The law rendered the use of French obligatory in commerce: 'in the designation, offer, presentation, publicity, both spoken and written, instructions for use, range and guarantee conditions for goods and services, invoices and receipts', and gave responsibility for implementation, not to a special institution nor to the police, but to the Ministry for Consumer Protection and those agents concerned with the suppression of fraud. Etiemble's proposals (Figure 5.1) had mostly been implemented.

This law was regarded as provocative by some members of the European Community, and the Commission entered into lengthy correspondence with the French in an attempt to change those of its provisions which could be regarded as preventing free competition among member States. The law had to be modified by ministerial circular in 1976 and again in 1982, in order to conform with the Treaty of Rome. By 1994 however, the 1975 law was universally regarded as ineffective. The fines imposed were small, the authorities charged with implementing it often found difficulties in interpretation and showed little enthusiasm for adding to their burdens in a difficult area, while it was difficult to identify an 'injured party' who might have the right to institute proceedings (Faure, 1986). Just to show that the Toubon Act was not simply a piece of right-wing symbolism, we should remember that several proposals for strengthening the 1975 legislation were made while the Socialists were in power, and work was actively proceeding on a new proposal before the 1993 election result gave Balladur the post of prime minister.

The official language

The law of 1992 adapting the Constitution was passed as a consequence of France's acceptance of the Maastricht Treaty on the expansion of the European Community and its conversion to a European Union. One new clause was inserted into the Constitution: 'The language of the Republic is French'. It is probably this clause that most clearly represents the identity concept in current legislation. Indeed, the first formulation ('French is the language of the Republic') showed that in the minds of the proposers French was a symbol of what it meant to be French, and they were put out by realising after protests that other countries which did not share the inward-looking view of the French Republic also used this symbol. Many of them took a dim view of the argument that the defence of the language should be put on the same level as the French national anthem and the French flag, as only a symbol. Much of the debate in France, though, repeated concepts we have shown to be widely accepted components of opinion about French in contemporary France, in particular those listed in Figure 6.3.

- French expresses national identity: not that of an ethnic group nor that of a political tradition, but that of the territory and of the culture.
- Language is an integral part of national culture.
- French is a symbol, together with the anthem, the motto, the flag and the liberties, of the French Republic.
- French is also and at the same time the language of Francophonie.
- French should be one of the official and the working languages of Europe.

There were some provisos, however:

- French should formally displace regional languages (which are used only in the village).
- Making French France's official language is an empty statement, unless there is also an independent foreign policy and an independent defence capability.
- French should be one of Europe's working languages, but making French one of the official languages of Europe should not allow access by foreigners to the French civil service (for example, to posts as teachers).

Sources: adapted from the 1992 debate recorded in the *Journal Officiel*, Débats, Assemblée Nationale, 12.5.1992: 1018-1022 and 1059-1060; Sénat, 10.6.1992: 1536-1541. See also the Introduction to the present volume, pp. 11-14.

Figure 6.3 French as official language

The issue of the ownership of French has led in later times to the clearer expression of the choices Poignant expressed in 1998: for Europe, for Francophonie, for multilingualism. The proprietorial attitude of the French towards French has disappeared, and dictionaries like the *Petit Larousse* specifically include non-metropolitan forms. Generally the fact that French is widely used overseas was seen as proof that French was still a major language of international importance, widely regarded as a language of culture. At the time however, 'This constitutional consecration was received with indifference in France, whereas overseas users of French, to whom this law is addressed as much as to the French, showed their satisfaction' (Szulmajster-Celnikier, 1996: 49).

One of the dangers that lie in this declaration of the official nature of French is the possible formal domination of French over other languages spoken in French territory. Participants in the Toubon debate, two years later, noted both that France was not bounded by the territorial limits of the hexagon, and that French for some in the overseas DOM and TOM had meant discrimination because people did not master French sufficiently well, and were now open to worse:

> I have one fear. If we (i.e. those living in Martinique) are, generally, bilingual, there is no doubt that a number of inhabitants do not always seize the subtleties of French, nor even its daily use...exclusive use of French in official offices and in the whole of the information and educational structure, particularly radio and television, is such as will generate incomprehension, if Creole does not help out. So I am afraid of the bad use to which civil servants and other cadres will put this Law, using it to confuse the worker, the taxpayer, those faced by the justice system because they will speak French, imposed as an official even superior language. (*Journal Officiel*, 3.5.1994)[54]

The first article of the Toubon Act of 1994 nonetheless took the basic concept of the official language and spelt out the consequences:

> Article 1. French is an essential element of France, the language of teaching, work, commerce and public service, and is the special link for the Francophone community.[55]

The insistence on the public service was underlined by the Constitutional Council's agreement , before the Act was signed into law, that the government had every right to insist not merely that French was used in all the state's work, but that an approved terminology could also be insisted on for use by the state. It was not until the implications of the Constitutional Council's decision sank in that the question of the definition of 'French' was seriously considered. Toubon himself, in the debate, had said that the proposal was not about defining the actual language itself. The Toubon Act was about status, not about corpus policy at all, even though Toubon made some interesting remarks about the incorporation of words like 'whisky'. The Constitutional Council's decision of 1994 had the direct result of confirming that the official terminology as laid down by the terminology commissions and as published in the *Journal Officiel* was, after the passage of the Act, now a legal requirement that the state could insist its servants used. At this stage it was the French as defined by state organisations that became the official language, and non-use or mis-use of it by state employees or by those dealing with the state was punishable by the criminal courts. The stage was now open to the language police, as the Socialist Party in Parliament had termed what they saw as this excessive provision.

Subsequent annual reports to Parliament by DGLF have homed in on the use of French by the public service mainly because considerable numbers of complaints from the public had been received. In some of these the fantasy element was evident: France Telecom, the national service, invented words like Tatoo or Wanadoo for some of its activities, provoking the ire of correspondents, but since the Terminology Commissions had produced no official equivalents for such expressions, the DGLF had no grounds for action! In some places the 1996 and the 1997 reports coyly mention 'difficulties' in the non-use of French by the public service; in others, and particularly where multi-nation bids had been submitted to European agencies or where public agencies like the Banque de France would otherwise be unable to work with (or in competition with) private sector firms, the law had been bent, or indeed modified by later legislation, to accommodate the reality of internationalisation. Nonetheless, the law has been taken seriously by nearly all ministries, who had nominated a senior official to take appropriate action. The training establishments, too, particularly ENA (the Ecole Nationale d'Administration) had made considerable efforts to improve instruction both in French and in other languages. Work on the readability of texts had been given a new emphasis in the Ministries of Finance and Defence, and new websites as they were established made sure French was being used.

Use of French by public servants is a requirement spelt out by a Prime Ministerial circular of April 1994, which threatened dire career consequences for individual functionaries not using good French. The need for such threats was pointed out by a survey conducted in 1978 (Fugger, 1979) which showed a considerable degree of ignorance among public servants of the terminology decisions then in operation: only 15% of the sample were prepared to implement them, 46% prepared to reject them, 30% ready to decide on use according to the context, and 9% simply not answering. In June 1998 Pierre Moscovici, the European Minister in the Foreign Office, together with Catherine Trautmann as Minister of Culture, published a 'Vade-Mecum in 10 points' in a guide to the use of French in the European Institutions (*Lettre d'Information*, 30, June 1998: 18. The Vade-mecum is reproduced here as Figure 8.5 in Chapter 8). Although couched in the language of the rights available to 'elected persons, civil servants, experts, heads of firms and professional organisations, academics...', this pointed out rather menacingly that 'in meetings, the representatives of France express themselves in French, whether or not translation is provided'.

Art 2	French is compulsory in commerce and in publicity.
Art 3	Public notices must be in French.
Art 4	Any translations of these must be in two languages.
Art 5	Contracts must be in French if drawn up by French public bodies or individuals working with public bodies.
Art 6	Any person attending a conference, congress or manifestation in French has the right to speak French; all participants must receive documents in French; officially organised congresses must have translation facilities.
Art 7	Official and subsidised publications must be in French.
Art 8	Employment contracts must be drawn up in French (and in the language of the worker if different).
Art 9	Internal regulations must be in French.
Art 10	If work cannot be described by a French term the French text must contain a suitable description in French.
Art 11	˙The language of teaching, examinations, theses and projects is French except for teaching of regional or foreign languages. Mastery of French and of two other languages is one of the basic aims of education.
Art 12	French is compulsory in radio and TV broadcasts.
Art 13	Broadcasting must respect French and francophonie.
Art 14	Trade marks must use the terms officially approved.
Art 15	Subsidies and grants by official organisations are subject to acceptance of these regulations.
Art 16, 17, 18	The consumer protection service is charged, along with the police, with implementing this Act.
Art 19	Approved associations whose objectives include the defence of the language may act as the aggrieved party in actions brought under this Act.
Art 20	The Act applies to contracts drawn up after its passage.
Art 21	Regional languages are not affected by this Act.
Art 22	An annual report must be presented to Parliament before 15th September.
Art 23	This Act is applicable after 12 months at the latest.
Art 24	The 1975 Act on French is abrogated.

Source: Loi 94-665 du 4 août 1994 relative à l'emploi de la langue française. This summary gives only the most significant parts of each Article.

Figure 6.4 The Toubon Act

The Toubon Act and its Implementation

The other provisions of the 1994 Toubon Act are, in summary, as shown in Figure 6.4. This French linguistic legislation is intended to raise the status of French, not merely by giving force to its symbolic labelling in 1992 as the official language of the Republic, but also by imposing its use in specified domains. In 1539, these were limited to written contracts and to the administration of justice in and through the courts. In 1794, 1833 and 1881-6, education was the main target. In 1975, French became compulsory in the work-place and in commerce. In 1994 however, although the Constitutional Council refused to allow the law to impose the use of official terminology on private citizens, five domains were formally identified for the use of French alone. The Constitutional decision was important because, in specifically banning state control of the language used by private citizens, it marked the limits of interference by the political community on the speech patterns of the speech community. Although the government and hence the state had a perfect right to dictate the use of language within the administration it had no such rights elsewhere.

In the following discussion of the domains of language use affected by the Toubon Act it is important to note that although the intention of the government to control the whole of the speech community was clear, the political community lost the ability to do so. The test of whether it lost altogether must lie in future statistics of language use, particularly in the domains which the Toubon Act specified and where private individuals as well as the state are concerned, as well as in consideration of attitude and opinion about language use in France.

Employment

One of the novelties of the Toubon Act had been its awareness of the remainder of the French legal and penal system. Whereas the 1975 Act had been drafted as though it was tackling a problem which had little connection with the rest of the penal code and hence remained largely symbolic, the Toubon legislators used the provisions of existing law both in devising the set of punishments appropriate for any violation of the new text, and for defining exactly which parts of the employment legislation should be affected. These were mainly those concerned with workers' rights in employment contracts. While employment contracts had been theoretically controlled already by the 1975 legislation, in 1994 the rules were extended to any document affecting health and safety, discipline, and internal arrangements such as conditions of work agreed by a collective convention. They applied to recruitment advertisements (any employment to be carried out in France had to be advertised in French whatever the nationality of the employer), and in theory all those placed by any French employer whether or not they concerned work to be carried out abroad. Nonetheless, they did not go as far as the Quebec legislation which requires that firms use only French in all internal communication, both written and spoken (Ager, 1996a: 36).

By 1997, although no case had been taken as far as the courts, the DGLF had received several complaints from individual workers, from the language associations, or as a result of its own monitoring of recruitment advertisements. In cases where French firms recruited abroad, and were nonetheless obliged to use French, some had got round the law by passing the advertisement through their overseas subsidiaries. In general the DGLF had become aware by 1997 that this whole area was extremely problematic. The 1997 report divided the problems up into those affecting individual contracts, where 'the Ministère du Travail has not been informed of any dossier and there is hence no case law'; job advertisements, where there is 'no permanent observation' but major infraction was 'very rare'; documents placing obligations on employees 'which was a notion foreign to the law on employment, and hence posed problems for inspectors'; the question of the internal working language, where the DGLF could simply note that it was becoming a tendency for firms to use English if they were subsidiaries of international organisations and sometimes in other cases where there was no commercial or international need.

> Such a tendency is particularly worrying...for social questions and the protection of employees, sometimes obliged to use a foreign language with other French workers, in receiving instructions and in training. (DGLF, 1997, 2, II, 3)[56]

The DGLF's response was to give advice to those making enquiries, but although a working group had met on the questions involved and submitted a report in 1995, it seems fairly clear that the area is one where French businesses are unlikely to change their practice. One was cited in 1997 as having published a second advertisement in French after an earlier one in English alone. The 1997 DGLF report in this section sounds rather more like a sad shaking of the head than a proactive legal pursuit: 'firms are showing a certain indifference to the relationships between language and the world of work or the economy'. One prize example was clearly shocking: 'in Vietnam, despite action over several years in preparation for the Hanoi Francophone Summit, the first advertisement seen on leaving the airport was an enormous poster in English for a large French firm'.

Education

In 1995 the programmes for French in education were reviewed and the importance of study of the language confirmed within the timetable allocations. Bayrou's new 'schools contract' of 1994 stressed the need to concentrate on French in the sensitive years - the last three of primary education, where there was substantial progress to be made. By 1997 the 'educational system has made mastery of the language a priority' (DGLF, 1997, 2, VI). Many reports other than the DGLF one on achievement in French schools remain pessimistic, but those quoted by DGLF on reading competence were said to be 'encouraging' and showing improvement: 19.5% below a satisfactory standard in 1992, 15.3% in 1995 at CE2 level (approximately age 9), 11.5% in 1992 and 9% in 1995 at age 11 (DGLF, 1996, IV, 3). The 1997 report was more cautious: it noted that the tests differed from year to year and thus direct comparisons were impossible. The comparison of results at the end of primary education obtained by children in 1923, 1924 and 1925 with a sample tested in 1995, was put forward as disproving the prophets of doom about the quality of modern education, but it nonetheless showed that although results in writing and in dictation (on understanding the text) are more or less the same or slightly better today, in spelling, grammar and verb forms today's children scored distinctly worse. But it is in teaching in French, rather than the teaching of French, that supporters of the law had seen the greatest problem. Many of them had in fact revealed their own concerns as being connected with the intellectual world, of conferences, colloquia and the submission of doctoral theses. The 1995 Report had threatened to pursue the Grandes Ecoles Commerciales which continued to teach business management in English. Anecdotal experience can confirm that some French Universities are quite determined to refuse any equivalence of doctoral level qualifications not written in French unless they were co-supervised by a French university. The DGLF report does not seem altogether convinced either about European doctorates or those in which summaries in French are allowed, with the main text in a foreign language. Indeed, the traditional impermeability of the French educational and qualification system, which has always appeared designed to prevent candidates with a foreign background from gaining employment with qualifications other than French ones, seems still to be important and to gain comfort from the legislation.

Publicity and commerce

Georgia Tech Lorraine, an offshoot of the Georgia Institute of Technology in Atlanta, based in Lorraine and at that stage using only English on the Web page advertising its courses, was taken to court in 1996 for violating the Act. It was not alone: the Body Shop in Chambéry had also been found guilty of 'cruelty to the French language by selling products labelled in English' (*The Guardian*, 19.11.1996). The Direction Générale de la Concurrence, de la Consommation et de la Répression des Fraudes (DGCCRF), the agency responsible for pursuing offenders against this 'protection of the consumer', showed new-found diligence after the Toubon Act. It carried out 1,918 checks in 1994 (796 in 1990, under the 1975 legislation), 2,576 in 1995 and 6,258 in 1996, with a further 2,704 in just four months of 1997. Court cases rose from 107 in 1994 to 366 in 1996. The courts themselves also became somewhat tougher: convictions rose from 22 in 1993 to 56 in 1996. Summarising the languages involved and the sector, the DGLF remarked that 65% of cases concerned packaging, labelling and directions for use in English, although German, Italian and Spanish were each responsible for at least 5% of cases. The DGLF, which set up a formal partnership to pursue these cases with the DGCCRF in October 1996, investigated particular sectors, making three specific checks in 1995 on garden and electronic equipment and on contact lenses and on other sectors the following year. Where garden equipment was mainly of European origin and from large international firms, there were few problems (19 in 365 outlets): most accompanying documentation was in a number of languages including French. CDs were more frequently sold without French documentation (21 court cases and 10 warnings in 85 outlets). In the field of contact lenses, imports were widely made from Britain, the United States and Japan. Warnings followed:

> leaders of the manufacturers and importers were made aware of the obligations imposed by the Act. They wish to adhere strictly to the regulations, and they will hence shortly be received by the administration so that the point can be made about the new linguistic instrument. (DGLF, 1996, 2, I, 1, appendix 6)[57]

The 1975 Act had been subject to a number of reserves by the European Commission in view of the issue of open competition. By 1996, unease about the effect of the Toubon Act on the spirit if not the letter of competition agreements had certainly been expressed by the British and German governments and by the Commission itself. Law on language is not systematic in Europe, covers only packaging, labelling and directions for use, and hence a number of problems have arisen. One concerned the notion of 'language readily understood by consumers' in the country of final sale, which has now generally been replaced, to the satisfaction of French legislators, by the expression 'official language(s)' of the country of final sale. The Commission has put a number of questions to France about its language legislation, including for example the requirement for a quota of songs in French required of radio and TV stations. Another area involved major insurance contracts, where France conceded the possibility that certain contracts be drawn up in other languages where the relevant legislation is not French, as may be the case in insuring major risks.

It is of course in the area of consumer information that cynical commentators were sure the Toubon Act intended to keep out competition from foreigners. _Libération,_ on 24. 2.1994, simply said it was intended for Italian makers of kettles and Japanese electronic firms. It is hardly surprising that the authorities targeted agricultural products in 1996, nor that agricultural imports from Spain was involved. There is undoubtedly an element of commercial protectionism and support of protesting French farmers involved:

> Professionals (i.e. retailers) seem to be exercising greater vigilance, which in turn is having an effect on suppliers. The establishment of checking procedures among these is no longer unusual: professionals are no longer hesitating after checking goods in sending back those which do not respect the 1994 legislation or in ensuring they do conform. Such awareness is lacking in some areas, however, as the sector analysis, the identification of sensitive sectors and the quarterly checks since 1996 show. Hence the _DGCCRF_ and the _DGLF_ will undertake... a major exercise in informing professional organisations about what is at stake, in terms of economics and the law, in this linguistic instrument, a major element in the policies of competition and consumer protection, on the national as well as the European Community level. (DGLF, 1996, 2, I, 1)[58]
>
> Because of the proximity of the Spanish frontier, some Spanish producers, importers and wholesalers make direct deliveries, at lower prices, to French distributors (hyper and supermarkets, retailers, restaurants) situated in border regions. (DGLF, 1997, I, 1)[59]

The effort by the political community to control the language use of commerce has certainly intensified, and the attempt to control economic behaviour through stressing pride in France and Frenchness is very clear. By 1997 more than 15,000 firms had been checked, and several thousand products. Most of these were in areas where French production was low (some cosmetics, motorbike accessories, some health products, software, video games) or where the service offered was one that traditionalists might feel was un-French such as fast-food restaurants, where 24% of establishments were taken to court, although this onslaught had led to formal agreements between the larger chains and the DGLF in an attempt to stop the repeated ad-hoc cases.   Indeed, one effect of case-law was that the Béziers tribunal decided on 2nd April 1997 that expressions like *Big Mac, Mac chicken* and *Mac bacon* did not contravene the law since they fell into the same set of exceptions as *chorizo, cookie, couscous* and *gin* which had been accepted as French words in the 19th March 1996 Circular of Application of the law. The 1997 report did show, also, that the general level of the punishments was fairly low: the Body Shop in Chambéry had been given ten fines of 100 francs; the largest single fine recorded was 5,000 francs.   Interestingly, one fine was for a faulty translation rather than the absence of one at all.

Media

Most of the provisions affecting broadcasting media have come from a different, parallel law of 1994 intended to ensure a quota of 40% of songs in French on private radio. Public radio stations already required 'a majority' of such material to be in French. The underlying elitist attitude, often expressed and certainly influential in French cultural policy, sees American cultural imports, from pop songs to films like Jurassic Park, as attacking the very basis of French culture. It has been most overtly stated in the 1993 GATT negotiations, when the concept of the cultural exception to globalisation was developed. It is this area which in 1995 and 1996 led to concern by the European Commission, and the government response has been to stress that the criterion is not the French nationality of the singer or the music, but the language used, despite the definition in the 1994 law of 'French or French-speaking artists' (artistes français ou francophones).

Media linguistic control also affects the 'quality' of language, which is said to have been a concern of television and radio authorities since at least 1968 - a significant date in itself. The observers who check on this, most of whom are members of Défense de la Langue Française, the approved language association housed by the French Academy, undertake random checks on grammar, vocabulary and pronunciation. What is particularly looked for is the use of the official terminology; attempts to translate Anglicisms (no other language is mentioned); corrections of mistakes as they are made; and what is said in programmes on language. TV channels usually have an in-house checking procedure, and interestingly the state contracts for the privatised TF1 and for M6 required the appointment of a qualified advisor in language. The contract signed with the supervising Conseil Supérieur de l'Audiovisuel in 1996 included a clause in which both committed themselves to ensure the 'correct use of French in broadcasts as well as adaptations, dubbing and sub-titling of foreign works'. The general outcome of these supervisory and controlling mechanisms seems to have been satisfactory, in that the DGLF reports of 1996 and 1997 find few problems, despite noting that the main complaint from radio stations aimed at young people had been the lack of French-language material. One should note, too, that despite the response to the European Commission, the only statistic mentioned in the 1997 DGLF report is based on singers' nationality rather than the language used. Despite these problems, there is little doubt that French media now broadcasts much more French language material than it used to and that this has given considerable financial benefit to French talent ('contributed to the development and renewal of Francophone artists' discs') (DGLF, 1997, 2, III, 2).[60]

The laws affecting media seem to reflect wishes by the political community to control the speech community, as well as a desire on the part of the elite to impose its view of culture on the mass. The net effect of the quota and the checks on language quality is certainly that media providers and journalists are aware of their presence. Interestingly, the difference with the British system is that the stress in France is distinctly on language quality in terms of correction and the avoidance of Anglicisms, while the British control system seems uniquely concerned with questions of decency. Either way, there are fears that open sky policies in the future may enable French citizens to receive television which has not been subject to state control in this way:

> Our quota system is nonetheless at risk in the future. The reading that the European Court of Justice has given of the Television without frontiers directive could mean that our broadcasting could be opened to European operators subject only to the legal control operative in their own countries, particularly insofar as quotas are concerned. (DGLF, 1997, 2, III, 4)[61]

Scientific meetings and publications

The precise formulation concerns 'manifestations, colloquia or congresses organised in France', which must allow French to be used, documents to be available in French and, at least, summaries of papers to be in French, as must publications, reviews and communications published in France. Possibly the most significant component of these measures is the fact that interpreting and translation agencies received a sudden boost in their income, and that subsidies for scientific meetings in particular could call on additional resources both to support the scientific work and also for translation and interpreting. Nonetheless the practical impossibility for organisers of large congresses with numerous workshops or parallel paper sessions to provide interpreters for everything, coupled with the innate impatience of the scientific American to listen to anything except English render the law very difficult to apply. If the scientific congress is to be worthwhile, too, it must report innovations and time is often lacking for large-scale processing of documents in advance, or for the training of specialist interpreters. In the case of only two large international meetings in 1995 was it financially possible to interpret and translate everything: in other cases the opening and closing speeches, only, were given in French.

The motive for this aspect of the legislation was 'to maintain for French its role as language of international communication', particularly through ensuring its continued presence in sensitive sectors among which science was foremost. The 1990 study which led to the inclusion of these clauses, against the almost unanimous opposition of the scientific community, showed 45% of scientific congresses held in France using English as their sole working language, while 55% of participants had merely a passive knowledge of the language and thus could not take part in debates. The DGLF continues to declare that these requirements are innocuous and inexpensive, but such protests hide the reality that they are in practice unworkable, given the attraction of a single global language for science and scientists including French ones. Indeed, it is not in the career interests of French scientists to insist on French, nor is there any formal organisation observing what goes on, as the 1997 DGLF report wryly notes. In these circumstances, the decision has been taken to concentrate on high-profile congresses which support the 'rayonnement' of French interests; but the amount of aid available (50,000 francs and no more than 50% of the total cost) renders the subsidies laughable in view of the costs of professional interpreters and equipment hire. The Institut Pasteur thus held half its 1996 meetings in French, the other half in English; other conferences provided translation only for the opening and closing sessions. Similarly, in the case of publications, although the DGLF 1996 report put a brave face on the situation, it is clear that English is and remains the main language of publication. In the case of computing, the Institut National de Recherche en Informatique et en Automatique published 420 reports between January 1996 and May 1997, 79 in French, 341 in English. The reports of its two conferences were in English with summaries in French.

Is the speech community falling into line?

The DGLF reports are of course destined to show how effective that organisation itself is, as well as to convey the actual facts of the situation. It is nonetheless clear that the political community, in the shape of the law and its state implementation agencies, has every intention of imposing its views on the speech community. The political aims of French language policy, as outlined by the Minister of Culture in March 1996, are repeated in the foreword to the 1996 report as if to remind readers of the authoritarian intent:

> French is a major element in social cohesion ... action in favour of French has three objectives: to ensure the presence and influence of French in our country, to maintain for French its role as a language for international communication, to promote multilingualism. (DGLF, 1996, Avant-propos)[62]

Responses by the speech community so far are somewhat ambiguous to the implementation of this 'attack on liberty', the law and 'the language police', as the enforcement agencies were termed by the Socialist Party which abstained from the vote on it in 1994. Requests for information and advice on specific cases rose from 550 in 1995 to over 700 in 1996, mostly on questions of publicity and commerce. Complaints about non-observance of the law gave rise to 'abundant' correspondence in 1995 and 1996, mainly about labelling or instructions for use. It is also clear that the speech community in France, despite a considerable amount of goodwill, is nonetheless not of itself inclined to do all the political community wants. The number of offences is still high; the DGLF is constantly intervening; some of the issues still continue to the stage of court cases, although as far as possible the DGLF is still apparently trying to ensure that the high profile ones leading to publicised fines affect French business less than English or American businesses, or imports of 'Asiatic' origin. In this, as in the protection afforded employment, the unsaid purpose of the legislation is clear: language policy advantages French economic interests. The protectionism is not motivated solely by fear of economic ruin: pride in France, and in the distinctive nature of French identity as exemplified in language, song and science, is a strong force.

Schiffman (1996: 123) considers that 'there are two high water marks for French linguistic culture and policy development - the development of the _Académie Française_ and the French Revolution'. This summary judgement needs to be expanded. Now, it is clear that in view of the deliberate and high profile Toubon Act and its determined application by the powerful Administration that it is not just these that lie behind present-day political and intellectual interpretations of concepts like the identity of France, the power of the state, and thus the issue of the status and prestige of French. The identity of France is much more complex than a simple transfer of the royalist and revolutionary ideals to the present day. Language policy, too, is not just a feature of the linguistic culture, the cultural and intellectual world of the bellettristes and the attitudes of the elite. It represents a larger political and social environment, in which commercial, industrial and social concerns involving such mundane matters as competitiveness are also involved. But it is time now to consider direct action by the state, not on the users of language, but on the language itself. How has the political community attempted to direct and manage the French language itself?

Chapter 7

Managing French to Serve the State: Stability, Elasticity and Polyvalency

We have noted that the major part of the Grégoire Report of 1794 was devoted to a plea for corpus policy aimed at constructing a language suitable for the new nation-state. The purpose was to work on the actual form of the language, its words and grammar, in a spirit of rational reform aimed at making the language 'pure'. Thomas's (1991) review of purist attitudes towards language, which as we noted above helps to understand language attitudes in France towards concepts of social exclusion, is also helpful here in analysing the nature of French corpus policy. Thomas's major division between 'external' purism opposing the influence of the outside world on one's own language, and which acts by attacking other languages or by trying to exclude borrowings from them, and the 'internal' language attitudes which have a range of motives, reflects the basic division we have made in this book between the motivation of insecurity (which leads to xenophobic purism) and that of identity, which relates to all four types of internal purist attitudes. In opposition to the rational reformist zeal of Grégoire aimed at producing a perfect language, and hence accepting that French is not at the moment quite that vehicle, most other internal purist attitudes take the view that French is, or has been, at one stage or another as near perfection as possible, and the aim is to preserve it. Archaising, elitist and ethnographic types of purism, the latter close to ethnic nationalism, identify types of French which must be preserved. Such attitudes, which Thomas distinguished as in Figure 7.1, are often present at one and the same time in French arguments and discussions on the language.

Assuming thus that the basic motivation for corpus work on French is in some way to confirm French identity, the purist attitudes aimed at doing so sought, before and during the Revolutionary period, to prioritise the rational (reformist) approach to language: it should be rational and logical, clear and precise. The logical grammar of Port-Royal of 1660 and the praise of French by Rivarol in 1784 had already provided examples of such attitudes before the Revolution. It is this attitude, too, which fostered three basic ideas about (the need for) codification of the language: the legitimacy of one (socially prestigious) variety of the language, the prioritisation of the written forms over the spoken, and the logical superiority of certain desirable forms. During the Revolution there were many proposals for reforming spelling, grammar and expressions. Then, with one type of French established, attitudes changed to prioritise the archaic approach, keeping the language stable and unchanging because perfection had been achieved and the greater danger was social disturbance. The ethnographic attitude (preference for what is 'truly French') and the elitist one (what is 'good usage' and elegant) also gained in importance. It is these three attitudes that stabilised the orthography, the morphology and grammar, and had major effects on vocabulary.

External perspective	Internal perspective
Xenophobic	Temporal plane:
	Archaising
	Reformist
	Social plane:
	Elitist
	Ethnographic

Source: Thomas, 1991.

Figure 7.1 Types of purism

The needs to ensure that French itself was rational, worthy of France and at the same time a vehicle appropriate for the communication of significant modern ideas were, and still are, main motives for attempts by the state to get involved in the process. These motives have clearer socio-political origins than either the archaic or the xenophobic attitudes, and are perhaps more important for managing change than for internal stability. But the archaic motivation has political connotations, too: in ensuring a stable educational foundation for society, and also in providing support for traditional social structures. Xenophobia, too, is a political motive, variously in favour at different times in pursuance of a range of political purposes. Purist attitudes are hence not a prerogative of the speech community, and the desire to control language may also have political motives. The involvement of the state has been taken farther in France than in most other countries for a number of reasons.

At first, under the Ancien Régime, the vehicle of state involvement was the French Academy, abolished at the beginning of the Revolution. Napoleon continued the abolition, but it was during the Empire that the mechanisms of state control over language started to appear. The centralisation of the Administration and its reliance on French, together with the gate-keeping work of the educational system resulted in a strong control mechanism ensuring the widespread use of the standardised form. But social control was as important: the desire of the growing middle classes was to seek safety in the known correction of an approved language. It was not until the twentieth century that the vehicle of state control was added to, as the Office de la Langue Française, requested by a significant group of linguists, was set up in 1937. Abandoned during the war, this became the Office du Vocabulaire Français in 1957. In 1966 President de Gaulle set up the Haut Comité pour la Défense et l'Expansion de la langue française, which had among other tasks that of ensuring that modern French vocabulary could match the requirements of a technological age. As this group changed its name, and to a certain extent its role, over the next few years, the task of managing terminology became ever more important, so terminology committees were set up in each ministry after 1970. The mechanism for implementing state 'interference' in the actual language was revised in 1984, again in 1989 and 1993 to give a somewhat complex range of committees, groups, associations and services which all felt they had a hand in managing French. The main ones at national level now, apart from the Academy, are the Conseil Supérieur de la Langue Française (CSLF) chaired by the Prime Minister and to which the Délégation Générale à la Langue Française (DGLF), attached to the Ministry of Culture, reports. An inter-ministerial group of senior civil servants ensures co-ordination among the many ministries involved (seven signed the 1995 Decree for the application of the Toubon Law), and the DGLF also has a remit to 'propose and implement an open and dynamic language policy to serve national unity and France's international strategy'. The DGLF also works with the terminology bureaux of other countries, such as Switzerland, Quebec and Belgium, on matters of corpus policy. In this chapter we are concerned with such matters of constituent or administrative policy only to the extent that the work the organisations do on language forms reflects the identity motive. The corpus work itself raises two major questions:

- what is the balance between keeping the language stable and allowing it to change? and, the sixty-four thousand dollar question:
- does it work?

Corpus work, in any language, seems to be a mixture of

- stability, trying to maintain and codify the standard language;
- elasticity, making sure the language can accept new terms and designations as the world changes; and
- polyvalency - making sure that the language 'must be capable of expanding its repertoire in order to fulfil all the social functions which it is required to carry out', so it can be used in the full range of social situations. (Thomas, 1991: 53)

These three aims of corpus policy conflict with each other: stability, or the least change possible, would mean that the language could remain for ever fixed, so the question arises as to whether codification has been taken too far in French. Elasticity is absolutely essential if innovations are to be named and if new senses for existing words are to develop, so the question is to know what is so bad about the particular mechanism, of linguistic borrowing from Anglo-American, which is so denigrated in France. Polyvalency works against both of these, which try to ensure as far as possible a one-to-one relationship between a word and a particular environment or context of use, and the issue here is to evaluate language policy actions against the stated aim of social integration.

Stability

The French Academy

The French Academy, founded at first as a discussion club, was adopted by Cardinal Richelieu in 1634, although its Constitution and aims were registered by the Paris Parlement in 1635 (Castries, 1985). Richelieu did not see its task as being solely conservation and codification: the job he gave it was to make French pure, eloquent and capable of treating the arts and sciences, which it was to do through publishing a Dictionary, a Grammar, a Rhetorics, or description of styles and manners of speech, and a Poetics, or description of the rules for writing acceptable literature. The Academy was a state organisation, and was given specific jobs to do in supporting Richelieu's policies: to publish negative 'views' on Corneille's 'le Cid', regarded by Richelieu as glorifying duelling (then officially banned) and the Spanish (against whom the French were at war). The Academy was abolished in 1793 and only partially recreated in 1795 as part of the Institut National charged with 'collecting discoveries and perfecting the arts and sciences'. It is, since 1816, the third Classe of the Institut de France which has four other 'classes' making five Academies in total: Academies of Inscriptions et Belles-Lettres, Sciences, Beaux-Arts, Sciences Morales et Politiques.

The French Academy is a group of forty 'immortals', chosen by other members for their eminence in literature and the arts. The youngest (in mid-July 1997) was 59 (Pierre-Jean Rémy), the oldest 96 (Julien Green), and there were eight members over 90 years old. The Academy itself meets weekly on Thursdays, and is supported by a Permanent Secretary (in 1998, Maurice Druon) and by a small professional staff. Only two experts in linguistics have been elected since 1900. Although not chaired by him, it is formally under the 'protection' of the President of the Republic. This means, of course, that it both is and is not part of the government machine, and its independence from direct control means that it is in a sometimes uneasy relationship with the DGLF and those parts of the Foreign Ministry dealing with language abroad. It awards literary and language prizes, and carries out regular work in discussing the meaning of words for its dictionary, which is constantly being revised. The Rhetoric, the Grammar and the Poetics have now fallen by the wayside, since the expertise available to the Academy is limited and certainly not up to the requirements of modern linguistics. The Academy has for long now taken the view that its role is to record usage (_greffer l'usage_) rather than attempt to prescribe it. In its preparation for the dictionary work, too, it tries to identify what current meanings are, but since it has deliberately excluded some levels and varieties of language from consideration from the beginning (familiar, vulgar, slang words; neologisms; most technical terms; regional words) it often seems fairly remote from the day-to-day (Batty and Hintze, 1992: 25). As a result, the codification the French Academy has been most familiar with has been a sort of exclusion and purification, removing words from the language rather than welcoming innovation. It is this role of the Academy which has given rise to or at least reflected the widespread attitude in the speech community which prioritises correctness, objects to novelty, seeks elegance and equates good French with the French of the past.

The Academy had gradually fallen into the periphery of the language world, particularly after the _Grammaire de l'Académie_ of 1932 was howled down as being scientifically poor, and despite constant updating of spelling in editions of its dictionaries over the nineteenth century. Littré had taken over as the standard dictionary in the late nineteenth century; grammar was defined in school text-books not produced by the Academy even as early as 1833. When de Gaulle set about modernising

France in the search for greatness, the fuddy-duddy old men of the Academy failed to fit the image, and the creation of the Haut Comité simply by-passed it. By the time of the creation of the terminology committees after 1970 it had even less it could offer, and next to no staff to do it with. Indeed, the committees were sometimes called alternative academies. But the poor public reception of the work of the celebrated terminology committee of 1986, on feminism in the language, and 1990, on spelling - even though this was done under the aegis of the Academy and formally approved by it in full session - was to provoke the policy-makers into realising that brash new organisational innovations possessed neither the respectability nor the intellectual weight to ensure that changes they proposed could be accepted by the speech community. It was probably one or two acid remarks by Druon as Secretary of the Academy, too, which brought the supporters of the Toubon Act face to face with the need to get the Academy and the speech community on board, and Druon's polite recommendation to 'spend six months getting the Academy to advise' sharpened the realisation (see *Le Figaro*, 4.8.1994). In 1996 therefore the Academy regained its role as supreme arbiter for the official vocabulary, with the passage of Decree 96-602 of the Ministry of Culture. This made terminology committees compulsory in every ministry, and placed a general committee in the Prime Minister's office with the task of approving the work of all the special committees and also that of examining words and expressions which did not fall within the remit of any one of them. M. Gabriel de Broglie was appointed as the general committee's first head for four years. Once the general committee had submitted the terms it wished to the Academy and the Academy had also approved them, they could be directly published in the *Journal Officiel*. Such direct publication means, of course, that the Academy now has direct control over new official terminology, even though this is currently limited to four or five thousand terms and even though its use is limited to state organisations or those dealing with them.

Language defence associations

Five associations were formally approved in 1995 as having the right to act as the aggrieved party in actions brought under the Toubon Law. From this point of view, since they have the right to act in court in 'criminal' cases, they are in effect part of the government mechanism for protecting and defending language, although the Tribunal de Police in Paris insisted in 1996 that only state agencies had this right. The five are listed in Figure 7.2.

- Défense de la Langue Française, founded in 1958 and supported by the French Academy (DLF).
- Association Francophone d'Amitié et de Liaison, an umbrella group founded in 1974 and restructured in 1983 (AFAL).
- Avenir de la Langue Française, founded in 1993, which acted as the main pressure group for the Toubon Law (ALF).
- Conseil International de la Langue Française, founded in 1968 (CILF).
- Association des Informaticiens de Langue Française, founded in 1981 (AILF).

Figure 7.2 Associations defending French

One has to say that generally the Associations are single-issue pressure groups, and share a much harder attitude towards language than even the most die-hard of politicians dared to express in 1992 or 1994. The Associations themselves have enjoyed public subsidies since well before the Toubon Act was passed. Their membership consists of individuals, it is true, but significant members are close to political circles: Salon, the leading light in the ALF, is in the Ministry for Co-operation; Guillou, also in the ALF, is a former diplomat. So one could conclude that the Associations are representative of the Paris Establishment, of the intellectual and educational world, of the world of state functionaries, and indeed seem to represent the 'policy community' and even the autonomous state in action (Ager, 1996b: 126-31). But one has to ask how representative of French public opinion the Associations are. The abstention by the Socialist Party, the public outcry, various newspaper comments and the publicly expressed concerns over freedom of speech during the Toubon debate showed both that there were strong objections to the idea of a state language policy and wariness about the mandarins and the elitism of the proposals. Two changes have hence taken place on the official side: the discourse of support for language policy adopted words like 'openness', 'legitimate', 'guarantee its place', 'modern', 'exchange' in addition to the usual patriotic fervour. The idea of the 'rights' of speakers of French to use the language has been raised in importance, and the commercial advantages to France of insisting on its own language were advanced, less and less discreetly. Secondly, the decision was taken to run a publicity campaign about the essential value of (this approach to) language matters, in an attempt to counter the accusations of authoritarianism, of unawareness of the reality of language, and of an inward-looking, defensive and closed approach to

France's role and to new developments like Europe. The concept of support for multilingualism, too, made its appearance as a key item in language policy. Some politicians went so far as to point out that the status of French, certainly on the international level, depended on the status France gave to other languages, although this new-found attitude did not then extend to the regional languages. The Associations did not seem overall inclined to modify their approach, however, and the public declarations and calls to arms remain. There is no doubt that there are many, very active, self-appointed guardians of the language both in and outside the Associations. An article on 6th January 1997 in *Le Monde* reviewed some of the spelling mistakes in the paper that had been picked up by readers, and was introduced thus by the editors:

> If one theme recurs with solid regularity in readers' letters, it is that of the defence of French, in all its forms: calls for grammatical correctness, battles against invasions by English words, denunciation of barbaric and inappropriate terms (*barbarismes et solécismes*), warnings against bad use of words, condemnation of spelling mistakes. Many correspondents, often members of Language Defence Associations, pick over our articles and let us know about their sad surprise, or their vehement indignation, at the errors which the speed of daily production prevents us correcting in time. (*Le Monde*, 6.1.1997)[63]

Has codification and control led to ossification?

Preserving the stability of any language is often likened to Canute's work: an impossible task. Usage will not be limited by diktat and private citizens cannot be prevented from saying what they like; social preferences for a group norm cannot be excluded; the whole point about the elite is that it has to mark its difference from what the mass say, so its language will inevitably change in order to maintain distance. Conservation by guardians like the French Academy can only take place in a small isolated community carefully protected from external reality; the social pressure required to force people to speak the same (variety of) language would only work in a tightly controlled environment. Although the purpose of codification is to ensure that the value of language is stable, pursuing the ideal of stability too far can lead to the language ossifying. Nonetheless, just like the currency, words must be safe and sure, their value readily understood and exchanged, without ambiguity and available to all. The legitimate language must be guaranteed, and in the French conception the guarantor has to be the state. The state then has to avoid the danger that stability implies archaic purism, and needs a repressive, controlled police state to work properly. If it does work properly, the inevitable consequence is that language makes no progress, and language, like society, would gradually be left out of desirable change.

Another argument is occasionally put forward, too. It is stated that French is inherently difficult to learn. Not merely this, but that this very difficulty is so valuable in training the mind, sharpening the faculties, that the language must be kept in such a condition that it is a mental test and training ground. Any attempt at simplifying French, at bringing the spoken and written codes closer together, at enabling Francophone countries outside France easier access to (a version of) the language, would thus destroy the very character and value of the language:

> our language is itself an institution: it is only living and fruitful by virtue of being well taught...French is not a lingua franca you daub yourself with in order 'to communicate'. Its norms are inseparable from the legislation which nuances and interprets them: a stock of shared literary texts and history...Well-taught French is more than just French: it is the human spirit placed in possession of a symbolic system which opens the door to all the others...the Latin of modern times is in itself a human education...Francophonie was from the beginning a wager on the quality, the singularity and the superiority of education in French. (Fumaroli in *Le Figaro*, 18.3.1996)[64]

State policy on codification has been located either at arms length, as with the Academy; or, if directly, through the education ministry, in the instructions on language use contained in the syllabuses at the different levels, and in the instructions to examiners in the range of official examinations which give qualifications or give access to employment in the public service. Such policy has not always been rigid, nor over-detailed. In 1901 the Education Ministry issued a set of *Tolérances*, forms which the jury of markers for public examinations did not have to consider as wrong, and tried again to stop the examination system and its markers being too dictatorial in 1910 and in 1975. The list is still valid, and republished frequently (Tolérances, 1997). Some of the rules for grammatical agreements were relaxed in the Academy's 1990 *Rectifications* to spelling. In this area then, micro policy has proved much tougher than macro policy. It has really been mainly in the area of borrowings, and fairly recently, that pressure to manage change has been at a high level, and then not through these agencies. Nonetheless, this type of policy, and these agencies, lie at the edge of elitism. The purpose of language control through state institutions giving access to socially prestigious employment and to social acceptability is thought by many to represent political (or economic) gate-keeping, rather than the social gate being guarded by the nineteenth century bourgeoisie with their preferred instrument, the baccalaureate. In this view, the examination process merely checks that the 'right' sort of education has been experienced: the child has received instruction in socially acceptable norms. As we noted above, success is predetermined: awareness of correct spelling, punctuation and expression only comes through having access to the sort of texts which are only freely available to the elite. Without public libraries, free school textbooks, some children have access only to poor quality journalism or the spoken media.

Government and state action has greatly intensified since the Toubon debate in an attempt to raise awareness of the issue of language as a living inheritance. After 1994 there was clearly a need to gain the support of the speech community for what had been openly called a Fascist policy, condemned by the Constitutional Council as contravening the fundamental freedoms of the Rights of Man. The DGLF spelt out the policy for promoting the importance of French as follows:

> No matter what the wish of the authorities, a linguistic policy cannot succeed without everybody's support... The aim is to ensure the public becomes aware that French is our most important inheritance. Every main part of the policy for French, from the Act of August 4th to multilingualism, from enrichment of French to the information society, needs actions to make people aware. (DGLF, 1996, 3, II)[65]

Numerous specific publicity arrangements have followed: a French Language Week is repeated every year, there is official support for manifestations such as the spelling contests held annually, brief adverts appear regularly on TV and radio. The purpose of such actions is to promote the idea of state control and particularly to make the new terminology acceptable. The danger, obviously, is that it might convince people that there is a real possibility of the disappearance of French when they never thought there was any.

But state involvement in control goes back two centuries at least, and there is some evidence that this has led to ossification. There has long been a current of French opinion which has sought control of the language by official means, although not in quite such blatant terms as those of a public notice of 1799: 'The Citizens of Paris must reshape and correct on posters anything which is contrary to the laws, to decency and to the rules of French' (cf. Brunot, 1967: 685). This has been most significant in the lexicon, where the French reverence for the dictionary is well-known and where, from the eighteenth century, 'The dictionary was to provide the benchmark for legitimate usage' (Posner, 1997: 171).

Legitimate usage in fact meant a paucity of new creations and a restriction of the word-stock. It has been claimed that the undeniable attempts from Malherbe and Vaugelas on to limit the word-stock of French had the effect of forcing lexical innovation to rely on borrowing from other languages since the processes of word-creation within French were frowned upon: 'borrowing is favoured by the timidity of language users who are deprived of dynamic inventiveness' (Hagège, 1987: 144). Other methods of word formation do exist (see below) but the range is small, and neither semantic shift nor affixation have been much used in standard French because users are terrified to seem too creative. It is this struggle between stability and elasticity that is the locus of the language legislation and the locus of the purists' battle. The purists will inevitably lose either way, in the view of some: either France itself turns its back on modernity, or the language collapses as internal methods of word creation are freed up to enable greater, more rapid and more imaginative developments.

In terms of grammar and morphology, there is mixed evidence about whether codification has led to ossification. Most new word creations fall into the simplest _-er_ or _-iser_ structures: _solutionner, crédibiliser, fidéliser,_ while new creations which do not follow this pattern, like _alunir_ (to land on the moon) are rare, so ossification might be said to have occurred. But most grammatical change - the disappearance of forms of the subjunctive, of the preterite, of interrogative inversion - can hardly be laid at the door of codification. The strict set of arrangements for written French, particularly the spelling of _-e, -es, -ent_ for verb tenses or _-e, -é, -ée, -ées_ agreements are just not relevant for the spoken forms, and the language has simply passed them by. The language has continued to change in other types of usage: left dislocation is much more frequent than it was in the period to 1950 (_Marie, sa cousine, elle la connaît?_); the use of _est-ce-que_ in questions, the loss of _ne_ in negatives, changes in adjectival position (_l'actuel Président_ rather than _le Président actuel_) all show that the codification which condemned such usages has not caused the language such terror that it has not developed. Indeed, it may be that the strictness of the codification process, its application to a strongly maintained stress on the accuracy of written forms and the purist attitudes that have led to such a strong apparent liking for the language of the past have affected, in the end, only one level of language: the formal, written variety whose use is more and more restricted. Much journalism, modern writing in literature, modern writing in such jargon-ridden areas as scientific articles all show less awareness of strict codification and correctness rules than the more formal style of the serious newspapers or 'good' literature.

Elasticity

Délégation Générale à la Langue Française and Commissions de Terminologie

Among its other duties, which include the general policing of the Toubon Law, the DGLF provides technical support for the terminology committees of each ministry which have the task of developing an official terminology for innovations. The role outlined for the Délégation in 1989 was to 'promote and co-ordinate the action of administrations and both public and private organisations which assist in the diffusion and good use of French particularly in the domains of education, communication, science and technology'. The DGLF's lexicological section accounts for four of the eleven administrators (chargés de mission) it employed in 1997, and it sees its role very clearly as ensuring the replacement of Anglicisms by French terms.

Innovating within French: borrowing is bad!

Most French language policy, reflecting the identity motivation, rejects linguistic borrowing, particularly from Anglo-American, as naturally bad, and bases this attitude on the views expressed by authors like Etiemble and those who have followed him:

> Purists make a great song and dance about the 'corruption' of the language caused by excessive borrowing from other languages. This is a feature of modern attitudes to language, which is seen as reflecting ethnicity and national culture, and therefore more narrow-minded patriots are resentful of any linguistic incursion by the 'outsider'. (Posner, 1997: 156)

Almost any other linguistic device is pressed into service in the terminology committees. Suggestions have been made for using regional words previously unknown to standard French (_bogue_, to replace 'bug' in computer terminology), inventing new senses for existing words (_poursuite_, to replace 'tracking' in satellite tracking), creating new words by inspired adaptations of existing roots (_mâchouillon_ to replace 'chewing gum', based on the French verb _mâcher_; _remue-méninges_ to replace 'brains trust' from _remuer_ 'to move' and _méninges_ 'cerebral membrane'). French, like any other language, has many ways of creating new words (cf. Guilbert, 1975; Mitterrand, 1992). Affixation, or the incorporation of bound morphemes into words, is particularly productive in French, both in the addition or use of prefixes like _auto-_ (_autodétermination_, created in 1955 with the political sense, _autogestion_ 1960), _hyper-_ (_hypersonique_ 1950), and, and this is the most frequent system, by the use of suffixes such as the verbal ending -er (*chuter, faxer, toaster*), or the ending -*icien* used to refer to a particular profession (*informaticien, esthéticien*). Changes in word-class are frequent: adjectives used as nouns (*un encadré*), verbs as nouns (*le va-et-vient*). New uses of existing words are also common. Particularly frequent in recent years have been the use of abbreviations as words (*un apéro, sensass,   la promo*) and that of sets of initials in the same way (*un CRS, une ONG, une OPA, les Vécés, une ZUP*, all given in the 1997 *Petit Larousse Illustré*).

Among all these methods, and with constant linguistic change and constant innovation in meaning and in meaning change, only one technique, borrowing, and that from one language, English, is the subject of condemnation by purists and politicians as we have noted in Chapter four above. There is of course some truth in what is said about the current effect of English on French. But overall it is highly unlikely that French is in any real danger from English. Perhaps the most significant feature of borrowing is its ephemeral nature: the churning (appearance and disappearance) of new words is amazingly rapid. We have noted above that half the 15 Anglicisms of a short extract from Etiemble, writing in 1966, had disappeared thirty years later. Hagège (1987: 29) comments on the disappearance of the prefix *self-* (*self-service* replaced by *libre-service*). Walter (1988: 306) comments on the replacement of 'compact disc' by the more French *disque compact* (rather than the *disque audio-numérique* proposed by the relevant terminology committee). The most normal outcome of the appearance of an English word, grammatical or stylistic expression is either that it simply disappears after a short period, or is absorbed into the system of the language to a greater or lesser degree. This might mean simply spelling the word 'in French' (*containeur*), adapting it into the French verbal or other system and also spelling it differently (*interviouvé*), creating new words based upon it (*gadgétiser*). This becomes rather more difficult in the case of linguistic preferences or grammatical styles (*bureau informations* said to be based on the English lack of 'of' where French would traditionally have used *bureau de renseignements*), or where the order of words is that of English (*air-conditionné*, although this is being replaced by *climatisé*). But we should perhaps also recall that English-sounding words are not necessarily adopted because the speech community wants to. If a French alternative can be invented this often achieves success, in much the same way that the fast-food revolution based on hamburgers has in much of France (and indeed elsewhere in the world) given way to *croissanteries* or *grilladeries*, without the need for a state-backed food policy.

Polyvalency

Conseil Supérieur de la Langue Française (CSLF)

The Vice-Chairman of this prestigious committee was in 1997 the distinguished linguist Bernard Quemada. His understanding of his duties in 1994 was to provide:

> Research, consultation and the development of proposals for action...It is well known that language laws are ineffective unless they receive, in addition to strong institutional measures, the support of civil society and the agreement of the public... It is up to the Council to promote French, give added value to it and render it illustrious. (*Brèves*, 2e trimestre, 1994)[66]

The CSLF was set up to be the supreme body for language matters in France, and hence almost instantly fell foul of the role the Academy thought it had. The task of the CSLF is to persuade the speech community to accept language policy and to oversee the work of the DGLF. Its task is not really management of the language itself, and in this it should be able to steer clear of conflict with the Academy. The DGLF was supposed to work under the CSLF's general direction, so the latter had access to resources the Academy did not. The present-day CSLF, created in 1989, has seen its membership of 25 personalities, plus ex-officio members such as the Minister for Education, modified in 1993 and again in 1997. It is chaired by the Prime Minister, and has the overall duty to study, within the general orientation defined by the President and the Government, questions relative to the 'use, management, enrichment, promotion and spread of French in and outside France and policy towards foreign languages'. It 'makes proposals, recommends forms of action and gives its opinion on questions referred to it by the Prime Minister or by the ministers for Education or Francophonie'.

Language policy and social integration: an elitist idea?

It is in this sense that policy actions have been conducted, particularly those concerned with illiteracy campaigns, to support French as an 'instrument for integration' and a 'social link'. These aspects of policy are aimed at ensuring that every child gets a satisfactory grounding in French; that illiteracy is combated, and that 'disadvantaged groups' can gain access to language training, in order to enable them to participate in society. Linguistically, one has to pose the question as to what sort of French we are talking about. The norm of French, as recorded in dictionaries and grammars, is for some linguists at least now quite far from the language as spoken on the streets. There is an increasing difference between written French and spoken French; between the French of today and the archaic, over-precise forms preserved in literature; between the staid and starchy French of formal life and superior uses of language and the dynamism, vitality and novelty of the French of the young, particularly as shown in the urban speech of the city centres. The French of other countries, particularly Quebec and part of Africa, and of social classes other than the elite, are also said to demonstrate increasing moves away from the French of the traditional norm. So is the purpose of language policy elitist, to impose the language of the superior classes on the lower classes, the language of the powerful on the language of the powerless? Is imposing standard French merely a way to ensure that society accepts the leadership of the elite?

The identity of France and French is closely associated by traditionalists with the idea of good French, French of 'quality'. The whole question is bedevilled by rhetoric, ideological assumptions, and attitudes towards language which transfer the issue of language quality to that of the quality of society. At one end of the discussion, high quality French tends to be regarded as so fixed and controlled, so rigid, that it is soon equated to 'written, outdated and formal' language. De Rudder went so far as to fear that standard French would become, like Latin or Classical Arabic, a 'language of reference, very far from what is actually used' (quoted in Battye and Hintze, 1992: 53). At this end of the debate, the point of view tends to be taken that if French is to change and develop at all, such changes will have to come from the non-standard varieties, which themselves form a sort of advanced French anticipating the changes that will inevitably come. Gueunier pointed out that the normal definition of quality is based on the linguistic performance of schoolchildren who cannot manage the correctness and precision of the norm but nonetheless are as expressive and intelligent as their forebears who could (Gueunier, 1985). Her view was that any decline in quality could not be detected by scientific research. The other end of the debate puts all the blame on modern French, considering it to lack any good qualities at all. This defensive attitude declares any change to the language to be degradation and decline.

Eloy, summing up the conclusions of a conference called by the DGLF to debate this very notion, pointed out that whether or not the idea of language quality lacked scientific validity, it was considered as serious by large numbers of the French and this very fact made it worthy of interest (Eloy, 1995). He pointed out that the concept quickly raised ideological passions, that practical problems were raised by it for language planners, and that for the citizen it involved questions of democracy, freedom, and the ability to participate in society. The conclusion he and the conference came to, was that purism is an inevitable component of the language debate in France. Condemnation of present-day language was far more prevalent than the opposite. The actual norm of language at any one time was a social construct, dynamic because it changed according to what was considered central to the society. It was a dynamic norm, too, because it was defined in relation to the language use which surrounded it. The language use of children; that of foreigners; and that of social classes other than one's own would always be condemned no matter what individual language elements they used. Purism, he considered, therefore had no basis: it consisted of judging, negatively, other people's language choices, by condemning terms which are in fact used, accepted by usage, and linguistically possible. Purism tended to the global condemnation of all children, all journalists, all teachers. Any analyst of purist discourse could rapidly point out how inaccurate, badly informed or prejudiced such purists were.

- They were ignorant of the idea of appropriateness of language to situation - if a journalist uses a familiar expression that may be because he wishes to establish familiarity with his audience. Instead of criticising this choice, purist discourse maintains he has committed a linguistic error.
- They were unable to recognise new uses and meanings, while purists of the past had condemned as horrors and grammatical crimes, forms nowadays widely accepted.
- They rigidly condemned even momentary lapses.
- They gave excessive importance to certain markers - subjunctives, borrowings, onomatopoeia, passives, adverbs. (Eloy, 1995: 396-7)[67]

The norm is the sociolinguistic variety of the language which is prestigious. In most societies this is the language of power, that used by the social, economic and political elite. In French this has usually been defined as the language of the Parisian bourgeoisie, with the language of intellectuals - a recognised group in French society - as perhaps a more conservative, even pedantic version of this. In today's complex society imposing such a norm is likely to provoke reaction, and one could instance 1968 and its linguistic consequences as demonstrating just such a reaction in, for example, the now much commoner use of *tu*. We have noted above (Chapter 2) the existence of language levels. The sociolinguistic shift that has taken place in French society since 1968 is not to reject the norms of careful (soutenu) and everyday (courant) French, but to accept wider use of familiar French in situations where, possibly before 1968, one of the 'higher' levels would have been employed.

> 'Certainly what at one time were regarded as almost unfit for polite company now forms part of the everyday vocabulary of even respectable matrons...omission of _ne_ in negatives, non-use of inversion in interrogatives, or of abundant use of _ça'_. (Posner, 1997: 75)

One could add even more blatant examples, particularly in the now common use of _merde_ as expletive, _con, conne_ and _connerie_ as simply meaning stupid/stupidity, or _je m'en fous_, now rarely replaced by the euphemism _je m'en fiche_.

So Is Corpus Planning a Chimera?

It would be nice to know whether attempts at manipulation and management of language like those outlined here are successful. If one takes the two centuries from 1600 to 1800 as the start point against which to measure change, an attempt could be made to see whether the legislation and attitudes which started to be established during this period and led to the desire for corpus policy have actually had much effect in France. As we have shown, this is quite difficult to do, although there are some examples on each side of the debate. Two directly opposing views are common in this debate: that of the purists, of many of the French policy community, of the state in its support for laws like that of 1994, who think it important to manage the corpus on the basis that if you don't you'll certainly lose, and that of the linguistic professionals like Eloy or Posner who generally think legislation pointless. Eloy's conclusion to the conference on language quality (Eloy, 1995: 411-2) was that the state actually operates in three ways: through its own usage; as legislator; or as organiser. In its usage, state discourse has established a particular type of speech and writing which can only be controlled to the extent that functionaries themselves agree to, and adopt these conventions. As legislator, the only area in which the state could sensibly intervene - it simply cannot affect the basic structure of the language but only some types of actual language production - is in terminology where technical norms are being set up; but even there if the proposals are poor they will simply not be used. The state as organiser supports and organises, for example the teaching profession or the public media, but can in no way control the action at micro level of every teacher or journalist. Overall, Eloy considers that the state can only affect such external aspects of language, and can have no effect on the corpus itself.

Others take much the same view. The main locus for change in language has not necessarily been in the forms themselves but in the selection of which forms to use, in the popularity and rejection of one type of expression or one form of discourse rather than another. Changes have followed fashion, even though they have done so against the rigid background of a general consensus of what is correct. But the changes in discourse, in language selection took place despite the 'stranglehold of academic French':

> In the nineteenth and twentieth centuries stances with regard to language have dogged aesthetic and social attitudes, with some loosening of the stranglehold of Academic French. So successively, we have had, for instance, Romantic colourful vocabulary, Parnassian linguistic precision, Symbolist linguistic obscurity, modern attempts to fashion a specifically 'arty', belletristic language or, alternatively, to incorporate popular idiom into literary style. (Posner, 1997: 28)

> ...while there is much continuity between standard written French of the seventeenth and twentieth centuries, many aspects of French pronunciation, morphology and syntax have also evolved during the modern period, whether we think of the new literary uses of the imperfect tense in *style indirect libre* (Text 38), or the narrative imperfect, or developments in the spoken language..., the preference for regular *-er* verbs (*solutionner* and *émotionner* rather than *résoudre* and *émouvoir*) or the use of the conditional form in both clauses of conditional sentences. (Ayres-Bennett, 1996: 230)

Many commentators nevertheless point out that codification, purism and the associated language attitudes, and deliberate language policy for the corpus did have undeniable effects. Firstly, in establishing and confirming these linguistic attitudes; secondly in some cases of holding back development in vocabulary, grammar or style, and more rarely in fostering or changing it in specific directions. Spelling was fixed, more or less successfully, from the sixteenth century, mainly by the practice of printers, and confirmed in the eighteenth century in the Academy's various dictionaries (Catach, 1992). Two major changes were adopted as late as 1835: the replacement of *-oi* by *-ai* (e.g. in *français*), and the use of the same spelling in plurals of words ending in *-ent* or *-ant* (*enfant*, *enfants*, instead of *enfans*). This thus represents, in Catach's phrase, a 'state spelling system'. Later attempts at change and improvement, usually in the direction of a more rational or more easily understandable and learnable system, have had somewhat less success. The most recent took place in 1990 and the recommendations ('_Rectifications_', published by the French Academy) are not part of the required official language for state servants. Its recommendations are not even included in the latest editions of the _Petit Larousse_, although these have carefully taken note of regional and overseas terms and new ones arising in scientific and technical French., and the dictionary itself is revised every year. In morphology and syntax, the intention to standardise is most obvious in the works by Malherbe and Vaugelas in the seventeenth century, although these were not written for the mass. Grammar books (more than ten different ones) were officially approved for education in 1835. Most importantly, perhaps, the models French speakers and writers were encouraged to imitate, up to the second world war, were:

> the observers and creators of the nation's French (i.e. from the middle of the period, the French of the Republic): the great authors from Boileau to Voltaire, to whom will later be added Musset, Vigny, Hugo, Sand, Balzac, Flaubert, Maupassant, Zola, Anatole France. (Molinié, 1991: 33)[68]

It is arguable whether such recommendations actually mean that a standard French grammar was authorised by the state. Nonetheless, the impression is widespread that the 'advice' incorporated into school syllabuses then and now was meant to be taken seriously, and children were enjoined to write French characterised by 'nobility, correctness, precision, naturalness, clarity, harmony, concision' (see Antoine and Martin, 1985). But it is in vocabulary that the codification processes of the Academy and other authorities have had the most long-lasting effect, left permanent scars. The aims were the straitjacketing, purification and reduction of variety, one was eliminating regional, social or technical varieties of language. As a result, under a thousand different words cover some 90% of a thousand written texts of the period from 1789 to 1965 (Molinié, 1991: 51), and neologism or the creation of new words was for long anathema to the spirit of French. The tendency was to seek always the abstract and the general, and to avoid the specific, the detailed and the narrow. Molinié was not in much doubt that the overall aim of standardisation and codification was the control of the language:

> It is indeed the practice of the language which is targeted. Not only is this practice policed, in its internal workings; it is also obligatorily imposed, in a totalitarian and dictatorial manner in its external or relational aspects. This French will little by little stifle any other linguistic expression. The movement is slow, but continuous and implacable. It reaches its height at the point of the Republican and

secular struggle, and indeed we will have to wait until 1950 before an opposing movement can be discovered. (Molinié, 1991: 34-5)[69]

The issue of language control through corpus planning has been of great importance to all parts of the political spectrum, and most parties in power in France have tried to manipulate both the language and language usage to reflect their own preconceptions. Developing an instrument designed to manage language became important at the time of the Revolution, and it is hardly surprising that language should have been on the agenda in 1993 and 1994 when the nationality issue was under discussion. Corpus policy reflects beliefs in the rights of mankind and in the fundamental liberties, but only in and through French and by contrast with other perceptions. It is as though the French identity structure stands up best when it is in clear contrast to its opposite, which many French politicians and others see as the 'Anglo-Saxon' tradition of laxism, allowing the language to go where it will.

Part 3: Image

Chapter 8
Gaining influence and prestige: Francophonie, cultural relations and French abroad

The stated aims of French language policy, as summarised by Douste-Blazy, Minister of Culture in 1996, are given in Figure 8.1.

- ensure the presence, prestige and influence (*rayonnement*) of French as the language of the Republic
- retain for French its role as language for international communication
- preserve cultural and linguistic diversity throughout the world by promoting multilingualism. (*Brèves*, 5, 1996)[70]

Figure 8.1 The aims of French language policy

The three aims reflect the mixture of motives we have identified in this book: insecurity, identity and image. While the first aim reflects pride in French identity, it also contains within itself the wish and the hope that people both inside and outside France will respect and accept this. Both the others, too, are concerned with the world outside France: the second is defensive and reflects insecurity about the future, while the third, which we shall examine in greater detail in the next chapter, is mainly designed to help French against the spread of English. Outside France itself, the influence and prestige of the country depends on a language policy, but also on gaining friends and allies through the creation of an attractive image of France:

The presence of French in the world accompanies the presence of France. The promotion of French and of its use as a means of international communication, at a time when globalisation favours monolingualism, are more than ever, for the position of our country in the world, for the acceptance of her ideas and conceptions, for the future of Francophonie, a priority which requires a determined and explicit language policy. (DGLF, 1997, preface)[71]

The image others have of a country reflects its identity, nature and characteristics. But every country hopes the image will be favourable and attractive, and most work hard to correct false impressions, give a favourable slant to events, present themselves in the best possible light. Image creation is in modern terms a deliberate construction of what one wishes others to see, think or believe about oneself, one's country, a product. Insofar as French and French language policy are concerned, government and state actions are aimed at generating exactly the same result in the 'client' as the advertiser and marketing expert aims at. Although it may be unusual in the subject area of this book to use approaches derived from the business world, there is a clear parallel between the processes involved for marketing a commercial product and those followed by the French state in persuading 'clients' to accept a 'product'. The key concepts for marketing are the marketing mix of the four 'p's: the nature of the product, its price or cost, its packaging or presentation, and the place of sale. These four aspects clarify what is required to successfully devise marketing strategies, and the main part of this chapter will be organised around them. The marketing strategies themselves, the language policies, will be assessed against this background.

The Product

French language

The product which is 'on sale' to overseas clients is, firstly, the French language. Its qualities as a saleable item hence need to be evaluated, and there are two clearly opposing views involved: firstly that the French language is now in a state of perfection and cannot be improved upon. This view has long been held, with some justification (see Chapter 9 below). Secondly that the French language could be improved in some way to make it more appropriate to the market. It could, for example be rendered easier to learn so that more students could be familiar with it and its 'sales' thus be improved. The _Français Fondamental_ (Gougenheim, 1958) produced in the 1950s for the overseas 'market', is not much talked of nowadays, though; French is presented as 'the language of the Republic', and it is on this basis that it figures in the policy aims. French is not just the language of the Republic: it is also the language of a number of other countries, an official language for many, and a means of communication available to many more. But France does not suffer from competition in international sales, as Great Britain does from American or Indian English. In terms of competitive advantage, too, it is not just language that is on sale: three content areas seem central in French official presentations. These are science and technology; culture; and education, although the latter is so tied up with the French educational system and the set of values involved in its design and implementation that it is often unclear whether it is education or the French system that is on sale. The conclusion must be that French language, as a product, is inevitably associated with the concepts of French society and culture it conveys: to the extent that these may be positive and sought by 'clients', greater popularity may ensue. Negative associations, particularly those of the difficulty of the language, its lack of utility in the modern world, its association with an elite or with its colonial past, must be avoided as far as possible. Buyers are expected to have an integrative, rather than instrumental, motivation.

French science and technology

Two views characterise the French scientific establishment: that there is such a thing as French science and technology which has significant national characteristics, and the opposing view that science is international and universal and therefore cannot be restricted by having to be expressed in French or tied to a specifically French world-view. Generally speaking, the first view has been that of the language activists, generally not themselves scientists, while the latter view is that expressed by most French professional scientists and by the organisations that represent them. The major attempt in language policy to promote French as a scientific language has thus had considerable problems in gaining acceptance, even among scientists. It is in science particularly that information is crucial and the rapid dissemination of articles, access to databases and communication by electronic means is as fundamental as well-equipped laboratories and the provision of basic requirements like uninterrupted electricity supplies and the availability of chemicals. A common international language is a great advantage, and it may be for this reason that the French scientific community gives only lukewarm support to efforts to impose French language on electronic communication like the Web and email. For French the need for international communication may nonetheless sometimes have unexpectedly favourable consequences. Nigeria, for example, is surrounded by French-speaking countries in Africa and projects like water management there may lead to greater need for French than for English, despite the predominance of the English language in water technology on a world-wide level. There is, too, a long history of scientific co-operation between France and other countries: 300 French researchers visit Brazilian universities every year, 30 are permanently employed there and some 800 Brazilian scholarship holders study in France (Etat, 1995-6: 257). In other countries, the level of scientific co-operation is currently decreasing (New Zealand, Israel). The French government has long financed a system of sending young people abroad for scientific 'co-operation', particularly as an alternative to military service. But the whole area of science and technology, and the language(s) in which it is disseminated if not created, is a major problem for a language policy.

French culture

The official defence of the specific nature of French culture has in recent times been most vociferous during the 1993 GATT Uruguay Round of negotiations leading to the establishment of the World Trade Organisation and the agreements on open access to global trade. At the time, the main success, from the French point of view, was in negotiating the cultural exception which allowed individual countries or groups of countries to provide support for internal cultural producers or industries and to protect these from imports, mainly of American cultural products and particularly in music, film and television. The net result of these protective and defensive actions has been a rise in sales, in France, of French language cinema and music, and, according to the 1995-6 report on the state of francophonie world-wide, they have increased the world-wide popularity of a range of Francophone cultural productions ranging from song (Céline Dion, inner-city rap) to film productions by Quebec and Maghreb organisations (Etat, 1995-6: 595).

There have been many attempts to provide positive support for exports of French culture. But it is in this area, of the commercialisation of cultural products, that French efforts have faced enormous competition from Anglophone and particularly American producers. In these circumstances, there is a continuing belief in Francophonie that only by regulation and control can any room be allowed in French-speaking markets for non-francophone producers. One view expressed in the 1995-6 report on the state of Francophonie encapsulates both the advantages and the dangers for French-speaking culture, and at the same time represents the nature of the debate over top-down governmental control versus free, unregulated cultural expansion:

> Francophonie...is extending beyond the bounds of the Francophone community...and henceforth intends not only to reinforce its unity and demand its place in the universal polyphonic concert but also to breathe into this world civilisation a spirit of organisation, of regulation, of management. It's not a matter of holding back creative energy and individual freedoms, firms and initiatives, on the contrary, but it is a question of ensuring that this flowering, meeting the explosion of face-to-face mass communication technologies, is not a jungle, anarchy, a new barbarity. Ethical regulation is needed by the universal civilisation. (Etat, 1995-6: 597)[72]

A less lyrical assessment of the strengths and weaknesses of the cultural market, of the possibility of French and French-speaking influence rising on the world cultural scene, may lie in the tendencies of book exports to different parts of the world as shown in Table 8.1.

Table 8.1 Exports of French books

Region	1994	1993	% change
N America	519434	464739	11.8
Far and Near East	73520	97232	-24.4
DOM-TOM	271163	233290	16.2
Africa	175316	213045	-17.7
Maghreb	109545	98547	11.2
Asia/Oceania	66861	58146	15
S America/Caribbean	46038	42329	8.8
Central and eastern Europe	33164	26508	25.1
Others	5110	7147	-28.5
Overall	2978501	2760558	7.9
1994 figures, in thousands of francs.			

Source: Etat, 1995-6: 169

Education

As in most other areas of consideration of the product to be promoted abroad, two opposing views conflict: the belief that education in French and of French represents a height of achievement that is valuable in itself, and, on the other side, that education is so difficult that if French is to be successfully promoted the education system, and its methods, have somehow to be made more accessible. The advantages and disadvantages of the French educational approach are possibly those outlined in Figure 8.2.

Advantages (which can also be disadvantages):
- nationally defined programmes and syllabuses
- nationally verified and accepted diplomas and certificates, awarded through an assessment system which itself is based on peer approval through assessment juries guided by nationally approved criteria
- clear progression through the educational system on the basis of achieving predetermined targets, rather than on age.

Disadvantages, particularly for 'export':
- the system was modelled on a belief in exclusion, aimed at preventing the mass from achieving success in the baccalaureate, itself seen as the gateway to social success
- methods and materials are devised for French metropolitan conditions. The classic example is that of school history books, which traditionally started off with phrases like *nos ancêtres les gaulois* (Our ancestors the Gauls) or were based on imaginary travels around a France with no poor, no social or religious problems and no conflicts.

Figure 8.2 For and against the French educational system

The problem of encouraging other countries to take up the French educational system has been rendered even more acute in recent years as the World Bank's espousal of structural reforms, and the Washington consensus about privatisation and economic systems which has inspired the policies of the International Monetary Fund, together had the result of destroying state educational systems, welfare systems and state support for essentially agricultural economies reliant on the production of primary crops, particularly in developing countries. In addition, although many countries are prepared to accept French establishments teaching for French qualifications, it is precisely the Franco-centredness of these that sometimes causes problems for parents abroad. If the baccalaureate has no value in the higher education or employment circuits of a country other than France there is little point in encouraging children to obtain it. Similarly, if the French educational system cannot certify studies in topics or languages which it does not recognise but which are central to the overseas culture or economy, it has few advantages. Nonetheless the export of French education has resulted in

300 establishments overseas, teaching in the French system to 150,000 children of whom 90,000 are not the children of French nationals stationed abroad (Etat, 1995-6: 313).

The Price To Pay

Continuing neo-colonialism

France ensured the spread of its language and culture in the same two ways most other countries used in the nineteenth century: force and diplomacy. Force is what built the second largest Empire of the last two centuries, and after the military, missionaries and merchants who built it have gone, (most of) the resultant French-speaking countries remain together in the organised international Francophonie meetings. Past colonialism, with all its brutality and exploitation is an unavoidable historic fact. The question for today is whether such colonialist attitudes persist, or whether French international ambitions for her language, her culture and her influence mean that purchasers would have to pay too high a price.

---

(1)   continuing arrangements between France and countries of the African bloc in matters of raw material supply

(2)   continuing security and defence agreements between France and countries which are former French colonies, since the French practice of deploying troops in support of particular regimes has led to many instances of military involvement

(3)   the relationships between the DOM-TOM and contemporary France. Although these regions are no longer exploited for their primary wealth and there is a net outflow of funds to them, the economic relationship is somewhat uneasy in a number of respects, in that:
  - their citizens do not fully enjoy all the social benefits of French citizenship, although this changed in 1997;
  - it is convenient that the salary arrangements for functionaries enable them to avoid paying income or other taxes. Although this is undoubtedly beneficial to expatriate civil servants, it is a factor affecting incomes in the DOM-TOM themselves, falsifies the labour market and leads to a dependency culture. (see Belorgey and Bertrand, 1994; Ager, 1996a)

Figure 8.3 Continuing neo-colonialism

Three points recur when the point is made that France seems to have retained many advantages for herself which remind some of colonialist attitudes, as Figure 8.3. indicates. The dominant role of France in Francophonie is responsible for much of the feeling that neo-colonialism is still an important factor in international relations. France itself counts for half of all the French speakers in the world and is far and away the dominant partner in the international Francophonie organisation. It is hence almost inevitable that other member countries of Francophonie, the international organisation, and even those in francophonie, the countries across the world who use French as a language, should occasionally feel somewhat overshadowed if not oppressed. France has struggled hard to shed the appearance of a former colonial power, but there is little doubt that some of her actions in Africa, or in the Pacific, are as much to be decried as those of other former colonising countries. France's high-handed action in restarting nuclear tests in the Pacific in 1995 had, at the time, major effects on French language learning in New Zealand and Australia, as well as on Tahiti. (Ager, 1996a: 158)

Packaging and Presentation

Product differentiation

Possible ways of presenting French language and culture, and positioning the product for the market, must be based on an estimation of possibilities. In this, comparison could be made with what has happened with a successful language like English, and/or with languages in a very similar situation to that of French: Spanish, Portuguese or Italian. A conveniently simplistic opposition between French and English is frequently made: English, despite its obvious cultural history, is decried as being a reduced form of communication suitable only for minimal exchanges with no cultural content, a sort of telegraphese available to enable two businessmen to conduct the lowest level of formal exchange. By contrast, French is presented as a rich language, representative of a rich culture and inheritance, and determined to be used for more than the simple exchange of simple truths. Spanish and Portuguese are seen as in a similar situation to French despite their obvious differences. Spanish is the rising language of the New World, spoken by millions of people outside Spain as their native language but characterised by its use by all social classes and particularly by the comparatively poor populations of countries close to the United States, and in the States itself where it is the language of the non-prestigious Hispanics in the South. Although it shares many features with the situation of French, by contrast, French is also presented as the language of culture, the elite and privilege. Portuguese is seen as a world language, and the language of the Brazilian masses with which there is much sympathy and fellow-feeling. But Portuguese is viewed as lacking the depth of culture associated with French: it is a language of holidays, music and joy, but not of serious high culture. In the case of both Spanish and Portuguese, the problem from which they both suffer, according to such an estimation, is the lack of unity. While French is one and the same everywhere, both the other languages have (at least) two forms, each claiming norms and each claiming equal prestige. The main contrast with these lies in the values each is said to convey. None has the claims to universalism implicit in Republican and Revolutionary thought.

The Place of Sale

A variety of situations

Outside France, French is rarely in the same situation as in the hexagon. In most countries it is one among competing languages, and often finds itself in a situation of conflict with them. Few countries (Belgium, Canada and Switzerland) have it as an official language and widely spoken as maternal tongue by large populations, and the purpose of the language policy of such countries is to ensure it is as much used as any other official language in a similar situation. French is here in societal bilingualism (or multilingualism), and each country contains two or more monolingual populations each using their own language. In these countries, France has little role to play in attempting to sell French language or culture, although it has made its political position clear in the Canadian situation where it would be delighted to see Quebec independence and there is considerable official co-operation in a number of fields. There is mutual help and the exchange of ideas in terminology with Quebec and elsewhere. Both official and more decentralised contacts take place, through international groupings such as the Association of French-speaking Mayors and in many even less official associations, clubs and societies uniting professionals, individuals and those with similar interests. Town-twinning sometimes takes place. In such countries, France can do little about the image of French, since that image is based mainly on the local situation.

In other countries French is in a variety of multilingual situations, ranging from those in which French is official and/or used by a significant number of people as either first or second language, to those in which it is a learnt language but is used only when communication takes place with a French-speaking country. The situations are very different from each other, in the extent to which French is used, the domains in which it is appropriate as a means of communication, and in the perceptions of French the population holds. Societal bilingualism does not exist: individual bilingualism or multilingualism is common, and people must usually learn a number of languages to operate effectively in society. In many African countries for example French is used by a minute proportion of the population who also use the language of their own ethnic group, a national language and possibly also English or another international language. The role of France must be effectively supportive, particularly in questions of language teaching, the dissemination of cultural products such as books and films, the use of cultural vehicles such as the media or the new technologies, and the careful avoidance of any appearance of interference with internal affairs. This latter is sometimes difficult in countries where history is full of examples of such interference in previous times. The African ex-colonial powers in particular are often sensitive to any suggestion of French influence. The position is particularly difficult in the remaining Territoires d'Outre-Mer and indeed in the Départements d'Outre-Mer as well, where accusations of neo-colonialism remain since French is the only official language and the official descriptions include such sensitive phrases as 'France of the Indian Ocean' or territories within 'the frontiers of the Republic' (cf. Ager, 1996a: 76-93; Aldrich, 1996; Aldrich and Connell, 1992).

The French government publication, *Etat de la Francophonie*, reviewed the range of situations in which French is used in its 1995-6 edition. As illustrations of the countries or regions where France might be able to exercise influence, three can be cited here: Tunisia, Niger, and Louisiana. French has always been important in Tunisia, where it is first language for about 30% of the population and much used in professional contexts and in relationships with Europe. French language media are well established, with newspapers, television and radio stations. France has always provided considerable financial and other support. But the main existing image is of French as 'language of culture, not only the traditional one of literature and humanist values, but also of scientific and technical research at a high level. Undoubtedly, this climate of tolerance and partnership favours francophonie'. The main conflict is with Arabic, both as religious language and as the most widely spoken colloquial and official language, and Arabic is heavily promoted as the preferred language of the country. In Niger, where French has traditionally been the official language and language of education, two influences are affecting the previous importance of the language: growth in awareness and pride in national languages, and the power of aid. Aid is principally derived from American, Dutch and German sources and these, together with international pressure from other donors including the World Bank, tend to suggest greater use of national languages. But greater use of the main language, Housa, spoken by 55% of the population, would apparently support this ethnic group and thus divide the country along ethnic lines. In Louisiana, French is the language spoken by Cajuns, most of whom have gradually lost active use of the language - it is estimated that few under 45 remain native speakers of this variety of French. Considerable investment has been made in recent years in reviving the French-speaking past, and France has been heavily involved in sending language teachers, subsidising materials and inviting Louisiana representatives to Francophonie summit meetings. But only 87,000 of 300,000 children learn the language at school, although 9,000 do so in immersion classes where all the teaching is in French.

Marketing Strategies

An analysis of the possibilities facing those who would create an image of French and France abroad, such as that above, is carried out annually, although not in these terms, in the report of the Haut Conseil de la Francophonie to which diplomatic services, international organisations and ministerial services in France contribute. As a result of such assessments, specific strategies are adopted, for example by the Foreign Affairs section responsible for linguistic policy abroad. Much of this is very mundane and practical, and usually remains as an internal report for senior civil servants or ministers, but is occasionally reviewed and reconsidered as a whole within the policy review activities of new governments. Perhaps in anticipation of such a new government, a glossy Foreign Office publication of 1996 spelt out the then policy strategies and priorities (Politique, 1996).

This specified the two geopolitical priorities which remain in this role in 1998: Africa and Europe. The demographic future for French lay with the former, policies for which came under a different ministry, but the future of French as an international language depended on the latter, together with the maintenance of relationships with countries with Romance languages and a new effort towards Asia. The first circle of importance is the countries of the European Union, where the policy was based on some strengthening but mainly on continuation. The policy saw the future of French as dependent on the generalisation of a policy encouraging the teaching of two foreign languages in educational systems, bilingual schools, early foreign language learning, together with strengthening efforts for the dissemination of books and audio-visual items. European initiatives such as the exchange programme SOCRATES should be a high priority. The urgency of not forgetting Europe is shown by the drastic reduction of French language learning in Germany, where a drop of 50% had taken place in ten years: somewhat late in the day, it was proposed to recognise the educational responsibilities of the Länder and decentralise such services as those of linguistic attachés. The countries of central and eastern Europe formed the second circle. Here, the strategy was to prioritise support for the countries likely to enter the Union, although with preference for the countries which have already joined Francophonie - Romania, Bulgaria and Moldavia. But the real situation was that since the end of communism, English was massively preferred, while German ran it a close second as foreign language. Strategy for French meant supporting a range of activities in teacher training and the preparation of learning materials. The third circle contained Mediterranean countries and also those officially participating in Francophonie. The strategy again consisted of support for the teaching of French through bilingual education, or in support for centres of excellence in primary bilingual education or in higher education. This presentation of French policy also incidentally showed how well the 1997 Francophone summit meeting in Vietnam had been prepared in advance, and how much training support the French government had provided, apart from building a new conference hall and repairing much else. 1,200 specialists were trained for the two-day meeting itself, and there had been a range of general training and educational initiatives with longer effect, together with training in translation, journalism, business and a range of other subjects. Other countries in the world also received support which varied depending on the local situation. In North America the image of French is deliberately associated with support for the new technologies in order to 'valorise the image of French as the language accompanying scientific and economic co-operation' (Politique, 1996: 70).

Overall, the strategy for marketing French and France relied on direct subsidy, but also on partnerships: with international organisations such as UNESCO and the European Union, where international finance was available; with the Francophonie organisation and its operators such as the Canadian-led organisation of the Francophone Universities (AUPELF-UREF) or TV5 (French-language satellite television); with regional and decentralised organisations, where the role of the ministry was merely to act as subsidy provider, spending 26 million francs in 1995. Three particular policy lines, established elsewhere but implemented by the Foreign Ministry among others, were important: support for the use of French in information highways; support for

French usage in terminology and neologism; and the diversification of language teaching in France.

Teaching French abroad

Deliberately teaching French abroad must be one of the main policy lines to follow. Like the British, France first set up a language teaching programme through cooperation between the state and an association, the Alliance Française. This is nominally a group of different associations, locally managed, which have affiliated to the Paris Alliance Française founded in 1883. In 1994 the organisation was teaching more than half a million students world-wide, most of them in South America. The French government itself has developed an external cultural and linguistic policy and set of organisations, described in Etat, 1995-6: 411-33 and Politique, 1996. Mainly, these have provided and supported teachers abroad. Some teachers are recruited and paid for by the Co-operation Ministry, and hence work principally in the former colonies, particularly in Africa, while others are recruited and supported by the Foreign Affairs Ministry. Overall, there are usually more than 20,000 such teachers working overseas, which compares with about 6,000 from Britain.

These figures are for the specifically recruited short-term assistants. Overall, nearly a million teachers of various levels deal with nearly sixty million learners of French at all levels in every country. Among these, some countries show a real concentration of language learners, among them Britain where the lack of diversification in foreign language learning in the schools means that several million schoolchildren concentrate on this language. Other countries with a high concentration of learners include the United States, Italy, Egypt, Canada and Algeria. In nearly all these countries there are historical reasons for the numbers, or the educational system finds it very difficult to change rapidly. The surveys conducted by the Haut Conseil de la Francophonie find little anticipation of change, and certainly none in a negative direction. Indeed, over the ten years from 1984 to 1994, numbers of learners increased by more than two million (Politique, 1996: 20). Support is provided in a number of ways other than direct teaching, or financing teachers or assistants: most Embassies have a linguistic attaché in their cultural section who can act in general support of language learning; journals and teaching materials are subsidised. _Le Français dans le Monde_, for example, officially published, first appeared in 1961. The internal administrative problems caused by the division of responsibilities between the Foreign Affairs Ministry and the Ministry of Cooperation have been, if not resolved then at least moderated by a number of actions since 1990: the foundation of the Agence pour l'Enseignement Français à l'Etranger which manages teaching establishments abroad on behalf of both ministries is one of the main ones.

Some teaching of French abroad is also done officially by Belgium, Canada and Quebec. The Francophonie organisation itself also supports the teaching of the language through its 'operators' such as TV5 or, at higher education level, the Agence Francophone pour l'Enseignement Supérieur et la Recherche. Support comes also from other, non-governmental quarters. The ninth Congress of the Fédération Internationale des Professeurs de Français (FIPF) was held in Tokyo in 1996 (Etat, 1995-6: 63-5). The Congress took considerable comfort from the statistics of French teaching world-wide, noting particularly that more than 55 million students were following courses in the language and that there were more than a million teachers of the language. The conclusions of the Congress underlined the absolute necessity of taking a sane and reasonable view of the conditions under which French was taught, and particularly of the fact that French was always in competition with other languages both within a foreign society and in terms of the languages available to the children and parents of that society. French, inevitably, would always be the second or third foreign language after English, and thus would be in competition with German in Europe, with Spanish in the Americas, with Japanese and Chinese in Asia and the Pacific countries, with Arabic in North Africa and with African languages in the rest of Africa. In these circumstances French would be best advised to support multilingualism and multiculturalism.

The DGLF now has oversight of the different official actions, although this area has been a good example of internal administrative disorganisation with a large number of official groups and ministries involved, unclear lines of demarcation and a variable control structure. One problem is to know who to teach the language to: who will influence the future. The Balladur Government of 1993-5, among other actions, instituted a programme of language support and training in the context of European Union enlargement, for up to 800 of the total of 2,000 functionaries. Programmes of this sort, which both enable the teaching of French and also ensure access to influential civil servants working for international organisations and particularly those associated with the United Nations and its agencies, are heavily supported by official channels. In 1996, the Ministry of Culture set up an Observatoire de la Langue Française one of whose tasks would be to set up running assessments of the use of French abroad, and this itself used the month of April 1997 to examine appropriate methodology and systems.

Cultural diplomacy

The importance of cultural diplomacy, and the maintenance of a high level of cultural activity abroad, should be a high priority for a country which prides itself on the level and reputation of its cultural productions. As with the teaching of French, the responsibility for implementing policy lies with the Cultural Relations section of the Foreign Affairs Ministry, and the Embassies abroad. Different policies have to be devised for different countries and regions. In many African countries, the educational system is in such a disastrous situation that often the only available cultural centre is that provided by the French government, and this is often besieged by young people eager to gain access to libraries. In many African countries, cultural productions however often attract expatriates, while the only way of attracting the local public seems to be to offer shows and productions more oriented towards local, rather than French, culture. But since this is counter-productive if the aim is to show the culture of France, the centres sometimes remain under-used (Etat, 1995-6: 115). Cultural policy was extensively revised in 1983, and the point made then, that cultural diplomacy worked best on a reciprocal basis, has generally been followed since. Over the last ten to fifteen years there has been less concentration on teaching the children of expatriate workers or on providing an overseas base to which such expatriates can gratefully escape from the barbarity of the culture into which they have been projected, and a more deliberate attempt to appeal to local populations. But the exact nature of the appeal varies from country to country.

Ensuring the use of French outside France

The pros and cons of the situation for French in the European Union are those of Figure 8.4. The 1994 proposal to limit the number of working and official languages in European Institutions to five, as the number of official languages rose with the growth of the Union from nine to eleven, met with strong opposition as we have noted. The suggestion provoked an instant, and quite violent response from the Greek, Danish, Netherlands and Portuguese delegates; the Swedish Prime Minister making a visit to Paris insisted on giving his speech in Swedish; on 19th January 1995 the European Parliament passed a resolution noting that 'any proposal aimed at limiting languages increases the distance between the citizen and the European Institutions' and condemned the suggestion outright. Following the presentation of French views on linguistic diversity to the European Council of

Ministers, a resolution was adopted by them in June 1995 approving the following points:

- diversification of foreign language learning;
- increasing primary school foreign language learning;
- offering two foreign languages during compulsory education;
- increasing bilingual classes;
- placing greater emphasis on spoken understanding;
- adjusting learning methods by adopting intensive short courses;
- stressing the linguistic diversity of Europe. (Etat, 1995-6: 99-100)

Advantages for French:
- French enjoys leading status, and preferential legal protection in European countries and institutions;
- it is one of the official and formal working languages, one of three informal working languages of the administrative institutions;
- French is the first language of institutions such as the Commission and the Court of Justice;
- until recently it had been the only language of Press conferences;
- French or Francophone civil servants still form the largest group of functionaries.

Disadvantages and problems for French:
- the legal position of French does not mean it is in practice used in the preliminary stages of discussion, or in working groups;
- in foreign affairs (discussions with member countries of the former eastern bloc, for example) English is often used;
- *AFP* (*Agence France Presse*) uses less French than Reuters in its news bulletins;
- the enlargement of the Union will inevitably introduce non-Francophone countries;
- future Commissions and supporting staff may not necessarily use French so much as those of the recent past.

Figure 8.4 French in the EU institutions

In 1995 the DGLF's special report on the position in the main other international organisations was summarised by the Haut Conseil de la Francophonie as follows:

In the UNO General Assembly, 30 delegations (27 in 1993) used French in whole or in part. But as a working language French was used only for 5% of the available time in New York, and for 20% in

Geneva. Its situation is under threat in some financial and technical organisations. Difficulties occur because of budgetary restrictions on the recruitment of French-speaking officials and on interpreting and translation services, but also sometimes depend on the political context. States newly joining international organisations from Central and Eastern Europe or from the Community of Independent States (mainly the former USSR), but also from the Far East, are more often than not English speaking and 'choose to speak English, or, and this is fairly recent, their own language'. (Etat, 1995-6: 98)[73]

The Olympic Games held in Atlanta during 1996 were particularly closely watched, and overall the DGLF congratulated itself on the 'very satisfying result' achieved. The pressure group sent to Atlanta in February 1996 would be followed by similar groups for the games in Nagano and Sydney.

As a consequence of these observations, France now has two rather different policy lines: insisting on the use of French by French officials, and, secondly, ensuring the use of French as an official language or preferably in less formal situations by all, not merely by French officials. The 1996 report had this to say on the duties of French officials:

General principles
(The circular of 30.11.1994 to all ministries from the Ministry of Foreign Affairs and the Ministry of Culture) presented an overall picture of the situations in which French must be privileged by government agents:
• relationships with foreign interlocutors residing in France
• participation in international meetings
• departure on a tour of duty or on a mission
• relationships with international organisations.
These instructions cover spoken as well as written communication. Correspondence and documents, those of diplomatic and consular posts, must be in French accompanied by translations if wished. The role of all public officials must be exemplary in illustrating the principle that French is 'the language of the Republic' as well as its status as a great language of international communication.
In the case of international meetings... organised abroad or in France but whose organisers are foreigners, officials must always take care to express themselves in French. (DGLF, 1996, 2, III, 2)[74]

By 1998, with a Socialist government no less insistent that French be used by the representatives of the state, the instructions had been rephrased to emphasise the linguistic rights conferred on French civil servants and citizens by European legislation, as in Figure 8.5. The rights were expressed just as imperatively, insisting that French be used in what can only be seen as a provocative way.

Vade-mecum in 10 points
(1) French is an official language and a working language of the European Union institutions
(2) In meetings, the representatives of France express themselves in French, whether or not translation is available
(3) Any situation making the use of French impossible must be at least reported to the French authorities
(4) In case of necessity, a request may be made to postpone the meeting
(5) Preparatory documents must have been distributed in the French version
. (6) It is possible to delay discussion of an agenda item for which French language documents have not been distributed sufficiently far in advance
(7) It is appropriate in any case to refuse any legally binding decision if a French text is not available
(8) The European Council of Ministers may only deliberate and decide on the basis of documents and projects written in the official languages and hence also in French
(9) In informal meetings French use their own language
(10) In informal bilateral meetings French must be prioritised.

Source: *Lettre d'Information*, 30, juin 1998: 18[75]

Figure 8.5 1998 instructions to civil servants

Outside Europe, this approach is not always appropriate. The purpose of the Toubon Act, of the Circular of 30th November 1994 and the Guide of 1998 was to ensure that the official situation was constantly brought to mind; that as far as possible the letter of the formal situation was operated; and that French would be used in reality as well as in this formal sense. The DGLF, conscious as ever of its obligations as watchdog, has ensured the publication of guides distributed widely to participants in international meetings, official as well as private, to remind them of this official position.

The use of French in the private sector

The majority of the effort devoted to the defence of French and the support of its image overseas goes towards the public sector. But those government agencies and politicians responsible for the policy have realised that one of the greatest needs in this whole area is both to gain wider public support for the actions undertaken, and to seek friends able and willing to support action by the state in pursuance of a whole range of policies. Large firms, particularly in the civil engineering field such as Bouygues, although heavily supported by the state, nonetheless must operate as private enterprise and in many parts of the world it is they and not public officials who best represent France. Much of the drive towards setting up organisations in which the ideas of Francophonie could be developed came from Quebec: the Forum Francophone des Affaires was set up in 1987 as a Quebec initiative, is formed from firms established in French-speaking countries and meets at the same time as the Francophonie summits. One of the group's main aims is to foster co-operation between firms in a variety of countries; it publishes guides to international activities and has a secretariat which manages its affairs between summits. In France itself, an association called Actions pour Promouvoir le Français des Affaires holds annual competitions, encourages young people to develop French words for new technologies and inventions, and awards prizes during the annual day of Business French which it has held since 1987. Because the private sector is by definition fragmented and varied, political policy has to be limited to providing support. In many cases, this is closely associated with decentralised bodies (municipalities, regions, organisations) and raises the question of how much official policy can do other than subsidise and set the overall direction. The money provided by France for this purpose is not inconsiderable: 5.8 billion francs in 1995 (Etat, 1995-6: 291).

In another area of commercial activity private industry gains considerable support from the French state, in terms of direct financial subsidy and diplomatic effort. French exports, particularly of luxury goods, are often regarded as in some sense symbolic of the country itself, so protection of trade names or descriptions is strongly pursued. Recent campaigns to protect names such as Champagne have resulted in withdrawal of its use by others as a generic term for sparkling wine, even when made by the méthode champenoise. Similar attempts have been made with regional names like Beaujolais and Bordeaux, although the protection of trade names is not always easy and, particularly in European fora, has often produced counterproductive results like the attempt to ban terms like chocolate or beer unless the product conforms to a minimal European norm. Protection of descriptions of agricultural products can also lead to problems when regional names are used in some countries to indicate, not origin, but the type of product or the nature of the treatment (Aylesbury duckling, Axminster carpet). But agricultural products are a major part of France's export trade and in this area, as in so many others, language policy is simply another description for commercial protectionism.

Organisations and services charged with delivering the policy

The Haut Conseil de la Francophonie is chaired by the President and forms part of the services directly attached to his office. Created in 1984, it was devised in order to enable the President to discharge the specific roles that office has in relation to (Francophonie within) foreign policy and followed the break-up of the organisations set up under de Gaulle. It is separate from the Conseil Supérieur de la Langue Française (Prime Minister's Office) and the Délégation Générale à la Langue Française (Ministry of Culture) which are directly responsible for policy-making on language matters in both the national and international domain. The other official services are directed by the Foreign Affairs Department in which, after 1997, a Secrétaire d'Etat (Charles Josselin in 1997) was appointed to head up both Coopération and Francophonie, possibly in an attempt to clear up the administrative chaos, although it was naughtily commented in 1998 that on setting up the new government in 1997 Jospin 'forgot to assign the ministerial portfolio for La Francophonie to anybody' (Fenby, 1998: 31). Foreign Office services consisted of a number of different groups with a range of responsibilities, loosely divided into multilateral and bilateral ones. The latter were as follows in 1996:

> In bilateral co-operation, support for the spread of French abroad goes through two distinct services: the Direction du Développement du Ministère délégué à la Coopération on one hand, who has competence for the so-called 'field' (du champ) countries (French-speaking Africa and the Indian Ocean in particularly) and the Direction Générale des Relations Culturelles, Scientifiques et Techniques (DGRCST) of the Foreign Ministry on the other, which is responsible for all other countries. (Politique, 1996: 3)[76]

The *DGRCST* is divided into three main branches (Science and Technology, Audio-visual, Cultural and Linguistic), each of which is further subdivided as required. An organisme relais or non-departmental body, the Agence Pour l'Enseignement Français à l'Etranger founded in 1989, works in partnership as do other subsidised

Associations such as the Alliance Française or the Association pour la Diffusion de la Pensée Française. The sub-direction of Linguistic and Educational Policy, restructured in 1994, was then the central point, responsible for promoting teaching and diffusion of French in overseas educational systems; organising co-operative programmes with other countries; and co-ordinating French cultural establishments abroad. It had a budget of around 800 million francs for these purposes in 1996.

The Francophonie organisation

The Francophonie organisation is not supposedly dedicated to projecting the image of France or even of French: it is an organisation of over forty independent French-speaking countries, provinces or regions who share a common perception of the world and who wish to exchange views (see Ager, 1996a). To a certain extent, like the Commonwealth, it takes its origin from the former Empire. The end of the French Empire could be foreseen in the second world war, as countries like New Caledonia or Indochina were torn between loyalty to Pétain, the Vichy régime and thus the Nazi side, or to the Gaullist and American one. The Brazzaville conference of 1944 tried to set out new organisational arrangements which would reformulate the Empire, but these foundered and by 1962 most of the Empire had gained independence, although this was often tightly controlled in France's interest. It was not until 1986, when Canada eventually agreed that Quebec could take part independently, that the formal Francophonic organisation could be set up, and not until 1995 that it achieved its organisational format. But from 1997, the organisation is conducted under a Charter for Francophonie, holds Summit Meetings every two years, has a Secretary-General (Boutros-Boutros-Ghali, former Secretary-General of the United Nations, elected at Hanoi in November 1997), an executive international agency (the Agence de la Francophonie), and 'together, we shall write a splendid new page in History', as President Chirac said in Hanoi.

The organisation conducts its work through a number of official sub-groupings and agencies. Its main secretariat is the Agence de la Francophonie, an organisation which was set up in 1970 as the Agence de la Coopération Culturelle et Technique (ACCT) and renamed in 1997. Its principal 'operators', through which its programmes are conducted, are the Agence Francophone pour l'Enseignement Supérieur et la Recherche (higher education), TV5 (satellite television), the Université Senghor (specific University institution), and the Association des Maires et Responsables des Capitales et Métropoles Partiellement ou Entièrement de Langue Française (AIMF) (international 'decentralised' cooperation).

In 1997, President Chirac picked out in his inaugural address to the seventh summit meeting in Hanoi what he saw as the guiding principles and lines of action for Francophonie as a political organisation (Figure 8.6).

- Francophonie is above all a political enterprise;
- linguistic, economic, scientific, cultural and media co-operation;
- consolidation of the rule of law (l'Etat de droit);
- intervention (at the request of the parties) in cases of crisis;
- respect for freedoms and human dignity;
- solidarity between members, particularly in the case of rich countries helping poorer ones;
- 'Francophonie is also, and perhaps in the first place, a certain vision of the world: a political grouping based on the language we share';
- priority for basic education;
- defence of French in international organisations;
- joint action with other languages against 'a world in which speech, thought and invention would take place in a common mould';
- multilingualism in information highways.

Source: adapted from President Chirac's inaugural speech to the 1997 meeting of Francophonie. This summary gives both principles and guidelines for action by the new Secretary-General, as well as for the organisation itself.[77]

Figure 8.6 Chirac's guiding principles for Francophonie

Some of Chirac's aims and purposes showed changes from what had been the practice in previous years, particularly the prioritisation of the economic. But Francophonie remained a priority: 'On becoming President, I announced that Francophonie would be one of France's overseas priorities', and 42 million francs of additional funds (17% extra) were allocated for each year to 1999. France still saw language and culture (including the media transmission of both) as the underlying purpose. There was cautious support from Josselin (Secretary of State for Francophonie and Co-operation), who nonetheless made it clear that

the notion of Francophonie is not imprisonment in French but covers also opening towards English-speaking countries. Francophonie must not be a recollection of things past but a future, on condition that one has a very open understanding of it and it is not reduced to the defensive battle for a linguistic citadel. (*L'Humanité*, 18.11.1997)[78]

Map 8.1
Francophonie. Source: Battye and Hintze, 1992: 358

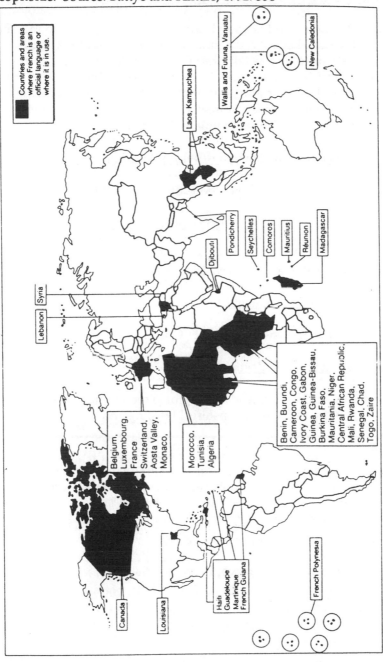

39 Member States of the Agence de la Francophonie

Benin, Bulgaria, Burkina-Faso, Burundi, Cambodia, Cameroun, Canada, Central African Republic, Belgium (French Community), Chad, Comoros, Congo, Democratic Republic of Congo (formerly Zaïre), Djibouti, Dominica, Equatorial Guinea, France, Gabon, Guinea, Haiti, Ivory Coast, Laos, Lebanon, Luxembourg, Madagascar, Mali, Mauritius, Moldavia, Monaco, Niger, Romania, Rwanda, Senegal, Seychelles, Switzerland, Togo, Tunisia, Vanuatu, Vietnam.

3 States attending Francophonie Summit Meetings not mentioned above

Belgium (Kingdom of), Cape Verde, São Tomé e Principe.

5 States associated with the Agence de la Francophonie, attending Summit Meetings

Egypt, Guinea-Bissau, Morocco, Mauritania, Santa-Lucia.

2 Participating Governments

Canada - New Brunswick, Canada - Quebec.

Observers at Summit Meetings

Albania, Macedonia, Poland and regional representatives from Aosta Valley, Louisiana, New Hampshire, New England.

Notes:
(1) The French DOM (Guadeloupe, French Guiana (Guyane,) Martinique, Réunion) and TOM (French Polynesia, French Austral and Antarctic Territories, New Caledonia, Wallis and Futuna) and other possessions (Mayotte, St Pierre et Miquelon) are not separate members of Francophonie.
(2) Algeria is not a member of Francophonie.
(3) Democratic Republic of Congo (formerly Zaïre) boycotted the 1997 Summit
Source: _Année Francophone Internationale_, 1998.

Figure 8.7 Members of Francophonie in 1998

Francophonie, and the summit meetings in particular, had become somewhat of a joke for the cynical observers who regarded them as one more international jamboree. President Mitterrand's son had for a time headed up the African cell in the Foreign Ministry, and Mitterrand's personal liking for some of the African dictators, in particular President Mobutu of the then Zaïre, had led some to question his judgement (McKesson, 1993). Under Chirac, too, the imposition of Boutros-Boutros Ghali as 'elected' Secretary-General, and the withdrawal of the alternative candidate (former President Zinsou of Bénin), provoked a near rebellion by African countries, who saw Chirac's realisation of his personal promise to the former Secretary-General of the United Nations as one more proof of the continuing strength of the 'old ways' (_Le Monde_, 14.11.1997). The defection of Congo (previously Zaïre), under its new Anglophone President Kabila, from the 1997 summit on the argument that it represented neo-colonialism sharpened the fear of many African countries that France's world role and importance would not suffice to counter American influence, and that the Francophonie organisation's meeting in Hanoi announced a significant shift in concerns away from Africa and towards the tiger economies.

The composition of formal Francophonie has in recent years added to the countries of the former Empire. Belgium, Canada, Quebec and Switzerland had participated from the beginning, while Algeria, 67% French-speaking, never has. Neither has Israel, which, despite its large population of Francophones, causes problems for potential members among the Arab states in the Middle East. Observers from areas such as Louisiana, New England and the Aosta valley have been gradually joined by non-French speaking countries like São Tomé e Principe, Moldavia, Romania and Bulgaria, while membership for Albania, Poland and other countries is likely. In these circumstances there is some doubt as to the purpose of the organisation. If such countries can join why not any country? How coherent could such an organisation be? For some commentators, the Hanoi meeting showed exactly how modern Francophonie had first to get rid of its previous nostalgia and fruitless combats with English based on elitist conceptions of culture. The future could lie with an expansion of Francophone media, as Hervé Bourges, President of the Conseil Supérieur de l'Audiovisuel, suggested in _Le Monde_ on 18.11.1997, or with strengthening the notion of cultural exception in world trade negotiations. It could lie in more direct responses to the needs of countries wishing to co-operate in the face of globalisation; those of eastern European countries for acceptance by the West; needs for development finance for the third world; the need to encourage secular institutions for those facing fundamentalist governments, particularly in the Islamic world. But there remained considerable doubt as to whether Francophonie had the means or even the will to provide such responses (Tréan in _Le Monde_, 14.11.1997). Jean Chrétien, Prime Minister of Canada, suggested in the closing session at Hanoi that Francophonie should follow the example of the Commonwealth by sanctioning countries it condemned; but Chirac was firmly opposed to any interference in the internal affairs of others.

The British press, of course, following the tradition of _The Sun_ in its anti-Frog mode, could and can barely contain its hilarity at Francophonie. The 1997 Francophone summit was

a grandiose but melancholy event... merely a folly...the French are obsessed with maintaining the purity of the tongue... French is no longer a world language in any significant sense (Ryle in _The Guardian_, 17.11.1997).

Chapter 9

Multilingualism: a policy for openness and diversity?

Change in the 1990s

The respect for multilingualism and diversity mentioned by Douste-Blazy in 1996 as the third aim of French language policy may seem rather strange. If one motivation for language policy is the projection of French identity in order to create a favourable image of France and French, policies supporting other languages and cultures hardly seem appropriate. But there are two very specific, logical and deliberate reasons for this policy aim: if French is to be promoted abroad, a favourable image of the identity of France is more likely if there is mutual respect and positive support for the cultures and languages of others. Secondly, there is strength in a collective defence with languages like Spanish or Portuguese against a common enemy seen as an otherwise superior foe (in this case, English). Historically, too, French has been promoted in the past in a fashion which has generated resentment rather than respect, and the poor impression left both by colonialism and by aggressive statements about the superiority of French culture and language have created negative impressions which need to be corrected. Hence, from the 1990s on, the rhetoric supporting French language and cultural policy started to stress support for linguistic diversity and respect for the languages and cultures of others. The contrast stands out:

In 1991: To promote the French of today and Francophonie means also patiently conducting, with our partners, a joint policy in favour of real European multilingualism. For one cannot help the future of our language except by ensuring that of the other great languages of Europe... Monolingualism would obviously happen in an Anglophone Europe; only multilingualism could ensure the maintenance of a cultural unity which would guarantee national identities. (*Brèves* 1, 1991)

In 1996: Openness towards others, respect for their language and culture are written into the government's policy and put into action by the different ministries concerned. (DGLF, 1996, 2, VI)[79]

The DGLF 1996 report outlines what has been done in pursuance of these aims in two areas we shall examine further below: the teaching of foreign languages in France, and the welcome offered overseas visitors to France through the use of their languages. There remain two questions: how real is this policy, or is it still just a cynical ploy aimed at ensuring support for French? and, if the policy is real, how far does it apply within France itself to the language diversity, not of tourists and visitors, but of resident groups who might be thought to be as entitled as they to respect and openness? First, let us recall the traditional way in which French and its culture used to be promoted: the *mission civilisatrice*.

La mission civilisatrice

The discourse of support for the teaching of the language abroad, and for the dissemination of French culture, has for long used the argument of the duty a civilised country has to bring enlightenment to others. Indeed, France had a mission to civilise others by insisting that they benefit from her language, her enlightened understanding of the world and her culture, which naturally required the extinction of their own in the pursuit of universality. France was of course not alone in this view of the benefits of civilisation, which was generally shared by the colonising powers and was indeed openly expressed in the Berlin conference of 1885 which shared out Africa among the European powers.

Le parti colonial of the late nineteenth and early twentieth centuries represents possibly the clearest statement of this type of attitude, although of course it dates back to the Revolution if not before, and the extremist attitudes of that period in no way represent overt current thinking in French political circles, except perhaps in the Front National or other extremist groups. The origin of the interest in colonial expansion lies in the 1871 defeat at the hands of the Prussians, when 'not only will France find in (colonial expansion) an increase in prosperity, it is above all the means of reconquering the prestige and the greatness the defeat had destroyed'. (Girardet, 1983: 86)[80] The tone of opinion among supporters of expansion can be gauged from quotations from two significant politicians of the era:

...our colonies will only be French in their understanding and their feelings when they understand French...For France above all, language is the necessary instrument for colonisation...Many French schools, to which we shall invite the natives, must come to help the settlers, in their difficult task of moral conquest and assimilation...when we take possession of a country, we should take with us the glory of France, and be sure that we will be well received, for it is pure as well as great, imbued with justice and goodness. (Jean Jaurès, 1884, quoted in Girardet, 1983: 94-107)[81]

For the superior races there is a right, because they have a duty towards the inferior races...They have the duty of civilising the inferior races...something else is necessary for France: she cannot just be a free country, she must also be a great country, exercising over the destiny of Europe all the influence which belongs to her, she must spread this influence over the world, and bear wherever she can her language, her customs, her flag, her arms, her genius. (Jules Ferry, 1885, quoted in Girardet, 1983: 94-107)[82]

The views of those aiming to bring the benefits of French civilisation to conquered peoples, although strongly opposed by those whose patriotism lay in France, gradually won the day and the 'exaltation of the colonial task of France' became widespread up to the 1950s in literature, economics and politics. Pressure groups sought public endorsement and presented their intentions for colonisation as supporting 'emancipation, morality and human development through productive labour' as a pamphlet for the French Colonial League put it in 1907. Such neo-colonialist views are still occasionally heard today. Although a rather special case, settlers in New Caledonia and Mayotte are on record as giving vent to somewhat similar views to those of the nineteenth century. Indeed, when in 1997 one island of the Comoran archipelago attempted to rejoin French Mayotte on the argument that it had been disregarded by its own government, and Mayotte was visibly better off, some French voices were even raised to say it should never have been granted independence in the first place. Much of the Algerian conflict, up to 1962, heard the same type of argument: a colonial situation was inevitable for underdeveloped peoples who could never aspire to self-government. Girardet, in his 1972 review of the development of the colonial idea in France, considered the colonial debate closed by then. By that time, a 'strange silence had ensued' and even if some of the original motives and justifications could still be heard, he considered that they hesitated to make themselves heard too loudly and insistently.

The superiority of French language and culture

In order to promote French language and culture, the object itself had to be thought of as superior. It is no surprise that such an attitude should be held by the speakers of any language: pride in the language and in the culture it symbolises is the most basic of language attitudes and is held by almost every language group. Indeed, it is when this pride decreases that language insecurity increases and that language shift becomes more likely. In France, the feeling is often traced to the essay by Rivarol, one of two awarded prizes in the competition organised by the Berlin Academy in 1784. This competition itself posed the issue in terms of seeking an explanation for the universal use and superiority of French in the eighteenth century and thus perhaps rather twisted the question. The other winner, the German philosopher Schwab, had written a serious tome seeking scientific reasons for the superiority of French. Rivarol's essay, a much lighter affair, was full of maxims, denigration of other languages and statements whose accuracy is debatable although they have continued to form one of the most long-lasting myths about French, particularly as opposed to English. Few linguists take the essay seriously; most have contented themselves with pointing out the obvious errors. But the phrases are widely known in French (an English version is in the Notes):

> Ce qui distingue notre langue des langues anciennes et modernes, c'est l'ordre et la construction de la phrase. Le français nomme d'abord le sujet du discours, ensuite le verbe qui est l'action, et enfin l'objet de cette action: voilà la logique naturelle à tous les hommes; voilà ce qui constitue le sens commun...
> la syntaxe française est incorruptible...
> Ce qui n'est pas clair n'est pas français.
> Elle est, de toutes les langues, la seule qui ait une probité attachée à son génie. Sûre, sociale et raisonnable, ce n'est plus la langue française, c'est la langue humaine. Quand on arrive chez un peuple et qu'on y trouve la langue française, on peut se croire chez un peuple poli. (Rivarol, 1784/1794/1991)[83]

There is a close connection between the superiority of French and the superiority of France. Sometimes the point is put with brutal simplicity, although with no tact and little sense of diplomacy. We have already noted in Chapter five above how the Permanent Secretary of the French Academy put it in 1994:

France cannot retain her rank as a great power, and conduct a policy affecting the world, unless she continues to have available a planet-wide military deterrent force and mastery of a universal language. (Druon, 1994: 23-39. See Note 46)

Caution, and even guilt as we have noted above in Chapter four, is nonetheless sometimes expressed at this type of triumphalism. De Beaucé, writing in 1988 a deliberate updating of the Rivarol essay, was rather more conscious of the degree of pessimism then prevalent about French and France and concerned to evaluate the reality of the decline. But he also saw a golden future for France in its language and culture:

Many ideas come together to evaluate this decline. There is the position of France, its political and economic weight. There is the prestige of its culture, the wealth of its creations, the mastery shown by contemporaries. There is disquiet at the strength of media and the forms of expression they impose. There is the idea of a special reserve of colonial preferences, the paradoxical fear that French as spoken by French speakers acts as intrusion. There is also the nostalgia for French humanism, for the leading role of our literature....So France should no longer have to suffer by its reduction in size. On the contrary indeed, since its many connections and its abilities, which favour flexibility in the way it behaves, could help to preserve many different possibilities for the future ...Its language and culture are of the highest value for this. (de Beaucé, 1988: 15 and 243)[84]

A year or so earlier Gabriel de Broglie had come to much the same conclusion: that for the good of France language and politics should be separated; that separating out the ideological message would give greater credibility to the language of France abroad; and that the civilising mission could be implemented better when France had a coherent cultural policy, a sound economy and an attractive international image. (de Broglie, 1986: 236)[85]

The concept of 'rank'

The continuing belief in the superiority of France, including but not restricted to its language and culture, can be traced in recent times to the persistence of the Gaullist pursuit of 'rank' (see Cerny, 1980; Cole, 1994). De Gaulle's foreign policy, and indeed much of his thinking in other spheres as well, depended on the view that in order for France to be truly herself she should occupy a leading independent role in world affairs. As a consequence, the 'reserved domain' of foreign affairs was conducted by the president's office; France acted as 'gendarme of Africa' in settling disputes; aid and defence policy were closely tied to the maintenance of influence; the jealous defence of French independence coloured a range of actions from diplomacy in the United Nations to the maintenance of the nuclear deterrent and, in later years, the retention of New Caledonia and French Polynesia as proofs of France's world role in the face of independence movements. Such Gaullist ideas were followed to a large extent by Mitterrand from 1981 to 1993, even though the strength of this policy line had already grown somewhat weaker through the 1970s and the brutal facts of cost and capacity meant that France could do less and less against the superpowers. The bases of Mitterrand's foreign policy, too, reminded many observers of the Gaullist line: the two shared a hatred of American dominance, of a world order based on free trade and economic liberalism, and of the English language. Mitterrand 'made himself the guardian of the temple':

> His last great anti-American combat was cultural...Europe was familiar to him. It was (the Europe) of language, which made him feel at home in French-speaking Africa and the Middle East. It was, he claimed, that of the spirit. He invited the planet's Nobel prize-winners, flattered the intellectuals who flattered him, refused to say a single word in a foreign language, was complacent in his mastery of language. He took around the world, without complexes, his pride in being French, deaf to those who didn't listen to him, ignoring those who ignored him. What France gains or loses through François Mitterrand's absence is principally that. (Tréan, 11.5.1995 quoted in FM, 1996: 175)[86]

Chirac, too, as the accepted descendant of the Gaullist tradition, deliberately imitated gaullist strategies and discourse after 1995. Again, the underlying conception was that of the greatness of France, mixed with a transfer of Frenchness to the ideals of Europe and associated with the ideas of the cultural exception and the need to keep Americanism at bay. The 'return to the Republican ideals', to confidence in the Nation and the State and in the lessons of history, was the theme of the general declaration of policies to be followed by the new Jospin government in June 1997: 'France is not just pretty countryside, a language enriched by spiritual works: it is above all, its history'. Although, by 1997, simple statements of the superiority in the world of France and of such values were no longer made by mainstream politicians, many of the underlying beliefs remained not far below the surface of their speech:

> Beyond our national space, changing our future means also participating in the future of the world. We must act everywhere in support of the rights of man and democracy. France owes it to herself

to be the voice of those who are deprived of them... Our second message is that of peace: maintaining or re-establishing peace, preventing crises, interference for humanitarian reasons: France has stamped her mark on such actions since 1988. Our third aim is co-operation for development...France will maintain a marked priority for Africa. (Jospin, 1997)[87]

A Policy for Openness and Respect for Linguistic Diversity

The 1994 'Global plan for languages', introduced during the early days of the Balladur government of 1993 to 1995, developed multilingualism as a specific policy aim (Figure 9.1). The policy was developed for the French chairmanship of the European Union in 1995, and was closely associated with consideration of language policy for Europe as a whole. It was based also, partly, on a rejection of any common European identity, particularly if this were to make easier domination by Anglophones who could be nothing other than a Trojan horse for the United States of America. Defence of French culture and language, in this interpretation, was seen as the same thing as defence of European specificity, while European specificity, in effect, was seen as taking the form of cultural and linguistic diversity, so not only could French be actively defended through a policy of multilingualism but this was the only way this could happen. Language planning would take place in Europe anyway, under the influence of existing policy on the free movement of people and commercial pressure such as the need to sell in the language of the client. Language planning could either be left to market forces or be conducted through conscious organisational effort. The 'global plan for languages' deliberately adopted the second route, and proposed that every European child should learn two foreign languages. At the same time, since France could clearly not insist on the use of French by others if it did not itself teach languages other than English, it must, at home, ensure that each child studied two languages in addition to French. Similarly, language learning should begin earlier in school life, at the primary or even kindergarten level. The plan involved 'reciprocity as well as precocity'.

Such policies could well be commended to, or enjoined on, other European Union members. But the 'global plan' would also need to build on preferential quotas for works of European origin in the media, encourage the development of European cultural industries and knowledge industries, ensure that the language industries could support multilingual translation and treatment of documents, and support co-operation between professional artists and writers.

- Recognition of the fact that French would be better protected by striking alliances with other language groups, particularly with the Romance languages.
- A language teaching plan for the generalised teaching of two foreign languages rather than one so as to advantage French teaching in countries where currently English was the only foreign language in education.
- Avoiding negative reactions from other countries, which might be likely if French alone was being defended. A better policy would be to present French purposes as defending diversity.
- A carefully reasoned strategy. The enemy was English and particularly its use by the USA, with the associated commercial exploitation, cultural difference and potential political and economic domination, but the grounds for preferring another language like French had to be carefully chosen. They could be cultural, but then English had as great a cultural inheritance as French; they could be elitist, but then English also had a high culture; they could be linguistic, but then the capacities of French as a vehicle of communication were not obviously better than those of English. It was hence better to advocate diversity rather than use any of these arguments in favour of French.
- Acknowledgement of multilingual facts. Even the best friends of French, in the Francophonie movement, lived in multilingual countries and it was difficult for them to accept that French was the only possible communication vehicle for themselves or others.
- Separating policies for French from policies for France. Misunderstanding the close association of French with France meant that policies to promote the French language were inevitably (mis)construed as policies for the promotion of France's own political or economic interests.

Source: adapted from Briand, 1994

Figure 9.1 The 1994 global plan for languages

The arguments were placed in the context of the GATT negotiating approach of late 1993 proposing the cultural exception. If cultural pluralism was essential for Europe, and indeed other parts of the world, in order to retain identity, then linguistic pluralism was equally necessary. This linguistic pluralism would ensure that Europe would be open and diverse, strong enough to resist domination in the future. But there were two specific points in favour of French which France should bear in mind. Much was at stake in commerce, sea and air transport, research and the protection of French consumers from massive imports from abroad. Secondly, in view of the potential for chaos in Brussels implied in the possible use of 15 working languages and 132 translation pairs, only 5 should be sanctioned, and French should be a main official and working language for all. Furthermore, to mark both France's central role in Europe and the fact that French was a, if not the, main European language, Francophone functionaries should be appointed to senior positions in preference to others.

The arguments, and the policy lines it suggested, had been developed in the Socialist government returned in 1988, perhaps as a contrast to the policy of the Right during 1986 to 1988. They appeared at about the same time as the restructuring of the language institutions in 1989 and were accepted by the Balladur government of 1993 before being proposed to the European Union by France in early 1995. Their rejection by other European powers, in a climate of considerable suspicion of French motives, was perhaps inevitable. The British saw no need to learn two foreign languages when for everybody else English was inevitably going to be one of them. Most other countries and particularly the smaller members of the Union could see nothing in the plan but complete surrender of their own identities, loss of work for their own interpreters and translators, and a further example of bullying by the large and powerful.

The French government continued during 1997 to see merit in pursuing the topic. President Chirac for example, in his opening speech to the Hanoi summit of November 1997, stressed the point about the purpose of the policy: it was not intended to dominate anyone but merely to make proceedings practical and workable. Indeed, Chirac claimed a policy of tolerance not merely for France but also as the policy of the whole Francophonie movement:

> Francophonie is not directed against any country and claims no hegemony. The message is one of openness and tolerance. And we Francophones can be proud of having been precursors of a winning movement: the just combat for the cultural diversity of the world. (Chirac, 14.11.1997 reported by Agence de la Francophonie website)[88]

The final communiqué of the summit, to which France subscribed, followed suit:

> ... enriched by the heritage of values and diverse expressions respectful of each partner's identity, and considering culture to be the basis of development, Francophonie declares itself to be open, plural,

a place for dialogue and exchange. (Reported by Agence de la Francophonie website)[89]

The Socialist government, of a different political persuasion from Chirac, put a slightly different gloss on it in the words of Josselin, Minister of Co-operation and Francophonie. These stressed the view of a new Francophonie, 'lively and attractive', that Jospin had outlined in June 1997, and showed even more clearly the combined effects of the reception of the 1994 Global Plan and the growing need to make and influence friends:

> Francophonie is a way of being non-aligned, a refusal of a single cultural and linguistic model in order to retain a world which is diverse and hence richer. (_L'Humanité_, 18.11.1997)[90]

Cynics may nonetheless continue to feel that French interest in European multilingualism, and in the recognition of linguistic and cultural diversity in the world, is self-interested and aimed at ensuring that French itself is used as widely as possible, as the revealing comment on motives for teaching foreign languages could indicate. Indeed Senator Jacques Legendre, author of the Senate report introducing the 1994 Toubon Law, put it succinctly in 1996: 'The place to be accorded French elsewhere depends on the place we give other languages here' (AELPL, 1997, 4). Everything points to the purpose being really the defence of French and of its international role, and through this, of the defence of France and her role as a world power. The presence of the French language accompanies the presence of France. Is this surprising?

Teaching Foreign Languages in France

Policy towards the teaching of foreign languages has developed in recent years in two ways. The early teaching of foreign languages has been confirmed as deliberate policy; and a formal basis has been given to the issue of which languages are to be taught in the system and why. Theoretically, twenty foreign languages may now be taught in French secondary schools: Arabic, Armenian, Chinese, Danish, Dutch, English, Finnish, German, Modern Greek, Modern Hebrew, Italian, Japanese, Norwegian, Polish, Portuguese, Russian, Spanish, Swedish, Turkish and Vietnamese, in addition to the special provision for regional languages and for the Languages and Cultures of Origin (Ager, 1996b: 70). Theoretically, too, if at least eight pupils can be recruited any language can be provided by correspondence courses. In practice the choice is limited to the thirteen most popular languages. In both secondary and primary education, governments have tried to get children to choose languages other than English through starting languages early and encouraging children to take more than one foreign language.

The new policies requiring every child to study at least one foreign language from the start of secondary education in the collèges (age 11) came fully into force in 1997. By 1998 pupils from the last two years of the collège should be studying two, although many already do. In fact 1,305,546 pupils of the 1,529,098 studying languages in secondary education in 1996 took two, while 137,194 took three. Enrolments in languages in secondary education, both public and private, for 1996-7 were as in Table 9.1. The take-up of languages depends on the regional situation as well as on perceptions of the relevant language by parents, estimations of career opportunities and numerous other factors. One of these is the closeness to frontiers: in Alsace it is hence hardly surprising that German is popular, and early teaching of the language is well established. Spanish is far more popular than German in Bordeaux, while Italian in Corsica is a popular choice. Regional languages are also widely selected in areas like Brittany and the South, in particular Toulouse and Montpellier. Nonetheless English is by far the most popular foreign language in education everywhere. As a proportion of enrolments, it regularly exceeds 95 percent.

Table 9.1 Secondary school enrolments in foreign languages

Language	Enrolments 1996
English	1,517,582
Spanish	734,561
German	571,127
Italian	104,966
Russian	12,777
Portuguese	5,863
Arabic	3,763
Modern Hebrew	2,112
Chinese	2,451
Japanese	1,386
Dutch	436
Polish	203
Total pupils	1,529,098

Note: pupil numbers in public and private education.
Source: Ministry of Education quoted in DGLF, 1997, Appendix

Teaching is offered in primary schools in Arabic, English, German, Italian, Portuguese, Spanish and Russian. In the first two years (Cours Elémentaire 1 and 2) teaching starts with fifteen minutes daily, using specially prepared audio-visual materials on a voluntary basis, progresses to more structured teaching and is done either by the class teacher, by secondary school teachers or by others paid by the local commune. English was again by far the most popular language (82% of children). 27% of children in the third year, and 56% in the final year of primary education were concerned in 1996-7. English was most popular, with 77.3% of children in the final year. German had 18.7%, Spanish 2.3%, Italian 1.3%, while all the others were taken by less than 1% of children. One of the main problems with this provision, as in other countries, is the lack of continuity in the learning of languages other than the main ones which might take place between primary and secondary education. The language chosen is sometimes not available in secondary school, particularly if it is a rarer one like Russian or even Italian (statistics from DGLF, 1997, 2, VII, 1).

Diversification of language choice, as a policy aim, has been part of the Ministry of Education's approach for a number of years (Ager, 1996b: 146). The main purpose of offering more languages has been to avoid domination by English, and a first attempt at avoiding this, by simply not making English classes available, had been so provocative in the 1970s that such an approach had to be hastily abandoned. As the education system became gradually more responsive to parental wishes during the 1970s and 1980s, the simple parental response has been more and more to choose English for instrumental reasons. In these circumstances the other foreign languages seemed doomed to practical extinction, so the invention of the two-language policy was to a certain extent the only way of saving them. The whole area of subject choice within education is sensitive both to parental and to pressure-group influence, and it is perhaps not surprising that there is now a clearer basis for the foreign languages available, expressed in the preamble to the annual syllabuses as from 1994:

> The languages which can form part of the Baccalaureate are made available on the basis of the following criteria:
> 1)   official languages of the states of the European Union
> 2)   languages widely used on the international level
> 3)   languages of foreign communities strongly represented in the national territory. (*Bulletin Officiel de l'Education Nationale*, 1994, 45: 3285)[91]

The sensitivity of the issue, and the extent to which the educational system still needs to inform parents about it, was underlined in a conference in 1996:

> The teaching of languages has always held a special place, always been a sensitive subject and has been the object of strong social pressures. Often criticised, derided, undervalued by comparison with other systems of foreign language teaching in Europe which are said to perform better, it also raises fears, since the general public is very aware of the importance of this subject area today, in the face of economic globalisation and the construction of Europe. (AELPL, 1997, 4)[92]

The motive for government policy now, however, is very clearly stated in the DGLF's annual report of 1997. Teaching more foreign languages at home is required since otherwise French might be less and less taught abroad:

> Reflection on the place of foreign languages in France cannot be distinguished from the major objective, which is the teaching of French abroad, closely followed by the DGLF and one of the Foreign Ministry's priorities...French is above all studied in foreign systems, even European ones, as a second language...In this place, its position is satisfactory overall, but very dependent on regulations governing the learning of a second language in schools, which France has been insisting on within the European Union. The promotion of multilingualism on national territory, whose importance is recalled by the 1994 Law, thus corresponds to this consideration, since France must practise at home what she is fighting for at the international level. (DGLF, 1997, 2, VII, 1)[93]

Translation and the Reception of Overseas Visitors

The idea that ministries should make documents available in a language other than French has not traditionally played any part in French administrative thinking. By contrast to many local authorities and central government departments in the UK, which have long produced documents in Welsh or the languages of settled immigration, only at local and regional level has France produced any official documentation in other languages. Even then, the victory of the Jacobins over the Girondins in the Revolution, and the abandonment of the translation policy in 1794, has meant that this policy of centralisation, uniformity and monolingualism has remained ingrained as the correct attitude to take. The DGLF report nonetheless, even if rather sniffily, does mention that the Ministry of the Interior is now producing documents, and, significantly, police documents, in a variety of languages including Arabic. Likewise the Ministry of Finance produces leaflets in 'four to six' European languages for those 'fiscally domiciled' outside France or for customs purposes, although it prefers not to produce translations on its Web site for fear of legal problems. The newly created Web pages for government sites sometimes produce translations, but only seven out of twenty-three gave, in 1996, the two translations required by the Law.

The two-language policy of the Toubon Act is by no means followed through, even in transport. In the railway system efforts are made to give material in English plus one other language chosen for geographical reasons. In 1996, a systematic survey was being undertaken by the railway system to ensure that there were always two foreign languages in stations or in security and safety information, but generally speaking the majority of stations outside the main ones remained monolingually in French. The Toubon Act was reported by DGLF to have been taken seriously by the Paris bus and metro system (RATP), where English, German, Spanish and Italian are prioritised and where a translation unit has adopted a systematic effort to improve the quality as well as the simple presence of translations.

France is a major tourist destination, with more than sixty million tourist visits annually. The Ministry for Tourism hence devotes considerable effort to campaigns in the tourist industry to improve reception facilities, and as part of this prizes are awarded for excellence in one aspect or another. The points tourists visit, too, were targeted: again a special survey was instituted by the DGLF in 1995 to encourage museums and great houses to provide information in at least two foreign languages. Versailles, for example, was 'encouraged' to add German to the signs it had erected at a high cost in French and English during 1993. Thirty-three museums were involved in 1996, and, as the DGLF coyly reports,

> In their concern for helping foreigners to gain access to French culture, these establishments are hence devoted to promoting multilingualism as soon as their means allow. The number of brochures or other actions being prepared demonstrate an increasing concern with this. (DGLF, 1996, 2, VI, 2)[94]

What would be interesting to know is the extent to which this programme is really being pursued, not merely by government departments, but by private operators also. Obviously the DGLF reports pass on the information which is submitted to them by the various ministries concerned, which are keen to show that they are following the requirement. Indeed, the activity level of the DGLF from 1995 has been very high. In conjunction with other agencies and particularly with the inter-ministerial administrative group it conducted a number of surveys, wrote to a number of services, exercised pressure on sensitive points. The effort put into replying to DGLF enquiries must have been time-consuming for busy civil servants. Overall, and added to the publicity campaigns the DGLF has conducted since 1994, and perhaps with the added power of the inter-ministerial group, the Toubon Law is clearly having an effect in the government service. Outside this, the DGLF goes no farther than saying that the signs are encouraging. As evidence it quoted a newspaper supplement in _L'Express_ published in five languages on 11th July 1996, and the multilingual publicity campaign conducted by Eurodisney and the metro service.

Cultural Pluralism in France

Accepting the undeniable fact that French outside France is always in a competitive situation with other languages, and that a correct strategy is to conduct a strong defence of the language, is one thing. It is also understandable that a policy of openness, acceptance of language diversity and tolerance towards others might form the best defence against the imposition of _de facto_ linguistic control from outside. But the logic of the situation is exactly parallel to what happened inside France itself in the extermination of the regional languages. How then, can any logical person accept that a policy of openness, diversity and cultural pluralism is unacceptable within France and only acceptable outside it? This contrast lying at the basis of official attitudes towards languages was frequently pointed out during the debates over the Toubon Act in 1994, and remains a major question which has been consistently avoided until the discussion of the question in 1998 in an opinion by the Constitutional expert Carcassonne on whether the Constitution, insisting on there being no minorities in France, actually prevented the signing of the European Charter for Minority Languages and Cultures (see _Libération_, 13.10.1998). In practical terms, as we have seen, there is now acceptance that regional languages may be taught within the state education system, and it seem likely that Carcassonne's positive opinion will allow ratification of the Charter. Image creation, of France as a plural society open to other cultures and languages, has until this point been just that: an attempt to portray France as she would like to be seen. Realisation that something has to be done about language policy to give some credibility to the image seems, in 1998, to have struck home.

Conclusion

We set out to explore the relationship between France and language, and particularly to examine the reasons and motives behind deliberate language planning and language policies. In doing this we have been led to examine both the nature of the language policies which different governments have adopted, and the relationship between these and the environment in which policy decisions in France have been made in the past and are made today. We started with three possible motivations: insecurity, or fear; identity; and image, or the promotion of this identity to others. In each case, there is little doubt that such motives have long been important in the political culture of France, not just in questions of language policy but in a wide range of other fields too. There is no doubt, either, that French policy-makers firmly believe in the importance of language policy and are fully aware of the connection between language and the society it symbolises. They also have a strong conviction that language is a matter of state; that governments and the political community are right to intervene in all the areas of language planning from defining the relative status of French, other languages and language varieties, to planning the corpus or form that approved language should take and to ensuring that language teaching for the young reflects the priorities of society. Three main considerations seem now to arise:

- the nature of French language policies as they have developed, and an assessment as to their intrinsic worth. On what basis can observers applaud or condemn French language policies?
- the issue of explanation for language policies: can they be explained as well as described, and if so, where is the explanation to be found?
- the question of the future: will French language policies change, and if so, in relation to what factors?

French Language Policies: an Evaluation

We have noted that the three aims of French language policy outlined in 1996 represent both the continuation of policies held since the Revolution or earlier, up to the time when de Gaulle renewed interest in language matters by creating the Haut Comité pour la Défense et l'Expansion de la Langue Française in 1966, and some change after about 1990. While the first aim assumes, almost without saying it, that French is a major component of the identity of France, it already contains within itself a certain amount of defensiveness, of fear that French may not be influential, prestigious or indeed the language of the Republic ('to ensure the influence and prestige of French as the language of the Republic'). The second aim is more clearly aware of possible loss of French influence and of attacks on French and the place of France in the world ('to retain for French its role as language for international communication'). The feeling of global insecurity it conveys is very obvious. Both aims show a desire to spread awareness of the language, and with it its cultural content, to others within and outside France. The third aim, 'to respect linguistic and cultural diversity and promote multilingualism', is rather newer than the other two. Its motivation is less plainly derived from questions of identity, insecurity or image creation; it is perhaps more instrumental and concerned with discovering an acceptable way of ensuring that the other two main policies stand a chance of being accepted, both within and outside the country.

What are the policies and how are they formally shown? The main legal instrument of recent times is the Toubon Act of 1994, elaborating a general statement in the 1992 Constitution. Like the majority of Acts of Parliament in France, this is a permissive instrument which gives general policy guidelines. Effect was given to its provisions in the decree of implementation of 1995 (85-240) and thereafter in a number of circulars and decisions which respond to difficulties of interpretation or make clear the lines of action which are to be followed in both general and specific cases. The detailed implementation and monitoring of this Act has been placed in the hands of a specific organisation, the DGLF, which has shown considerable zeal in implementing the requirements of the law, particularly in relation to the civil service itself. The inter-ministerial group of senior officials, too, has demonstrated teeth and a degree of determination in impressing the law's requirements on the administration. There has been perhaps high profile conformance work by the Direction de la Concurrence, de la Consommation et de de la Répression des Fraudes, but not towards ordinary French citizens, although the traditional xenophobia of the French civil service has brought foreign institutions like the Body Shop and an American University to the courts. While not a formal part of the Administration, the French Academy has a specified role to play, and the law has also seen fit to approve five language defence associations to take the role of the injured party in questions arising under the Toubon Act, although there clearly remains some reluctance within the justice system to see such amateurs intervening in the due process of law. The Toubon Act, on the face of it, applies only to the status of French in France.

The less obvious aspects of these status policies are not necessarily recorded in legal texts or statutes. They exist in written form in the annually revised syllabus and other requirements of the Ministry of Education; in the stated policies and actions of a number of agencies which deal, no matter how indirectly, with groups and communities like the socio-economically deprived or immigrants; in the policies described and implemented by the Ministry of Foreign Affairs and particularly its European desk; in the treaties, forms of co-operation and aid offered by France in relation to her former Empire, the overseas Territories and Departments for which she is still responsible, and the group of countries to which she is most closely allied in international Francophonie. Policy of a more symbolic type is expressed in the range of statements, speeches and other declarations, formal and informal, made from time to time by responsible politicians or officials from the President to Ministers, and, at a less exalted level, by individual administrators and significant personalities. It lies also, particularly in a field where behavioural change may be the aim of the policy, in the atmosphere produced by presidents, prime ministers and ministers of culture and represented in the speeches, writings and responses they give in trying to encourage an attitude or support an opinion about France's welfare or her future. Micro policy, too, can be tracked, in a country in which the representatives of the state are many, in the actions, indeed in the beliefs and attitudes, of public servants. Policy can also exist in the very absence of legal instruments, in the fact that there is no document, no speech, no comment even on certain aspects of behaviour. Policy towards sexist language is one example where government tried to develop a written view; but there are others where either a policy initiative has been tried and failed (spelling reform) or where no initiative has been made (minority language support).

Policies are not just about the status and prestige of French. The status and prestige of regional languages has received a major boost from the reception of the Poignant Report in 1998 and the rapid submission of the Carcassonne opinion in the same year. Immigrant languages have no formal status and this is unlikely to change.

Acquisition policy, state and government actions on the teaching of the country's standard language, the regional languages, the languages of immigration and foreign languages have all been considered and are generally clear. Sometimes these are less well implemented than the status policies: not every Académie or school has developed an implementation plan. Policies for managing the French language, too, are well established. Not merely has the French Academy been to some extent brought back into the mainstream of language control and language change, the government agencies facing up to problems of modern terminology now have more backing than they did and can call on greatly improved resources. But their work has not been rendered compulsory for private citizens, and the Parliamentary debate on the matter followed by the reference of parts of the Toubon Act to the Constitutional Council made it clear that there is considerable concern that policies like these, if pushed too hard by pressure groups and particularly by the Blimpish, elitist, forces at work in many areas of politics, might be perceived as nearly Fascist and certainly as contravening rights to free expression.

What are the positive points about France's language policies? French language policies have the advantage, by comparison with many countries, that they are usually open and clearly recorded in public documents. There are two major legal instruments, an annual report to Parliament on their operation, and at least two official organisations (the French Academy and the DGLF) dedicated to policy development and implementation. The policies apply to all areas of language planning. They are aimed at improving the status and prestige of the language, mainly by ensuring its use in every domain of life in the country. They apply also to the language corpus. Care is taken over changes which are discussed and approved by eminent bodies, not made up of politicians or interested experts but representative of the best of intellectual , economic and creative life. Policy applies also to ways in which French can and should be taught: the relevant ministry develops an annual review of guidance to teachers, specifies what to teach and often how; gives extensive instructions and help in the difficult task of education. Policies also encourage the teaching of other languages used within France, which, as we know, is not limited to the hexagon of metropolitan France but includes a number of overseas regions which are either considered as parts of the Republic or for which the Republic has retained responsibility, without always asking the native inhabitants. In each policy area the decisions have included the nomination of responsible agents for implementation, ranging from those which are part of the government machine like the DGLF, to those whose position is a little detached from it (the Conseil Supérieur de la Langue Française, the Observatoire de la Langue Française or the Conseil National des Langues et Cultures Régionales, although the latter has met only three times since its formation in 1983). Indeed, responsibility for implementing policy has been given to Associations who are, at least on the surface, not part of government at all, although they are in fact heavily subsidised by it. In this, France is almost alone: only Quebec has as sophisticated a mechanism for following language developments although private associations play no official role, while some other countries (Belgium) have elements of a similar approach.

Have these recent policies been effective? The 1975 Bas-Lauriol Act certainly was not. It was loosely drawn up; did not have the support of an effective implementation agency; caused endless problems for the agencies and services charged with implementing it; became in the end a mere nuisance for the legal system. Its replacement by the Toubon Act was developed in the full knowledge of these deficiencies and supported by a government which saw language as a major component in implementing a policy of greatness, itself driven both by a desire to follow in the footsteps of the great de Gaulle, and to outdo those aspects of gaullism which Mitterrand had taken over. In particular the Balladur government of 1993-5 wished to go farther than Mitterrand in pursuing the Mitterrandian desire to associate Frenchness and Francophonie, to give preferential support to French-speaking parts of the world, and to retain French influence in specific parts of the world such as Africa, the Pacific, the Caribbean where the logic of decolonisation dictates that France should have disappeared long ago.

The DGLF reports have shown since 1994 that the new law has been much more effective. Court cases have been ridiculed less; there has been much more emphasis by the enforcement agencies on supplying information and making people aware of what the law requires, on negotiation, on consultation with industrial sectors or organisations, and on threats, than on dragging cases to the courts. One particular innovation has been the number of surveys and special studies which have gone out to look for and assess the situation in particular branches of industry or institutions, and to inform the organisations and leaders of these of the law and of what they should do about it. In addition, there has been a great stress on the presentation of the policy, on propaganda, on trying to get the population involved. Competitions have been devised, publicity days have been set up, public support has been given to TV campaigns, to advertising, to the wide dissemination of information in an accessible and market-oriented form.

The creation of the DGLF, as part of the government machine, has changed things drastically from what they were under de Gaulle, when a highly prestigious organisation was set up but had to search for a role. Under Mitterrand, the organisation was restructured, but it was soon obvious that placing it under the leadership of a personality in the Arts (Philippe de St Robert), or of a professional linguist (Cerquiglini) merely enabled the professional civil servants to ensure it did nothing. It has not been until the Délégation has been incorporated into the professional service, and until the inter-ministerial group of senior civil servants was set up, that effective action has followed. Another useful clarification has been that of the role of the Academy. Its present task, of giving formal approval to terminology decisions, ensures it continued status but gets it away from the real work of implementing the law or changing hearts and minds among the general public. The real worry is whether the Academy is adequately staffed or sufficiently expert: but that is of course the point. It is precisely because the Academy is made up of representatives of the speech community without special political or technical expertise that its role is important.

Implementation of the policy has benefited also both from the Balladur circular of April 1994, including competence in French as one criterion in the promotion requirements for civil servants, and from the surprise decision of the Constitutional Council, when in July 1994 it decided that the Toubon Act did not really apply to the general public. The decision forced the public service to realise that the instructions were now no symbolic policy of interest only to the elite, to professional politicians and career diplomats, to the literary figures and the intelligentsia of Paris, but were a matter of direct interest in constructing, retaining and shaping the culture of the Administration. The second factor is that the economic stakes have become clearer since the 1993 discussions on the exclusion of cultural industries from globalisation and its effects. If France lost out in other fields, in the policy of protectionism and home preference which has always been her first wish, then the cultural domain rose in importance as a symbol of economic aims, and also coincided well with France's traditional belief in the supremacy of her artistic performance. Current language policy then is clearly stated; has risen in importance; is effectively implemented; and is associated with other policies.

Are French language policies then to be admired? Are they in some sense good? For whom? French language policies show that generally governments, the policy authorities, pressure groups and elitist groups have been leading public opinion, rather than following it. Both socialist and right-wing governments have discovered how risky this is on the rare occasions they have lent support to provocative suggestions like spelling reform or attacks on sexist language. Indeed, the elitist policies currently adopted do not seem to be helping the four social groups we have examined: the young, women, immigrants or the poor, to develop their own identities or social roles. The overriding desire to enforce equality by repressing group identity has a negative side to it. Although one must generally admire a set of policies based on establishing, confirming and maintaining a coherent approach to a unifying socio-political identity, the reverse side of this is the need to accept that all other identities must in the end disappear. There appears little compromise between majority and minority cultures, and assimilation is still the only possible outcome. France has a strong sense of identity, which has served her well over two centuries, and the current thrust of language policy is clearly intended to support what seems to be a general consensus among political Left and Right that this identity is to be respected and maintained.

Many Anglo-Saxon commentators have ridiculed the policies which react to feelings of insecurity, whether these are directed against regional languages or against English. There is little doubt that policies directed at killing off minority languages are generally objectionable, in that they so often represent attempts to harm the speakers as much as the language and may frequently be symbolic of feelings of superiority or of enmity. But the policy towards France's regional languages is long-standing; it has effectively done its work and few realistic observers could expect either that a language like Breton could regain its former role as the main means of communication for an entire region in every domain of use, or that France could accept that a language like Basque or Corsican could be used by France's representatives as an official language outside the country. Furthermore, an assimilation policy is the logical consequence of a belief in equality and the elimination of difference. The Poignant report of 1998 is crystal clear that French is the official language and that regionalists would do well to accept it in this role. Even less is it likely that a language like Arabic could be used in official roles, although the treatment of indigenous minorities of recent origin leaves much to be desired, even if other countries are little better at absorbing immigration than France. The social varieties, too, can hardly replace standard French in the official role or in its role as the mechanism for social cohesion.

Image projection, as a policy, is of recent origin. It is professionally crafted, carefully targeted and long-term, aimed at changing behaviour and convincing both French and foreigner. How good it will turn out to be is questionable. Certainly few of France's partners seem yet prepared to be persuaded of its sincerity, or of any real desire on France's part to see cultural diversity. Neither do many European partners easily accept a policy of multilingualism in the way it has been presented. Inside France, the annual festivals and French language weeks raise polite interest, although the more popular and broadly based manifestations like the spelling competitions have developed a considerable following. Only perhaps, in the annual festivals of games and music celebrating Francophonie can one see the glimmer of popular support for diversification.

Overall, policies are both good and bad. One of the main characteristics of French language policies is that they seem to be fairly consistent over a long period of time; that they generally have the support of most political opinion; and that even their strongest supporters have not gone to the lengths of xenophobia, hatred of minority groups, or arrogance that some countries have openly adopted in recent years. And there is some evidence that the new emphasis on the economic advantages of keeping French and avoiding English is slowly becoming evident: language behaviour is slowly changing and the blind acceptance of international English in all domains including everyday life has slowed, even if it has not disappeared.

Motives for Language Policies

Language change - the adoption of a new language, language loss, acceptance of a new language variety or rejection of a variety felt to be inferior or unacceptable - is a reflection of social change. It is generally agreed that in order to understand the actual use of one language rather than another, and specific language choices like these, linguistic explanations are insufficient, and the reasons must be sought in socio-political motives:

> Describing languages and linguistic situations is relatively simple...but remains on the surface of the facts...To understand the why of these situations, the why of language change, of attitudes and strategies, one must go to the root - the social root - of phenomena. (Calvet, L.-J., 1996: 110)[95]

> In my definition, language change must always be social in origin and to some extent willed, or at any rate recognized, by the community in which it occurs. (Posner, 1997: 106)

It may also be that much linguistic change, too - change in the subsystems of language such as a change in pronunciation, adoption of a new morphological form, change in lexis, change in syntax - often reflects social change. The examples are not numerous in French, but they are significant. One has only to think of the development of new terminologies, the creation of neologisms and the extent of borrowing to accept that changes in the meaning of terms often derive from changes in the structure of society, in the nature of social resources or in socio-economic trends. It is less clear that change in other linguistic subsystems always correlates with social change. But the adoption of the uvular [r] in the seventeenth century in many countries, not just France, is a clear indication of a linguistic change in pronunciation arising for social reasons. Similarly, the current tendency among young women in particular to stress, or even add, a final [e] in pronunciation may have social origins in a desire to differentiate the speech both of the young and of women from that of the Establishment. The language mixing now noted in urban speech has a direct social origin: Arabic is available to provide either a grammatical substratum or a range of discourse components, as well as lexical items, for use in French, and many young people adopt Arabic forms even if they themselves are not of Arab-speaking origin. Even English newspapers have noted this:

> Tu es un khomar, tu es kho-kho (You are a donkey, you are worth nothing)
> Ralouf, tu es shooté? (Pig, are you on drugs?). (*The Observer*, 28.4.1996)

Posner (1997: 138) mentions at least four other factors likely to cause linguistic change: a default movement towards simplification, whims of fashion, 'some sort of heave from outside', and/or pragmatic requirements. Our question in this book is not about unconscious linguistic change nor (solely) about unconscious language change. Some of the language policies we have been discussing are aimed at producing or preventing language shift. Thus for example the traditional and long-lasting shift towards French from the regional languages, and the more recent aim of preventing a shift from pure French towards Franglais or English. Policy-makers are clearly of the opinion that since language change and some linguistic change may have social origins, then specific language policy can provide the 'heave from outside' that could be needed to ensure it. It is partly our contention, too, that language policy can work; that it works because it is in essence political; and that the political community has every right to work on the basis of the importance of language to society. The speech community works by unconscious language and linguistic change, but the political community is aware of what it is doing and why.

Many commentators think language policy is essentially different from any other policy. Schiffman (1996: xi) 'puts language, and everything associated with language, at the centre of language policy' and 'eschews theoretical constructs of a formalist, post-modern, or neo-Marxist kind'. Schiffman's main thesis is that 'language policy is a belief system, a collection of ideas and decisions and attitudes about language. It is of course a cultural construct, but it is either in tune with the values of the linguistic culture or it is in serious trouble' (p. 59). This is tantamount to saying that policy is not the business of politicians, hardly a tenable proposition. Neither can we see much difference between policy about language and policy about social welfare or taxation: any policy will only work if the community accepts it. Language policy, like any other policy, is the result of a political assessment of the realities of the day and an estimation of what can be done about them. Language policy, often a short-term construct of the political community, is not the same as language attitudes, mainly the long-term beliefs of the speech community, although it derives from them.

Schiffman's view is essentially that language policy is a construct of the speech community, rather than of the political community, and that if the political community's actions are not in consonance with those of the speech community, they will fail. In the case of France (pp. 75-147), the evidence he produces, of the existence of the French Academy and the belief structures of the French Revolution shows success:

> French language policy, believed by some... to be the most explicit and restrictive in the world, is more of a cultural construct than an explicit policy. Its power rests in what people imagine it to consist of, rather than on actual statutes or rigid codes. In other words, policy is not as explicit as French people think it is - but it is every bit as restrictive as they believe it is, as long as they think it is. (Schiffman, 1996: 123)

These examples are not policy, in Cooper's definition ('language planning done by governments'), but language attitudes. Schiffman's manuscript was probably completed before the Toubon Act (references are to the 1975 Bas-Lauriol Act), the creation of the DGLF and the subsequent tightening-up of the Terminology Commissions and the role of the Academy, and before the present turmoil over questions of nationality. But French language policy is now, as we have shown, both explicit and overt, and a political construct, not a cultural one nor a bellettristic one. The key to explanations for it lies less in a linguistic culture and set of attitudes typical of the language defence associations and the cultural pressure groups, even the regional ones, than in the wish of the political community to influence the speech community by making reference to the imagined community. The imagined community, linked by myths, taboos, a supposed common origin and common values, is a community of reference: a notion to which members of a group refer in recognising others as sharing their identity, and in refusing acceptance to those whose identity lies outside the boundaries of the group. France is notable for the durable wish to make the geographical, political, speech and cultural communities coincide, as we have seen in relation to the 'myth of the hexagon'. The consequence of this desire is to assimilate all within the hexagon to a single model, and to erect barriers around the citadel. The wish to base French identity on shared social practices, even where these are difficult to describe and circumscribe, is similar. Such shared social practices, the culture of the society, or the set of meanings it collectively holds, are visible and, generally, have been strongly approved in France. Policy issues arise both in formalising them and at the boundaries, where French culture differs from other sets of beliefs and values, yet that culture is represented on French soil. Geography, as with the question of regional identities, hence forms part of the issue. So too do the attitudes of those 'within' and those 'without'. 'Inclusion' seems to be a positive value for those 'within' French society. The strength of these beliefs in the benefits of social integration and the dreadfulness of social exclusion is evident in contemporary French discussion of exclusion and its effects (cf. Ferreol, 1994), in the public debates over the Pasqua laws on immigration in 1986-88 and after 1993, and on the decision by the Socialist government not to rescind them in 1997. Beliefs are strong in the debate in France over feminism, in the nature of the Presidential election campaign in late 1994 and early 1995, and in the generally sympathetic public reaction to the more obvious indications of exclusion. Beggars on the streets or in the Métro, homeless action groups squatting in empty flats, or, to a lesser degree, violence in the suburbs, supposedly caused by the young or by immigrants, are not instantly rejected by all French people as antisocial. To judge by the Press at least, the general public reaction to these phenomena has been a strong wish to help rather than to condemn. The strength of the feeling of nationality may be judged by an opinion poll on possible changes in the nationality code. A survey of 28th and 29th November 1997, published in *Le Figaro* on 1.12.1997, part of which is reproduced as Table Conc.1, makes the point that individuals feel they are involved personally in the nationality issue. From all these points it is clear that most language policy as we have described it demonstrates that the

French political community had, and has, considerable effect on the French speech community in France.

Why should it be that the three motives, of insecurity or fear that the coherent nation-state might be destroyed, together with pride in the nature of French identity and the desire to encourage its spread, should be the main motives for French language policy? Partly because the creation and defence of the citadel has long been an aim of French society, and these three motives separately and together work to continue it. Partly, also, because the underlying concepts derive from all three communities: the political, but also the speech community which has standardised its manner of expression on one form, and the ethnic community which, despite its evident multicultural origins and practice, regards itself as united in the territorial, hexagonal basis for its identity. Partly because of the tradition of universalism, which regards all humanity as enriched by the mere presence of France. Partly, too, because the underlying voluntarism of French democracy continues to affirm the power of the individual, and his or her right to control all three communities through deliberate acts. The motives operate both in isolation from each other, and together, in inspiring specific acts of policy. These would never work unless the policy formulators devised them, and presented them, as following the underlying belief systems. But in this, language policy is again no different from any other policy.

Table Conc.1 Opinions on French nationality

Question 1: In thinking about children born in France of foreign parents, with which of the following opinions do you agree?

	Left	Right	All
Such children should be recognised as French provided they demonstrate their willingness:	64%	89%	76%
Such children should automatically be recognised as French:	33%	7%	19%
Neither of these:	2%	3%	4%
No response:	1%	1%	1%

Question 2: If major modifications were proposed in the French Nationality Code, would you personally wish to be consulted in a referendum?

	Left	Right	All
Yes:	70%	84%	75%
No:	29%	15%	24%
No response:	1%	1%	1%

Note: 'Left' and 'Right' indicate support for left or right-wing political parties.
Source: *Le Figaro* 1.12.1997

The myth of inclusion is based on voluntarism. In fact very few French citizens have ever made a specific voluntary act of joining nation or state. The state's servants sometimes take advantage of their special position by regarding themselves as the group to whom all should assimilate, and hence becoming an almost autonomous force in society. The other side of this is corporatist selfishness. The state's servants, not just the bureaucracy but all functionaries, influence policy-making as well as implementation. Such functionaries can then be seen by citizens as themselves outside society, so opposition to social norms can take the form, paradoxically, of opposition to the state. Organs of the state, particularly the police force and enforcers of law and order, commonly regard social deviance as unacceptable behaviour which can be treated as though the offender had no human rights at all, and both offenders against social norms, and those who regard themselves as having social rights but who may not be able to exercise them (particularly the unemployed) similarly regard the police, and any state bureaucrat, as fair game. Individuals are either completely within, or completely outside, the nation-state and hence society. In relation to foreigners but also to any marginalised group, the state considers it part of its purpose to ensure that the boundaries of inclusion and exclusion are maintained: its legitimacy depends on the boundaries being recognised. Probably the nearest comparable situation is that of Japan, where excluded groups also feel no compunction in their attacks on the state.

The central importance of the state and its power has been a constant feature of France since before the Revolution, and has overwhelmed French civil society, leading to a situation in which the differences between citizenship, nationality, culture and the nature of society have been obscured. It is for this reason that the French nation-state and its elite have fought against the regional languages and all they symbolise, and that they still, in what is confusedly realised by many to be a rearguard action, struggle against globalisation and Americanisation. The force of the identity concept and the neat bundle of beliefs that go with it - the Republican values, centralisation and Jacobinism, concepts of universality and Rights - has long been a bulwark against the rest of the world. But this is said to be changing, under pressures like immigration, the changing role of women, the need to internationalise, the creation of Europe. The very Americanisation which is said to be a danger brings with it the need to ensure that the inevitable changes are controlled and managed - not by the state so much, now, as by the technocrats and the managers, working within a pluralist market-place in which the interests at stake, and the players on the field, are less often the representatives of power (the monarchy, the Republican ideology, global capitalism) than representatives of the powerful (Le Pen, Tapie, Bill Gates, Rupert Murdoch). It is the individual able to participate in the game who ensures that policies are implemented.

The other main change in recent times has been the extent to which French ethnic nationalism has strengthened. The growing strength of the Front National is just one indicator of this. It may be that this is a reaction to the weakening of the concept of unity and inclusion. Nonetheless, the ethnicisation of the definition of belonging to the state, and the closer association between the French nation and the French state, have changed the nature of the discussion over the last twenty years:

> the breakdown of a unitary national state formation and its legitimizing discourses has led to a wide-ranging debate about questions of nation, state, culture, the market and citizenship, and holds out the prospect of a major reformulation of the relationship between individual and society. (Silverman, 1996: 157)

Language policy is not just a reflection of the dilettante interests and attitudes of the elite of the Parisian speech community. Indeed, the speech community within metropolitan France is much closer to the political community than perhaps in some other societies, as can be seen by the generally positive reaction by such everyday organisations as the opticians to the DGLF's 'conversations' with them. If the legitimising discourses of the unitary national state are breaking down, then the reaction of the political community in trying to direct the nature of social discourse is not surprising. The motive of insecurity may have recently changed its direction, but the belief that there is a close connection between language use, language policy and the security of the state, and an absolute necessity that the speech and the political communities work together to defeat fragmentation and to promote the coherence of the social identity, is reinforced.

Theories of policy formulation

Current theories of policy formulation envisage a number of approaches to government manipulation of society (Ager, 1996b: 9). They include the institutional, group, elite, systems, process, rational, incremental and game theory models of policy-making. Our examination of French society shows fairly convincingly that the elite have played a strong part in the development and implementation of all aspects of language policy. The long history of the imposition of standard French on the whole country, based on the elitist fear of possible break-up of the state, is a clear example of the importance of the leading regional Parisian network, in the same way as the rejection of socially undervalued language varieties demonstrates the power of leading social classes. The autonomous state, too, in the form of the corporatism of the bureaucrats, has had much to do with policy in France, and here the best example of slow, incremental policy-making is probably that of the delays to the implementation of the Deixonne Act of 1951 permitting the teaching of regional languages. By contrast, the institutional model and, notably, the group model which bases its approach on the battle between social classes, do not seem to have great explanatory power in relation to French society. We have examined elsewhere the nature of the French policy-making process (Ager, 1996b), and in this area the effect of the numerous pressure groups and particularly of the Paris-based intellectual network on the process is interesting. The interest is less based on the idea that such networks are influential as they undoubtedly are, as on the undeniable fact that they are generally poorly informed about their own society and often seem to lack awareness, particularly political awareness, as the examples of the reception of both the Toubon Act and the previous anti-sexist legislation of 1986 show. Although the remaining policy formulation models offer insights, none of them seems to have the same illuminating force as the three we have found to be particularly helpful: the elite model, the incremental model, and the process model.

The Past, the Present and the Future

How does the current scene compare with previous periods? We have observed some fairly clear correlations between language policies and the political or social environment in which these have been developed. Under the Ancien Régime, language policy was of little concern or interest except insofar as the state needed from time to time to ensure that the royal message was clearly understood: if not by all, then at least by those whose task it was to interpret the royal will to loyal or unwilling subjects. Language policy, such as it was, was part of the legal framework and applied to discourse in the courts. The Revolution changed all that. Its policies insisted on the use of a common language, insisted that this had to be taught to everybody, and tried to ensure that the common language was itself shaped, improved and controlled for the greater good. It developed a mentality of centralisation and interference by the state in the actions of individuals; recognised only such individuals, on whose individual adherence to general principles of human rights it relied; and developed an aggressive if somewhat confusing ideology based on the concept that the universalism of such roles for individual and state were unarguably right, unarguably universal, and also unarguably French. The Revolution brought language and politics together, in two ways: language became the fundamental way in which politics was conducted (rather than simple force and violence, although these were certainly used) and the politics of language were designed to create the state. Language policies were aimed at building unity, developing a universal means of communication, and preventing fragmentation.

In the nineteenth and twentieth centuries a different type of nationalism has been developed, which combines a more ethnically based view of the state and its role with a more defensive belief in the indissoluble link between a certain type of French state and the French language. Language policies concentrated more on education as the nineteenth century enabled a practical policy of schools to be developed, and the bourgeois state erected barriers and gate-keeping mechanisms, like the baccalaureate, to retain privilege and keep acquired rights for those who had jumped the right hurdle. As the twentieth century has moved on, different socio-economic groups have tried to maintain the same approach, and language policies have aimed more at ensuring that identifiable barriers are erected to keep out undesirables, whether these be women, the poor, immigrants, new technologies, the uneducated or the yet-to-be educated. The overall banner for these types of policies has been a form of Republican socio-ethnic nationalism, quite different from the universalism of the Revolution but unable to see the difference, and frequently adopting a very similar discourse. All political parties subscribe to the same shibboleths; but what the Front National, the Parti Socialiste, the Parti Communiste Français and the Rassemblement pour la République mean by the words is very different.

In the future, language policy may change to respond to different threats and opportunities. It is likely to become on the one hand even more 'Republican', in line with the first of Jospin's 1997 priorities to 'return to the Republican spirit' and reinforce the nation-state. But the concept of the nation-state itself may depart from the Jacobin, centralised form as the decentralisation option becomes more Girondin and regional strengths are recognised. Signing the European Charter for Minority Languages and Cultures may be one indication of this, as well as conveniently underlining the European option. Secondly policy may become even more international, and particularly aim to respond even more sharply to the threats from globalisation and the opportunities arising for French and France. The choices France has made for Europe and for Francophonie are indications of this: both are bolt-holes in which to get away from the world super-power as well as positive, deliberate choices of future orientations. The two commitments are fundamental in much more than language policy.

Francophonie is much more than the former colonial empire, too. It is that, and indeed includes the remnants of that empire, in the DOM and the TOM. Francophonie is now world-wide, and France seems to have every intention of retaining a global strategy and global importance, even if her actual possessions overseas are small. Her influence, epitomised through the language-based Francophonie movement, is deliberately fostered. But the problems are real: the poverty and backwardness of many of the French-speaking countries, in Africa above all; the inability of France to maintain her control of African ex-colonies; the lack of any real international spirit in an organisation so dominated by France; the lack of any real economic or political unity between countries of disparate location and interests. Linguistic unity, even, is skin-deep in an organisation where most participants use French only at the official level, where some also belong to the Commonwealth or to other international organisations and where some are clearly members only for so long as membership of Francophonie delivers advantages. Language policy aimed at internationalising and perhaps simplifying French so it could be learnt more freely and act as a replacement lingua franca of international communication seems to have been ruled out by the guardians of the citadel. Europe is an equally fundamental commitment, but with greater likelihood of success. France does not intend her dominant role in the construction of the European Union to be forgotten; nor does she see herself as taking a smaller role in the future as the Union is enlarged. But the policy of trying to bully her way to a continuing role for her language in the official institutions has produced negative reactions, and the reversal of policy to encourage European cultural pluralism and diversity has seemed shallow and cynical. The better solution might be to develop the idea of the cultural exception, unless this also degenerates to traditional protectionism. If it does not work, language policy will accept the inevitable and give way to international English.

Language policy is likely to remain at the centre of French concerns. For the Left, it will be described as even more Republican, Revolutionary in origin and supportive of human rights. For the Right, the same policy may be described as French, pure and solidly based in defending the identity and true nature of France. The discourses may be different, but the intention is the same: to ensure continued close interaction in language between the political, the cultural and the truly French.

Notes and source texts

Introduction

1 Article 1er. Langue de la République en vertu de la Constitution, la langue française est un élément fondamental de la personnalité et du patrimoine de la France. Elle est la langue de l'enseignement, du travail, des échanges et des services publics. Elle est le lien privilégié des Etats constituant la communauté de la Francophonie. (Loi 94-665 du 4 août 1994 relative à l'emploi de la langue française)

Chapter 1

2 En France, l'intervention de l'Etat en matière de langue est plus ancienne que la notion même d'Etat, apparue au début du XIVe siècle. Celle du pouvoir central sur les langues vernaculaires date du règne de Saint-Louis (XIIIe siècle) ... (qui) recommande ... à (sa) chancellerie d'éliminer le 'latin grossum' des documents diplomatiques et juridiques. (Szulmajster-Celnikier, 1996: 39)

3 avec l'oeuvre des générations qui ont créé la France - la Nation; avec l'idée laïque et républicaine de la création de la citoyenneté française; avec le grand oeuvre de l'éducation nationale. ...confondent le respect que nous devons aux traditions provinciales et des assauts délibérés sur l'unité républicaine; elles sont en effet un désir de déchirer la Nation. (Debré, M. in *Le Figaro*, 9.8.1985)

4 Ce sur quoi on bute au ministère de l'éducation nationale...c'est l'absence de statut spécial des langues régionales...Depuis la loi Deixonne de 1951, qui constituait une avancée mais qui ne définit pas de statut spécial, il n'y a rien eu, en fait...L'ambition qui est la nôtre pour la langue française va de pair avec la nécessité de ne pas laisser disparaître la richesse que constituent nos langues et cultures régionales. ((M. Ivan Renar, *Journal Officiel*, 15.4.1994. Sénat, Débats Parlementaires, 20 S (CR): 1090)

5 J'exprime mon hommage au système scolaire laïc et républicain qui a souvent imposé l'emploi du français contre toutes les forces de l'obscurantisme social et même religieux... il est temps pour nous tous d'être Français dans cette langue. S'il est nécessaire d'enseigner une autre langue à nos enfants, ne les faisons pas perdre leur temps avec des dialectes dont ils ne se serviront que dans leurs villages (Roger Pandraud, *Journal Officiel*, 15.4.1994. Sénat, Débats Parlementaires, 20 S (CR): 1090)

6 Article 6. L'enseignement public est partout dirigé de manière qu'un de ses premiers bienfaits soit que la langue française devienne en peu de temps familière de toutes les parties de la République.

Article 7. Dans toutes les parties de la République, l'instruction ne se fait qu'en langue française (Decree of 30 vendémiaire an II (21 October 1793). Quoted in Brunot, 1967, 9, 1: 148)

7   la plus belle langue de l'Europe, celle qui la première a consacré franchement les droits de l'homme et du citoyen, celle qui est chargée de transmettre au monde les plus sublimes pensées de la liberté et les plus grandes spéculations de la politique...

Les hommes libres se ressemblent tous; et l'accent vigoureux de la liberté et de l'égalité est le même, soit qu'il sorte de la bouche d'un habitant des Vosges, des Pyrénées ou du Cantal...

les premières lois de l'éducation doivent préparer à être citoyens; or, pour être citoyen, il faut obéir aux lois, et, pour leur obéir, il faut les connaître...Nous avons révolutionné le gouvernement, les lois, les usages, les moeurs, les costumes, le commerce et la pensée même; révolutionnons donc aussi la langue, qui est leur instrument journalier...

Le fédéralisme et la superstition parlent bas-breton; l'émigration et la haine de la République parlent allemand; la contre-révolution parle l'italien, et le fanatisme parle le basque. Cassons ces instruments de dommage et d'erreur. (Rapport Barère, quoted in Certeau *et al*. 1975: 291-9)

8   Mais on peut au moins uniformer le langage d'une grande nation, de manière que tous les citoyens qui la composent puissent sans obstacle se communiquer leurs pensées. Cette entreprise, qui ne fut pleinement exécutée chez aucun peuple, est digne du peuple français, qui centralise toutes les branches de l'organisation sociale et qui doit être jaloux de consacrer au plutôt, dans une République une et indivisible, l'usage unique et invariable de la langue de la liberté.

Tout ce qu'on vient de dire appelle la conclusion, que pour extirper tous les préjugés, développer toutes les vérités, tous les talents, toutes les vertus, fondre tous les citoyens dans la masse nationale, simplifier le méchanisme et faciliter le jeu de la machine politique, il faut identité de langage. (Rapport Grégoire, quoted in Certeau *et al*., 1975: 300-17)

9   La féodalité...y conserva soigneusement cette disparité d'idiomes comme un moyen de reconnaître, de ressaisir les serfs fugitifs et de river leurs chaînes...l'unité de l'idiome est une partie intégrante de la révolution...que le zèle des citoyens proscrive à jamais les jargons, qui sont les dernières vestiges de la féodalité détruite. (Rapport Grégoire, quoted in Certeau *et al*., 1975: 300-17)

10 Si dans notre langue la partie politique est à peine créée, que peut-elle être dans des idiomes dont les uns abondent, à la vérité, en expressions sentimentales pour peindre les douces effusions du coeur, mais sont absolument dénués de termes relatifs à la politique; les autres sont des jargons lourds et grossiers, sans syntaxe déterminée. (Rapport Grégoire, quoted in Certeau *et al*., 1975: 300-17)

11 Penserez-vous, m'a-t-on dit, que les Français méridionaux se résoudront facilement à quitter un langage qu'ils chérissent par habitude et par sentiment?...Ne faisons point à nos frères du Midi l'injure de penser qu'ils repousseront une idée utile à la patrie

la connaissance des dialectes peut jeter du jour sur quelques monuments du moyen âge...il faut chercher des perles jusque dans le fumier d'Ennius
la crainte de voir les moeurs s'altérer dans les campagnes...Des moeurs! Sans elles point de République, et sans République point de moeurs.
En avouant l'utilité d'anéantir les patois, quelques personnes en contestent la possibilité...Dût-on n'obtenir qu'un demi-succès, mieux vaudrait encore faire un peu de bien que de n'en point faire. (Rapport Grégoire, quoted in Certeau *et al.*, 1975: 300-17)

12   l'enrichir, le simplifier, en faciliter l'étude aux nationaux et aux autres peuples.

(2)   notre langue est remplie d'équivoques et d'incertitudes; il serait également utile et facile de les fixer

(3)   il serait utile de faire une revue générale des mots pour donner de la justesse aux définitions

(4)   la richesse d'un idiome n'est pas d'avoir des synonymes

(5)   on peut permettre quelques heureuses acquisitions...expressions énergiques ...qu'il serait important de faire revivre...emprunter des idiomes étrangers les termes qui nous manquent et de les adapter au nôtre, sans toutefois se livrer aux excès d'un néologisme ridicule...faire disparaître toutes les anomalies résultantes soit des verbes réguliers et défectifs, soit des exceptions aux règles générales. (Rapport Grégoire, quoted in Certeau *et al.*, 1975: 300-17)

13 Article 1. A compter du jour de la publication de la présente loi, nul acte public ne pourra, dans quelque partie que ce soit de la République, être écrit qu'en langue française.
Article 2. Après le mois qui suivra la publication de la présente loi, ne pourra être enregistré aucun acte, même sous seing privé, s'il n'est écrit en langue française. (quoted in Brunot, 1967, 9, 1: 186)

14 Au total, la Révolution et ses suites n'auront pas bouleversé réellement et immédiatement les comportements linguistiques quotidiens des Français, et donc maintenant des Provençaux. Mais elle aura inscrit profondément toute une mentalité linguistic-culturelle centraliste dans la société française. Cela produira ses effets progressivement au cours du XIXe siècle et plus brutalement pendant le XXe siècle. (Blanchet, 1992: 72)

15 Ces propositions étaient en contradiction avec les choix politiques des socialistes...Le Conseil National des Langues et Cultures régionales ...a été réuni trois fois en six ans et son influence a été négligeable...les cultures régionales ont cessé d'être considérées comme des facteurs de dégradation de l'identité nationale. (Giordan, 1992: 138-9)

16 (1)   les Droits de l'enfant et de l'élève sont la priorité

(2)   la langue française est la langue officielle

(3)   la République française reconnaît les langues et cultures régionales sur son territoire

(4)   la politique en matière de langues et cultures régionales doit s'inscrire davantage dans le cadre de la décentraliation

(5)   l'école républicaine est une école d'intégration

(6)   apprendre une langue régionale est un acte volontaire. Cette faculté doit être ouverte à tous

(7)   apprendre plusieurs langues est une richesse

(8)   le même niveau de langue française doit être atteint par tous les élèves

(9)   l'état s'engage à assurer la continuité d'apprentissage d'une langue régionale

(10)   l'état reconnaît le pluralisme des méthodes pédagogiques. (Poignant, 1998: 31-3)

Chapter 2

17 L'imaginaire et le pouvoir, deux clefs de notre compréhension de l'histoire humaine et française en particulier, ont été méconnus par les fondateurs de l'histoire républicaine, parce que leur culture, leur nationalisme, leur perception de la 'nature' humaine n'en percevaient ni la portée ni le ressort. Ayant sécularisé et laïcisé la conception de l'histoire, ils pensaient en avoir éliminé le sacré qu'à leur manière ils réinséraient dans le culte de la nation et de l'Etat. (Citron, 1987: 12)

18 leurs émules de 1848, qui applaudirent à Edgar Quinet quand il annonça que 'la France a pour misssion de conduire l'humanité vers la brillante aurore'...Jules Ferry a clairement exprimé en pleine Chambre, en 1885: 'qu'il faut autre chose à la France: qu'elle ne peut pas être seulement un pays libre; qu'elle doit aussi être un grand pays, exerçant sur les destinées de l'Europe toute l'influence qui lui appartient, qu'elle doit répandre cette influence sur le monde, et porter partout où elle le peut sa langue, ses moeurs, son drapeau, ses armes, son génie...André Malraux: 'La France n'est la France que lorsqu'elle se charge du destin de l'humanité'. (all quoted in Mordrel, 1981: 206)

19 la France, s'étant constituée à l'aveuglette et à la fantaisie des circonstances, est devenue un hexagone comme elle aurait pu devenir un trapèze ou une sorte d'étoile. Dans ce dernier cas, le symbole eût à coup sûr évoqué une intervention directe du ciel.
La France n'est pas une République, comme le fut Athènes, comme l'est un canton suisse ou un Etat des Etats-Unis. C'est une dictature collective exercée par l'appareil de l'Etat, déguisé en démocratie. Une démocratie qui se limite à un ensemble de concessions au citoyen isolé - mais jamais au groupe auquel il appartient...Son système politique, qui place tous les pouvoirs dans les mains de l'Etat, est une magnifique machine de guerre, et qui a été conçue par des régimes ayant besoin d'obéissance pour la faire. (Mordrel, 1981: 183 and 323)

20 postulat d'une langue unique dont les parlers d'Oc sont des dialectes, objectif de normalisation et normativisation de 'la' langue (création d'un 'occitan standard' archaïsant à base languedocienne, élaboration d'une orthographe complexe et archaïsante destinée à englober tous les parlers d'oc au sein d'une même 'langue occitane', admiration de la civilisation des troubadours, albigéisme revanchard et nationalisme 'occitan' anti-français, existence d'une nation occitane qui n'a pas pu exister politiquement à cause de l'intervention française en Languedoc, lutte contre le 'colonialisme français', admiration du modèle catalan). (Blanchet, 1992: 39)

21 Le mot 'provençal' désigne donc ici le réseau d'idiomes, la langue, appelé(e)(s) 'provençal' par ses locuteurs, c'est-à-dire uniquement les idiomes de la Provence, et éventuellement de certaines zones limitrophes. Blanchet, 1992: 43).
Le régionalisme provençaliste, très actif depuis les années 1950 ... sont fondés, en plus du Félibrige, lou Provençau à l'Escolo ('le provençal à l'école') et lou Group d'Estùdi Provençau ('groupe d'études provençales') qui seront des foyers d'action, de réflexion et de publication très efficaces...L'Astrado Prouvençalo ('la destinée provençale') qui reste aujourd'hui le plus grand éditeur provençal, Parlaren ('nous parlerons') dont l'action est beaucoup plus politique. L'Unioun Provençalo(('union provençale') ... a notamment mis au point, avec l'aide de juristes, un 'Statut pour la Provence'...La plupart des mouvements régionalistes provençaux agissent au niveau international, à travers des associations internationales comme l'Association Internationale pour la Défense des Langues et Cultures Menacées, et auprès d' instances telles que le Conseil de l'Europe... la C.E.E. ou l'U.N.E.S.C.O. (Blanchet, 1992: 87)

22 Le fait est qu'après l'échec des Félibres, on n'a pas réussi à définir une norme générale acceptée par toutes les variantes et on observe la préparation continue de grammaires et de graphies partielles, qui morcellent le sens d'identité culturelle compacte sous-jacente, présent dès le moyen âge. (Ferrer, 1990: 11)

23. Le Gouvernement encouragera l'affirmation de l'identité culturelle de la Corse et l'enseignement de sa langue. (Jospin, 1997)

Chapter 3

24 c'est la maîtrise des enseignements fondamentaux, langue française, orale et écrite, méthodes de travail personnel en lecture et écriture, calcul, repères pour la vie personnelle et sociale, qui crée l'égalité face à l'école. La première priorité est la langue française, orale et écrite. (Bayrou, F., quoted in DGLF, 1996, 2, IV, 3)

25 L'école est le berceau de la République. Outre sa mission d'instruction, elle doit assurer l'apprentissage du civisme. Dès l'enfance, il faut faire naître et vivre durablement un profond sentiment d'attachement aux valeurs républicaines au premier rang desquelles la laïcité, le respect de la chose publique, l'adhésion à une citoyenneté active et responsable, ensemble indissociable de droits et de devoirs .
... Faire participer les jeunes, en particulier les 'jeunes des quartiers', à la vie démocratique représente un enjeu d'une particulière importance. L'inscription de chaque citoyen sur les listes électorales sera rendue automatique l'année de sa majorité. (Jospin, 1997)

26 Des progrès nets ont été réalisés dans les apprentissages linguistiques fondamentaux, aidés par la prise de conscience, à partir des années 90, de l'enjeu du combat contre l'illettrisme, qui est une des formes de l'exclusion. (DGLF, 1997, 2,VI, 2)

27 Les femmes sont toujours professionnellement cantonnées dans les secteurs les moins qualifiés, les moins rémunérés, et ceux qui bénéficient des moindres chances d'avancement. L'écart des salaires entre hommes et

femmes reste important, comme demeure importante l'inégalité devant le chômage...Aucune des lois votées durant les années Mitterrand, nous l'avons dit, n'a posé explicitement le droit à l'avortement comme droit civil ni le remboursement de l'IVG comme faisant partie intégrante des droits sociaux. (Jenson and Sineau, 1995: 342-7)

28 Il faut d'abord permettre aux Françaises de s'engager sans entrave dans la vie publique. Dans ce domaine, le progrès passe d'abord par l'évolution des mentalités et le changement des comportements. Les Socialistes et la majorité ont montré l'exemple, tracé le chemin. Il faut aller plus loin. Une révision de la Constitution, afin d'y inscrire l'objectif de la parité entre les femmes et les hommes, sera proposée.
Quant au mouvement en faveur de l'égalité professionnelle entre les femmes et les hommes, il sera repris. (Jospin, 1997).

29 'nous devons nous battre pour que la France reste la France'
Pierre Bernard justifie son action par sa fidélité au catholicisme auquel le bulletin municipal se réfère sans cesse.
  'le taux de naissance des étrangers rapporté à la population est plus de quatre fois supérieur au taux de naissance des Français'
'Nous sommes assiégés, serons bientôt dominés...la plupart des immigrés ne cherchent pas à s'intégrer mais à nous exploiter '
Le racisme combine alors deux principes fondamentaux. D'une part, en effet, il naturalise l'Autre pour tenter de marquer son infériorité, il construit une hiérarchie raciale qui pallie plus ou moins une hiérarchie sociale menacée, disparue ou renversée. D'autre part, il postule une différence irréductible, pour marquer une incompatibilité supposée entre la culture nationale française et celle de l'immigré ou de l'étranger. (Wievorka, 1992: 295; 296; 300; 293; 341-2)
Note that the analysis of police discourse is from Wievorka, 1992: 225-75.

30 une telle réforme, aussi sympathique soit-elle, est impossible à mettre en oeuvre dans un contexte de chômage massif: on courrait le risque, entre autres inconvénients, de mettre à bas, par la concurrence d'une main d'oeuvre nombreuse prête à toutes les concessions, le dispositif de protection sociale dont bénéficient aujourd'hui les salariés résidents, français et étrangers .(Joffrin, *Libération*, 27.8.1997)

31 C'est pourquoi le droit du sol est consubstantiel à la nation française...Rien n'est plus étranger à la France que le discours xénophobe et raciste. La France doit définir une politique d'immigration ferme et digne, sans renier ses valeurs, sans compromettre son équilibre social...L'immigration est une réalité économique, sociale et humaine qu'il faut organiser, contrôler et maîtriser au mieux, en affirmant les intérêts de la Nation et en respectant les droits de la personne. Une politique d'intégration républicaine, déterminée et généreuse, propre à recueillir l'assentiment de nos concitoyens, sera mise en oeuvre...L'immigration irrégulière et le travail clandestin, - dont je sais qu'il n'est pas le seul fait des étrangers - seront combattus sans défaillance parce que l'un et l'autre compromettent l'intégration et parce qu'ils sont contraires à la dignité des immigrés. (Jospin, 1997)

Chapter 4

32 Le monde courtois est constitué de personnes qui se reconnaissent à des valeurs communes que chacun honore et cherche à mettre en pratique, et parmi elles, les qualités d'expression...Pour être admis comme personnage de la société courtoise il fallait savoir prononcer de belles paroles. (Chaurand, 1995)

33 For a classification and discussion of these terms see Otman, 1995. The majority of them derive from the essay on the advantages of French by Rivarol, 1784. It need hardly be said that such qualities are difficult to define and that few linguists accept them as being other than social judgements.

34 Le français est un bijou inestimable qu'il faut préserver comme on le ferait d'un trésor fabuleux.
Il n'est pas toujours aisé de distinguer le linguistique du politique, au moins du polémique. Quotations in this paragraph from Glatigny, 1995.

35 Si nous reculons sur notre langue nous serons emportés purement et simplement. (Pompidou, G., quoted in Legendre, 1994: 1)
Nous avons ensuite des devoirs à l'égard de l'ensemble de la nation: la langue française est celle de la République; c'est la langue de l'intégration nationale, celle qui garantit à tous l'égalité, qui assure le lien social. ..La langue française est une langue de liberté, de démocratie. C'est la langue du rêve pour de nombreuses personnes emprisonnées qui, pendant des années, ont rêvé à la démocratie, à la liberté, à l'indépendance! Le rôle du Gouvernement et du Parlement français est de dire à tous ceux-là que la France ne faillira pas à son devoir. (Toubon, 12.4.1994 in _Journal Officiel, Débats, Sénat_, 18 S (CR): 950)
Quelle que soit la volonté des pouvoirs publics, une politique de promotion de la langue française ne peut réussir que si elle obtient le soutien de la société civile et l'adhésion de tous...Une meilleure prise de conscience, en France même, des enjeux liés à l'emploi et au statut du français, ainsi qu'à la promotion du plurilinguisme, est indispensable. (DGLF, 1996, 3, II)
L'analyse des courriers reçus par la délégation générale à la langue française...une montée de l'intérêt pour les enjeux liés à l'emploi national et international de la langue française (et non plus seulement à sa qualité)...forte diminution des lettres portant sur les médias, qui visent essentiellement la qualité de la langue utilisée par les journalistes...et qui constituaient presque la moitié des courriers reçus avant 1994. (DGLF, 1996, 1, I, 1)

36 (1) L'alignement sur l'anglais;
   (2) Le vocabulaire abusif (Les emprunts enrichissent les langues, mais la situation actuelle crée un raz de marée de termes anglo-saxons qui n'a plus rien à voir avec le phénomène classique)
   (3) Le glissement de sens et l'anglo-saxon larvée;
   (4) Le jargon informatique;
   (5) La diffusion audiovisuelle;
   (6) L'enseignement;
   (7) Faiblesse des bases;
   (8) Une pédagogie pernicieuse;
   (9) L'absence d'une politique de la langue;

(10)   Le manque de mobilisation de la classe culturelle. (*Le Figaro Littéraire*, 8.2.1996)

37 le français est trop compliqué, élitiste, non démocratique (Richard Millet). Il faut que les Français arrêtent d'avoir honte de leur langue...L'école devrait inculquer aux enfants l'amour du français en leur montrant que c'est une très belle langue, nuancée. C'est ainsi qu'ils retrouveront la fierté du français et le désir de le promouvoir (Geneviève Dormann). Si le français veut survivre, il lui faudra, de toute urgence, renouer avec ses racines régionales et populaires (Raphaël Confiant). (*Le Figaro Littéraire*, 8.2.1996)

38 jusqu'à une période relativement récente, l'entourage familial, l'école et les Eglises se chargeaient d'enseigner aux enfants leurs 'valeurs; le système de valeurs apparaissait comme une tradition. Il semble désormais que jeunes et adultes ne disposent plus de ces guides traditionnels. Et par exemple, deux personnes sur trois pensent que 'il ne peut jamais y avoir de lignes directrices parfaitement claires pour savoir ce qui est le bien et ce qui est le mal; cela dépend entièrement des circonstances'...Et ceci a pour conséquence de créer deux morales, l'une à l'égard de soi et des proches, l'autre à l'égard 'des autres', que l'on traitera avec circonspection pour ne pas dire avec méfiance. (Riffault, 1994: 298-9)

Chapter 5

39 Que la radio et la Télé...soient invitées - je m'entends - à parler français...mots et tours interdits; interdits sous peine d'amendes.
Que les ministères de l'Education et de la Culture ...fassent une démarche conjointe auprès de tous les journaux français ... pour obtenir que la presse française...proscrive elle aussi tous les mots, tous les tours anglo-saxons interdits à la radio ainsi qu'à la télé.
Que le ministre de l'Industrie obtienne que les noms de produits français, que les marques déposées en France soient désormais libellés en français...pourquoi ne pas taxer toutes les 'enseignes sabirales'?
Que le Ministre de la Guerre...poursuive la campagne qu'il a timidement amorcée pour suggérer que l'armée française parle de nouveau français.
Que le ministère des Affaires Etrangères...obtienne des gouvernements étrangers que les placards de publicité proposées à la presse française soient rédigés soit en français, soit dans la langue originale, mais non point en sabir. ..Il pourrait aussi demander que les emballages de produits importés soient *tous*, sans exception, rédigés en français.
Que le ministre de la Culture, celui de l'Education nationale et celui de l'Industrie agissent en commun auprès des éditeurs, des agences de nouvelles, de tous ceux qui emploient des traducteurs, afin que ceux-ci, pourvu que leur compétence soit confirmée par un organisme sérieux...reçoivent une rémunération digne de ce beau métier malaisé. (Etiemble, 1964: 339-43). Other quotations from this source in the preceding and following paragraphs are in order from pages 345, 234, 237, 238 and 243.

40 il demeure que le vocabulaire courant du français moderne n'offre pas l'image d'une invasion. Dès lors, et puisque la situation objective ne justifie pas pleinement tant de fracas, il faut se demander quels facteurs ont pu conférer au débat le tour dramatique qu'on l'a vu prendre. (Hagège, 1987: 74)

41 on chasse la consonance anglaise mais non l'ambiguïté - voire le confusionnisme - conceptuel du terme. On érige en concept unique (en science?) une pluralité de concepts opératoires qui n'en demandent pas tant. (Pergnier, 1989: 194)

42 Le franglais satisfait le désir plus ou moins conscient d'une partie de la population française de s'identifier à un modèle mythique et unidimensionnel de la modernité. (Pergnier, 1989: :203)

43 un nombre considérable de communications commerciales internationales, avec tous les pays du monde, se font soit en anglais, soit dans un français émaillé de formules anglaises (on ne compte plus, dans les journaux, les annonces de recrutement en anglais). Le nombre de magasins, organismes, studios de radios privées...adoptent un sigle anglais ou anglicisé...les jeunes Français accordent massivement leur préférence aux chansons de langue anglaise...beaucoup de Français se trouvent en contact sinon avec l'anglais, du moins avec 'de l'anglais' à l'intersection de ces différents centres d'intérêts. (Pergnier, 1989: 131)

44 on a du mal à percevoir clairement quel bénéfice un tel pays peut retirer d'une généralisation du jargonnage et de l'aliénation de son idiome. On ne voit guère non plus ce que le monde, dans son ensemble, aurait à gagner de l'appauvrissement de son patrimoine linguistique, par réduction de la diversité des modes d'appréhension du réel que représentent les langues - et notamment les grandes langues véhiculaires de culture - sur le modèle standardisé d'une seule langue, à supposer même qu'il soit démontré que les mérites de cette langue sont supérieurs à ceux des autres... (Pergnier, 1989: 208)

45 Le latin est la seule langue de travail et de culture des élites intellectuelles, d'ailleurs en nombre restreint, alors que l'anglais, maîtrisé souvent superficiellement par un nombre croissant de cadres, techniciens, ...est une langue auxiliaire de travail...
La formation intellectuelle des élites au Moyen Age...s'était faite en latin...
la légitimité du latin reposait sur la croyance en un 'classicisme' né d'une 'secondarité culturelle'...(le latin était) véhicule d'un capital symbolique commun à toute l'Europe...l'anglo-américain qui, comme toutes les autres langues nationales , a aussi son corpus culturel... auquel on ne cherche pas à avoir accès en usant de ce médium. (Baggioni, 1997: 329-30)

46 L'irrespect de la langue traduit l'irrespect de tout.
La vulgarité des mots révèle la vulgarité de l'âme.
Depuis quand, dans quelle civilisation, le langage des gamins est-il devenu celui des adultes?
Quand entendrons-nous rappeler que la France est la troisième puissance du monde, pour l'étendue de la souveraineté maritime? Mais le moindre groupuscule lointain qui revendique la sécession d'un de nos territoires d'outre-mer, a droit aux envoyés spéciaux et aux doubles colonnes.
La France ne saurait conserver son rang de grande puissance, et mener une politique mondiale, que si elle continue de disposer d'une dissuasion militaire planétaire et de la maîtrise d'une langue universelle.
C'est la grandeur du pays qui permet d'assurer le bien-être social, et non l'inverse. (Druon, 1994: 23-39)

47 Question 3: Diriez-vous que vous êtes très attaché, plutôt attaché, plutôt pas
    attaché ou pas du tout attaché à la langue française?
    Question 8: Selon vous, qu'est-ce qui menace le plus la langue française:
    Le mauvais niveau de l'enseignement du français à l'école; Le manque de
    vigilance des Français eux-mêmes pour défendre leur langue; Le fait que
    beaucoup de Français doivent utiliser l'anglais pour leur travail; L'influence
    excessive de la culture américaine en France; Le mauvais usage du français
    dans les medias; La mondialisation de l'économie; Sans opinion.
    Question 5: A qui faites-vous le plus confiance pour défendre la langue
    française?
    Question 11: A propos de l'utilisation de mots anglais ou américains dans la
    langue française, laquelle de ces deux opinions correspond le mieux à ce que
    vous pensez? C'est une mauvaise chose pour la langue française qui risque
    ainsi de perdre son caractère propre...Ce n'est pas une mauvaise chose car
    une langue doit intégrer des mots étrangers pour s'enrichir et se développer.
    Question 13: Estimez-vous choquant ou pas choquant que des organismes
    publics utilisent des mots anglais pour nommer certains de leurs produits
    (comme le Shuttle pour la navette du tunnel sous la Manche ou Euronews
    pour la chaîne européenne d'information?
    Question 12: A propos de l'utilisation d'expressions ou mots anglais dans la
    vie de tous les jours, diriez-vous que c'est: moderne, utile, amusant, snob,
    gênant, agréable, abêtissant, choquant, sans opinion. (SOFRES, 1994)

48 Parmi les tendances négatives qui affectent la Francophonie, au cours de ces
    dernières années une tendance s'est manifestée tout particulièrement, que le
    grand auteur Milan Kundera a appelé 'l'anti-francophonie'. Il s'agit d'un
    courant de pensée, d'une attitude, de comportements qui consistent à
    critiquer ou à fustiger la construction d'une Communauté francophone
    internationale et surtout à tourner en dérision la volonté des francophones de
    se doter de législations linguistiques et de défendre leur identité culturelle,
    notamment en soutenant la thèse de l'exception culturelle dans le libre
    échange des marchandises. (Etat, 1994: 514)

49 Dans le domaine scientifique, notre langue est de plus en plus absente, voire
    chassée des colloques. Est-il acceptable que des manifestations scientifiques
    de haut lieu, tenues en France à l'initiative ou avec le concours d'institutions
    ou de collectivités publiques bannissent explicitement l'usage de notre
    langue?
    ...certains cinéastes français ...envisagent sans hésitation de tourner leurs
    films en version originale anglaise parce que cette langue est la clef d'accès
    au marché américain?
    Que penser d'un peuple qui pourrait bientôt ne plus chanter dans sa langue?
    Mais c'est aussi un souci essentiel que de vouloir continuer à penser en
    français, à chanter en français, à voir le monde en français. (Legendre, 1994:
    5-6)

Chapter 6

50 Cette idée française de la nation et de la République est, par nature,
    respectueuse de toutes les convictions, en particulier des convictions
    religieuses, politiques et des traditions culturelles. Mais elle exclut
    l'éclatement de la nation en communautés séparées, indifférentes les unes

aux autres, ne considérant que leurs propres règles et leurs propres lois. (Bayrou, quoted in Conrad, 1996: 216)

51 C'est vrai que j'aimais bien la IVe. Elle correspondait à l'esprit profond de la France. Je regrette pourtant qu'elle n'ait pas su concilier deux choses: les divisions des Français sur ce qui est secondaire et l'unité nationale, profonde, qui est celle du peuple et qui doit se traduire par un Etat fort. (Michel Charasse, quoted in Ferney, 1992: 69)

52 Pour décrire la société française de 1990, le vocabulaire le plus commode, le plus juste, c'est celui de l'Ancien Régime...querelles entre barons qui ne songent qu'à agrandir leur fief...les partis politiques...ont recours aux indulgences et aux excommunications...les seigneurs élus des provinces ou des villes, à force de clientélisme et d'esprit de clocher, arrachent peu à peu à l'Etat ses prérogatives, viciant les règles d'équité et menaçant à terme les principes de la solidarité nationale...une justice du Roy, magnanime envers les puissants, dure aux faibles...les corporatismes du Moyen Age, les manifestations des paysans et les révoltes suburbaines prouvent que, au coeur de la société industrielle, les jacqueries sont de retour. (Joffrin, quoted in Ferney, 1992: 135)

53 En France, l'Etat au contraire a été appréhendé de manière plus philosophique et plus politique...La principale caractéristique de l'Etat français après 1789...réside d'abord dans la tâche inédite d'ordre sociologique et culturel, qu'il s'assigne pour produire la nation, combler le vide provoqué par l'effondrement des structures corporatives et trouver un substitut à l'ancienne 'concorde' du corps politique traditionnel. (Rosenvallon, 1990: 99)

54 Mais j'ai une crainte. Si, appréhendés globalement, nous sommes bilingues, il est sans conteste que nombre de Martiniquais ne saisissent pas toujours les subtilités de la langue française, ni même sa pratique quotidienne...De toute évidence, le parler exclusivement français dans les administrations ou dans toute structure d'enseignement et d'information, singulièrement la radio et la télévision, est de nature à entretenir l'incompréhension, lorsque le parler créole ne vient pas à la rescousse. Alors, j'ai la crainte du mauvais usage qu'à la Martinique feront de la loi des fonctionnaires, et autres cadres, tardigrades, qui la brandiront comme leur bonne conscience, pour étourdir le travailleur, le contribuable, le justiciable à force de leur parler français, un français imposé comme langue officielle, voire supérieure. (Darsières, Journal Officiel, 3.5.1994, *Débats*, Assemblée Nationale AN26 (3) AN] (CR): 1397)

55 Article 1er. Langue de la République en vertu de la Constitution, la langue française est un élément fondamental de la personnalité et du patrimoine de la France. Elle est la langue de l'enseignement, du travail, des échanges et des services publics. Elle est le lien privilégié des Etats constituant la communauté de la Francophonie.

56 Une telle tendance est particulièrement inquiétante à divers titres, et notamment pour la qualité du dialogue social dans les entreprises et la protection des salariés, parfois ainsi contraints par leur direction, sans nécessité due à la nature de leur travail, à s'exprimer dans une langue étrangère, y compris avec les autres salariés français ou à recevoir des instructions et des formations en langue étrangère. (DGLF, 1997, 2, II, 3)

57 Sur l'insistence des opticiens contrôlés, les responsables du syndicat professionnel des fabricants et importateurs de lentilles de contact ont pris conscience des obligations faites à l'ensemble de la profession par la loi précitée. Ils sont désireux de se conformer strictement à la réglementation. A cet effet, ils seront prochainement reçus par l'administration pour faire le point sur le nouveau dispositif linguistique. (DGLF, 1996, II, I, 1, appendix 6)

58 Il apparaît que les professionnels exercent une vigilance de plus en plus grande, qui se répercute en amont sur le comportement des entreprises. Ainsi la mise en place d'un autocontrôle au sein de ces dernières ne paraît plus exceptionnel; les professionnels n'hésitent plus, après vérification des marchandises, à réexpédier celles qui ne respectent pas la loi de 1994 ou à prendre les mesures nécessaires pour les mettre en conformité avec celle-ci. Cette prise de conscience, néanmoins, tarde dans plusieurs domaines, comme le montre l'analyse par secteur et le repérage des secteurs sensibles, ainsi que les enquêtes trimestrielles ciblées mises en place depuis 1996. C'est pourquoi la DGCCRF et la DGLF mèneront, au cours de la prochaine période, une importante action d'information auprès des organisations professionnelles sur les enjeux économiques et juridiques de ce dispositif linguistique, qui constitue un élément majeur des politiques de concurrence et de protection des consommateurs, tant au plan national que communautaire. (DGLF, 1996, II, I, 1).

59 du fait de la proximité de la frontière espagnole, certains producteurs, importateurs et grossistes espagnols en conserves et surgelés viennent démarcher directement, à des prix moins élevés, les distributeurs français (hyper et supermarchés, détaillants, restaurateurs) situés dans les départements limitrophes. (DGLF, 1997, I, 1)

60 contribué au développement et au renouvellement de la production discographique des artistes francophones. (DGLF, 1997, 2, III, 2)

61 Notre système des quotas risque toutefois d'être fragilisé à l'avenir. En effet, la lecture que la Cour de Justice Européenne fait de la directive Télévision sans frontière pourrait se traduire par l'ouverture de notre espace audiovisuel à des opérateurs européens qui seront contraints au seul respect des dispositions en vigueur dans leur pays d'émission, notamment en termes de quotas. (DGLF, 1997, 2, III, 4)

62 Patrimoine que nous partageons avec l'ensemble de la communauté francophone, le français est un élément essentiel de notre cohésion sociale et l'un des vecteurs majeurs du rayonnement de notre pays...L'action en faveur de l'emploi de la langue française a trois objectifs: assurer la présence et le rayonnement du français dans notre pays, conserver au français son rôle de langue de communication internationale, promouvoir le plurilinguisme. (DGLF, 1996, Avant-propos)

Chapter 7

63 S'il est un thème qui revient avec une belle régularité dans le courrier des lecteurs, c'est celui de la défense de la langue française, sous toutes ses formes: appels à la correction grammaticale, lutte contre l'invasion de l'anglais, dénonciation des barbarismes et des solécismes, mises en garde contre le mauvais emploi des mots, condamnation des fautes

d'orthographe...De nombreux correspondants, souvent membres d'associations de défense de la langue française, épluchent avec soin nos articles et nous font part, tantôt de leur surprise attristée, tantôt de leur véhémente indignation, devant les erreurs que la précipitation de l'édition quotidienne ne permet pas de corriger en temps utile. (*Le Monde*, 6.1.1997)

64 Notre langue...est elle-même une institution: elle n'est vivante et féconde qu'à condition d'avoir été bien apprise...Le français n'est pas une lingua franca dont on se barbouille sur le tas 'pour communiquer'. Ses normes sont même inséparables d'une jurisprudence qui les nuance et les intérprète: un fonds de textes littéraires et de mémoire historique partagés....Le français bien enseigné, c'est plus que le français: c'est l'esprit mis en possession d'un système symbolique qui ouvre la voie à tous les autres...Le latin des modernes est en lui-même toute une éducation d'humanité...La francophonie a été, dès l'origine, un pari sur la qualité, la singularité et la supériorité de l'éducation en français .(M. Fumaroli, member of L'Académie Française, in *Le Figaro*, 18. 3.1996)

65 Par delà la volonté des pouvoirs publics, une politique de promotion de la langue française ne peut réussir que si elle obtient l'adhésion et le soutien de tous. ..L'objectif est de leur faire prendre conscience que le français est le premier de nos patrimoines ...Chaque grande orientation de la politique pour l'emploi de la langue française, de la loi du 4 août 1994 au plurilinguisme, en passant par l'enrichissement de la langue française et la société de l'information, appelle des actions de sensibilisation. (DGLF, 1996, 3, II)

66 Instance d'étude, de consultation et de proposition...Nous savons de longue date que les édits linguistiques demeurent sans effet s'ils ne trouvent pas, au-delà d'une ferme volonté des institutions, le soutien de la société civile et l'adhésion du public...Il appartient au Conseil de proposer au Gouvernement des actions pour promouvoir, valoriser et illustrer le français. (*Brèves*, 2c trimestre 1994).

67 l'ignorance des niveaux de langue, ou, pour mieux dire, de l'adaptation situationnelle: si tel journaliste de radio a employé une expression familière, c'est bien souvent parce qu'il veut établir une familiarité entre l'auditeur, ou l'invité, et lui-même...au lieu de critiquer ce choix, le discours puriste évoque une faute contre la langue;
l'incapacité à reconnaître, ou le refus d'admettre, l'apparition d'usages nouveaux; il suffit pourtant de relire les écrits puristes du passé, qui, par exemple, dénonçaient naguère comme horreurs et crimes grammaticaux des usages aujourd'hui admis;
La rigidité du jugement sur des erreurs de performance;
les marottes: l'importance démesurée accordée au subjonctif, ou à l'emprunt, ou à la phrase nominale, à l'onomatopée, aux verbes passifs, aux adverbes etc. (Eloy, 1995: 396-7)

68 Les écrivains témoins et créateurs du français de la nation (ce qui veut dire, et ce n'est pas un vain mot, à partir du milieu de la période, le français de la République): les grands écrivains depuis Boileau et Voltaire, auxquels s'ajouteront essentiellement, au fil du temps, Musset, Vigny, Hugo, Sand, Balzac, Flaubert, Maupassant, Zola, Anatole France. (Molinié, 1991: 33)

69 C'est bien une pratique du français qui est visée. Non seulement cette pratique est gendarmée, dans son fonctionnement interne; elle est aussi obligatoirement imposée, de manière totalitaire et dictatoriale, dans son fonctionnement externe ou relationnel: ce français peu à peu va étouffer toute autre expression linguistique. Le mouvement est lent, mais continu et implacable; son apogée est à l'époque du combat républicain et laïque; et il faudra, effectivement, bien attendre environ 1950 pour qu'un mouvement inverse se fasse concrètement sentir. (Molinié, 1991: 34-5)

Chapter 8

70 assurer la présence et le rayonnement du français langue de la République; conserver au français son rôle de langue de communication internationale; préserver la diversité culturelle et linguistique dans le monde par la promotion du plurilinguisme. (*Brèves*, 5, 2e trimestre 1996)

71 La présence du français dans le monde accompagne la présence de la France. La promotion du français et de son utilisation comme langue de communication internationale, à une période où la mondialisation favorise le monolinguisme, sont plus que jamais, pour la place de notre pays dans le monde, pour la prise en compte de ses idées et de ses conceptions, pour l'avenir de la francophonie, une priorité qui appelle une politique linguistique, volontaire et explicite. (DGLF, 1997, avant-propos)

72 La Francophonie dépasse en rayonnement les limites de la communauté francophone...et désormais elle entend non seulement se souder et réclamer sa place dans le concert polyphonique universel mais encore insuffler dans cette civilisation mondiale un esprit d'organisation, de régulation, de management...il ne s'agit pas de brider les énergies créatrices, les libertés individuelles, les entreprises et les initiatives (bien au contraire), mais il s'agit de faire en sorte que ce foisonnement qui rencontre l'explosion des technologies de l'information immédiate et massive ne soit pas la jungle, l'anarchie, la nouvelle barbarie; oui, c'est d'une régulation éthique dont la civilisation universelle a besoin. (Etat, 1995-6: 597)

73 à l'Assemblée générale de l'ONU, trente délégations au lieu de vingt-sept en 1993 se sont entièrement ou partiellement exprimées en français...Mais la place du français comme langue de travail reste de 5% à New York et 20% à Genève; sa situation est menacée dans les organisations à vocation financière ou technique...Les difficultés tiennent aux effets des restrictions budgétaires sur le recrutement des fonctionnaires francophones et sur les moyens des services d'interprétation et de traduction; elles tiennent aussi parfois au contexte politique: les nouveaux Etats adhérant aux organisations internationales - ceux d'Europe centrale et orientale, ceux de la Communauté des Etats indépendants (CEI) mais aussi ceux d'Extrême-Orient, sont plutôt anglophones et choisissent de s'exprimer en anglais, soit, phénomène récent, dans leur propre langue. (Etat, 1995-6: 98)

74 Les principes généraux.
(La circulaire du 30 novembre 1994)
Ce texte a présenté l'ensemble des situations où le français doit être privilégié par les agents: rapports avec les interlocuteurs étrangers résidant en France, participation à des réunions internationales, départ en poste ou en mission, relations avec les organisations internationales. Il est rappelé que ces

instructions, qui ont été reprises dans la plupart des circulaires ministérielles, couvrent tant la communication orale qu'écrite: la correspondance et les documents des administrations, ceux des postes diplomatiques et consulaires, doivent être en français, accompagnés éventuellement de traductions. Ici encore, le rôle de l'ensemble des agents publics doit être exemplaire pour illustrer le principe du français 'langue de la République' et 'langue des services publics', ainsi que son statut de grande langue de communication internationale.

La participation à des réunions internationales...organisées à l'étranger ou sur notre territoire par des tiers, les agents doivent avoir le souci permanent de s'exprimer en français. (DGLF, 1996, 2, III, 2)

75 Vade-mecum en 10 points
- (1) Le français est langue officielle et langue de travail des institutions de l'Union européenne
- (2) Dans les réunions, les représentants de la France s'expriment en français, qu'il y ait ou non traduction
- (3) Toute circonstance rendant impossible l'emploi du français doit faire l'objet, à tout le moins, d'une observation au procès-verbal et d'un compte rendu aux autorités françaises
- (4) Au besoin, le report de la réunion peut être demandé
- (5) Les documents préparatoires doivent avoir été diffusés en version française
- (6) Il est possible de surseoir à la discussion d'un point de l'ordre du jour pour lequel les documents en français n'auront pas été distribués en temps utile
- (7) Il convient, en tout état de cause, de refuser qu'une décision juridique soit prise sur un texte dont la version définitive en français ne serait pas disponible
- (8) Le Conseil des ministres de l'Union ne délibère et ne décide que sur la base de documents et de projets établis dans les langues officielles et donc en français
- (9) Lors des réunions informelles, les Français s'expriment dans leur langue
- (10) Dans les relations bilatérales informelles, il convient de privilégier le français. (*Lettre d'Information*, juin 1998, 30: 18).

76 En matière de coopération bilatérale, le soutien de la diffusion du français à l'étranger passe par deux services distincts: la Direction du développement du ministre délégué à la Coopération d'une part, ayant compétence pour les pays dits 'du champ' (Afrique francophone et Océan indien en particulier) et la Direction Générale des relations culturelles, scientifiques et techniques du ministère des Affaires Etrangères d'autre part, ayant compétence pour les autres pays. (Politique, 1996: 3)

77 La Francophonie est une entreprise résolument politique;
Il lui (au Secrétaire Général) incombera d'intervenir (à la demande des parties concernées) pour la consolidation de l'état de droit, dans l'esprit d'entraide fraternelle et dans le strict respect de nos souverainetés;
L'aspiration unanime des peuples à voir respectées les libertés et la dignité de la personne humaine ne peut être ignorée;

la Francophonie est solidarité. Cette solidarité répond à un impératif moral pour les pays prospères, en même temps qu'elle rejoint leur intérêt bien compris;
La Francophonie c'est aussi, et peut-être d'abord, une certaine vision du monde.   Nous bâtissons un ensemble politique fondé sur une communauté unique, cette langue que nous avons en partage et qui nous rassemble au-delà de nos diversités culturelles;
Dans tous les pays, donnons la priorité à l'éducation de base;
Dans les organisations internationales, dans les congrès scientifiques, faisons mieux respecter l'usage du français;
soyons solidaires des défenseurs, ou des promoteurs des autres espaces linguistiques.   Notre combat commun permettra de conjurer le risque d'un monde où l'on parlerait, penserait, créerait dans un moule unique;
Défendons et imposons le pluralisme linguistique sur les autoroutes de l'information! (Chirac, Discours inaugural au VI Sommet de la Francophonie, 14.11.1997)

78 La notion de francophonie n'est pas l'enfermement dans le français mais recouvre aussi l'ouverture vers les pays anglophones. La francophonie ne doit pas être un souvenir mais un avenir à condition d'en avoir une conception très ouverte et de ne pas la réduire à une bataille défensive d'une citadelle linguistique. (Josselin, *L'Humanité*, 18.11.1997)

Chapter 9

79 Promouvoir le français de notre temps et la francophonie, c'est aussi mener patiemment, avec nos partenaires, une politique concertée favorisant un véritable plurilinguisme européen. Car on ne pourra conforter l'avenir de notre langue qu'en assurant celui des autres grandes langues de l'Europe. L'unilinguisme se réaliserait avec évidence par une Europe anglophone; le plurilinguisme peut seul garantir le maintien d'une unité culturelle qui respecte les personnalités nationales. (Cerquiglini, *Brèves* 1, 1er trimestre, 1991)
L'ouverture aux autres, le respect de leur langue et de leur culture sont inscrits dans la politique du Gouvernement et mis en oeuvre par les différents ministères concernés. (DGLF, 1996, 2, VI)

80 Non seulement la France y trouvera l'occasion d'un accroissement de la prospérité, mais c'est aussi et surtout, pour elle, le moyen de reconquérir dans le monde le prestige et la grandeur que la défaite vient de compromettre. (Girardet, 1983: 86)

81 Nos colonies ne seront françaises d'intelligence et de coeur que quand elles comprendront un peu le français...Pour la France surtout, la langue est l'instrument nécessaire de la colonisation...Il faut que des écoles françaises multipliées, où nous appelerons l'indigène, viennent au secours des colons français, dans leur tâche difficile de conquête morale et d'assimilation...quand nous prenons possession d'un pays, nous devons y amener avec nous la gloire de la France, et soyez sûrs qu'on lui fera bon accueil, car elle est pure autant que grande, toute pénétrée de justice et de bonté. (Jean Jaurès, Discours pour l'Alliance Française, 1884)

82 Il y a pour les races supérieures un droit, parce qu'il y a un devoir pour elles. Elles ont le devoir de civiliser les races inférieures....qu'il faut autre chose à la

France: qu'elle ne peut pas être seulement un pays libre; qu'elle doit aussi être un grand pays, exerçant sur les destinées de l'Europe toute l'influence qui lui appartient, qu'elle doit répandre cette influence sur le monde, et porter partout où elle le peut sa langue, ses moeurs, son drapeau, ses armes, son génie. (Jules Ferry, Débats parlementaires, 28.7.1885. This and the preceding quotation are taken from Girardet, 1983: 94-107)

83 What distinguishes our language from both ancient and modern languages is the order and construction of the phrase. French first names the subject, then the verb which is the action, and finally the object of this action: that is natural logic for mankind; it is common sense
French syntax is incorruptible
What is not clear is not French
It is, of all languages, the only one which has probity attached to its nature. Sure, sociable and rational, it is the language of mankind. On arriving among a people and finding French in use there, one may believe oneself to be in polite society. (Rivarol, 1784/1797/1991)

84 Diverses notions se combinent qui mesurent le relâchement. Il y a la position de la France, son poids politique, économique. Il y a le rayonnement de sa culture, la richesse de ses créations, le magistère de ses contemporains. Il y a l'inquiétude devant les puissances audiovisuelles et les formes d'expression qu'elles imposent. Il y a l'idée d'un pré carré de préférences coloniales, la crainte paradoxale que le français des francophones serve à des instrusions. Il y a aussi la nostalgie d'un humanisme à la française, du premier rôle de notre littérature. (de Beaucé, T. 1988: 15)
...Ainsi la France n'aurait-elle plus à souffrir de son amenuisement. Au contraire même, car la multiplicité de ses parentés et de ses compétences, favorisant la souplesse de ses comportements, préserveraient plus d'avenirs possibles...Sa langue et sa culture y comptent au plus grand prix. (de Beaucé, T. 1988: 243).

85 Il faut commencer par séparer les questions linguistiques de la politique. L'abandon du message idéologique commande la crédibilité du discours français à l'étranger...Elle remplira d'autant mieux sa mission civilisatrice qu'elle se conjuguera avec une politique culturelle cohérente, une économie solide et une image internationale attrayante. (de Broglie, 1986: 236).

86 Son dernier grand combat anti-américain fut d'ordre culturel...L'Europe lui était familière. C'était celle de la langue, qui le faisait se sentir chez lui dans l'Afrique et l'Orient francophones. C'était, du moins le prétendait-il, celle de l'esprit. Il convoquait les prix Nobel de la planète, flattait les intellectuels qui le flattaient, refusait de dire un mot dans une langue étrangère, se complaisait dans son verbe. Il promenait sans complexe de par le monde l'orgueil d'être français, sourd à ceux qui ne l'entendaient pas, ignorant de ceux qui l'ignoraient. Ce que la France perd ou gagne à l'absence de François Mitterrand, c'est d'abord cela. (Claire Tréan, 11.5.1195 in FM, 1996: 175)

87 Au-delà de notre espace national, changer notre avenir, c'est aussi prendre part à l'avenir du monde. Il nous faut partout agir en faveur des droits de l'homme et de la démocratie. La France se doit d'être la voix de ceux qui en sont privés...Notre deuxième message est celui de la paix. Maintien ou rétablissement de la paix, prévention des crises, ingérence humanitaire: la

France a marqué de son empreinte ces champs d'action depuis 1988. J'en viens maintenant au troisième grand objectif de notre action internationale: la coopération pour le développement...Mais la France conservera une priorité marquée en faveur de l'Afrique. (Jospin, 19.6.1997)

88 La Francophonie n'est dirigée contre aucun pays et ne prétend à aucune hégémonie. Message d'ouverture et de tolérance. Et nous pouvons, nous les francophones, être fiers d'avoir été les précurseurs d'un mouvement qui gagne: le juste combat pour la diversité culturelle du monde. (Chirac, 14.11.1997 reported by Agence de la Francophonie website)

89 (5)   Conscients toutefois que, riche du patrimoine de valeurs et d'expressions diverses respectueuses des identités de chaque partenaire, et considérant la culture comme fondement du développement, la Francophonie s'affirme ouverte, plurielle, lieu de dialogue et d'échanges. (Déclaration finale du VIIe Sommet de la Francophonie de Hanoï, reported by Agence de la Francophonie website)

90 La francophonie est un moyen de non-alignement, un refus d'un modèle culturel et linguistique unique pour conserver un monde divers donc plus riche. (_L'Humanité_, 18.11.1997)

91 Ces langues évaluables au baccalauréat sous formes d'épreuves obligatoires répondent aux critères suivants:
    (1)   langues officielles des Etats de l'Union Européenne
    (2)   langues largement utilisées au plan international
    (3)   langues appartenant à des communautés étrangères fortement représentées sur le territoire national. (_Bulletin Officiel de l'Education Nationale_, 8.12.1994, 45: 3285)

92 L'enseignement des langues a toujours eu, en France, aux yeux des familles, une place spécifique, a toujours été un thème sensible et fait l'objet d'une pression sociale forte. Souvent critiqué, décrié, dévalorisé par rapport à d'autres systèmes d'enseignement des langues en Europe qui passent pour plus performants, il soulève aussi des inquiétudes car le grand public est bien conscient de l'enjeu que représente cet enseignement aujourd'hui, face à la mondialisation des échanges et la mise en place de la construction européenne. (AELPL, 4, 1997)

93 La réflexion sur la place des langues étrangères en France ne peut être dissociée de l'objectif majeur que représente l'enseignement du français à l'étranger, que la DGLF suit très attentivement, et qui est une des priorités du ministère des affaires étrangères...Or le français est surtout étudié dans les systèmes éducatifs étrangers, même européens, comme deuxième langue, à l'exception évidemment des pays anglophones. A cette place, sa position est globalement satisfaisante, mais très dépendante des règlementations sur l'apprentissage d'une deuxième langue vivante à l'école, que la France encourage avec insistance au sein de l'Union européenne. La promotion du plurilinguisme sur le territoire national, dont l'importance est rappelée par la loi du 4 août 1994, correspond ainsi à cet enjeu, car la France se doit de pratiquer sur son territoire ce qu'elle prône sur le plan international. (DGLF, 1997, 2, VII, 1)

94 Dans le souci de faciliter l'accès des étrangers à la culture française, ces établissements se sont donc attachés à promouvoir le plurilinguisme dès que leurs moyens le permettaient, et le nombre de brochures ou d'actions en préparation montre que ce mouvement s'intensifie progressivement. (DGLF, 1996, 2, VI, 2)

Conclusion

95 La description des langues et des situations linguistiques est en effet une chose relativement simple...mais qui reste à la surface des faits... Pour comprendre le pourquoi de ces situations, le pourquoi du changement linguistique, des attitudes et des stratégies, il faut aller à la racine - sociale - des phénomènes. (Calvet, 1996: 110)

References

AELPL. (1997) *Bulletin d'Information de l'AELPL*. Paris: Association Européenne des linguistes et des professeurs de langues.

Agence de la Francophonie. Website. www.Francophonie.org.

Ager, D. E. (1990) *Sociolinguistics and Contemporary French*. Cambridge: Cambridge University Press.

Ager, D. E. (1995) Immigration and language policy in France. *Journal of Intercultural Studies* 15 (2), 35-52.

Ager, D. E. (1996a) *Francophonie in the 1990s: Problems and Opportunities*. Clevedon: Multilingual Matters.

Ager, D. E. (1996b) *Language Policy in Britain and France. The Processes of Policy*. London: Cassell Academic.

Aldrich, R. (1996) *Greater France. A History of French Overseas Expansion*. London: Macmillan.

Aldrich, R and Connell, J. (1992) *France's Overseas Frontier. Départements et Territoires d'Outre-Mer*. Cambridge: Cambridge University Press.

Allum, P. (1995) *State and Society in Western Europe*. Cambridge: Polity Press.

Anderson, B. (1991 2nd ed) *Imagined Communities: Inquiries into the Origin and Spread of Nationalism*. Norwood, N.J.: Ablex Publishing Corp.

Année Francophone Internationale. (Annual from 1991) *Année Francophone Internationale*. Québec: Faculté des Lettres, Université Laval, Québec and Paris: La Documentation Française.

Antoine, G. and Martin, R. (1985) *Histoire de la Langue Française, 1880-1914*. Paris: Editions du Conseil National de la Recherche Scientifique.

Ashford, M. and Timms, N. (1992) *What Europe thinks*. Aldershot: Dartmouth.

Ayres-Bennett, W. (1996) *A History of the French Language through Texts*. London: Routledge.

Baggioni, D. (1997) *Langues et nations en Europe*. Paris: Editions Payot et Rivages .

Ball, R. (1988) Language insecurity and State language policy: the case of France. *Quinquereme* 11 (1), 95-105.

Battye, A. and Hintze, M.-A. (1992) *The French Language Today*. London: Routledge.

Baylon, C. (1991 2nd ed 1996) *La Sociolinguistique*. Paris: Nathan.

Beaucé, T de. (1988) *Nouveau Discours sur l'Universalité de la Langue Française*. Paris: Gallimard.

Belorgey, G. and Bertrand, G. (1994) *Les DOM-TOM*. Paris: La Découverte.

Bengtsson, S. (1968) *La Défense Organisée de la Langue Française*. Uppsala: Almqvist and Wiksells.

Berrondonner, A. (1982) *L'éternel Grammairien. Etude du Discours Normatif*. Bern: Lang.

Blanchet, P. (1992) *Le Provençal. Essai de Description Sociolinguistique et Différentielle*. Louvain-la-Neuve: Peeters.

Borkowski, J.-L. and Dumoulin, D. (1994) Illettrisme et précarisation. In G. Ferreol (ed) *Intégration et Exclusion dans la Société Française Contemporaine* (pp. 219-45). Lille: Presses Universitaires de Lille.

Boyer, H. (1996) *Eléments de Sociolinguistique*. Paris: Dunod.

Braudel, F. (1986) *L'identité de la France*. Paris: Les Editions Arthaud.

Braudel, F. (1989) *The Identity of France*. (S. Reynolds, trans.) London: Fontana.

Brèves. (Annual 1991 to 1996) *Brèves. Lettre du Conseil Supérieur et de la Délégation Générale à la Langue Française*. Nos 1 to 7. Paris: Délégation Générale à la Langue Française.

Briand, S. (ed) (1994) *La Francophonie et l'Europe. Actes de la 10e session du Haut Conseil de la Francophonie*. (2 volumes). Paris: Haut Conseil de la Francophonie.

Broglie, G. de (1986) *Le français, pour qu'il vive*. Paris: Gallimard.

Brun, A. (1923/1973) *Essai historique sur l'Introduction du français dans les Provinces du Midi de la France*. Paris: Champion et Genève: Slatkine Reprints.

Brunot, F. (1967 1st ed 1899). *Histoire de la Langue Française des Origines à nos jours*. Paris: Armand Colin.

Bulletin Officiel du Ministère de l'Education Nationale. (Monthly) Paris: Ministère de l'Education Nationale.

Caldwell, J. A. W. (1994) Provision for minority languages in France. *Journal of Multilingual and Multicultural Development* 15 (4), 293-310.

Calvet, L.-J. (1993) The migrant languages of Paris. In C. Sanders (ed) *French Today* (pp. 105-19). Cambridge: Cambridge University Press.

Calvet, L.-J. (1996 2nd ed) *La Sociolinguistique*. Paris: Presses Universitaires de France (Que sais-je 2731).

Castries, Duc de. (1985) *La Vieille Dame du Quai Conti. Une histoire de l'Académie Française*. Paris: Editions Perrin.

Catach, N. (1978 4th ed 1992) *L'orthographe*. Paris: Presses Universitaires de France.

Cerny, P. (1980) *The Politics of Grandeur. Ideological Aspects of de Gaulle's Foreign Policy*. Cambridge: Cambridge University Press.

Cerny, P. (1990) *The Changing Architecture of the State*. London: Sage.

Certeau, M. de, Julia, D. and Revel, J. (1975) *Une Politique de la Langue. La Révolution Française et les Patois*. Paris: Editions Gallimard.

Cesarinini, D. and Fulbrook, M. (eds) (1996) *Citizenship, Nationality and Migration in Europe*. London: Routledge.

Chambers, J. K. (1995) *Sociolinguistic Theory*. Oxford: Blackwell.

Charlot, B. (1994) De l'éducation nationale à l'insertion professionnelle: les mutations du système scolaire. In G. Ferreol (ed) *Intégration et Exclusion dans la Société Française Contemporaine* (pp. 345-79). Lille: Presses Universitaires de Lille.

Chaudenson, R. (1991) *La Francophonie: Représentations, Réalités, Perspectives*. Paris: Didier.

Chaurand, J. (1995) La qualité de la langue au Moyen Age. In J-M. Eloy (ed) *La Qualité de la Langue? Le Cas du Français* (pp. 25-35). Paris: Champion.

Chirac, J. (14.11.1997) *Opening Speech to Hanoi Francophonie Summit*. Paris: Agence de la Francophonie website.

Citron, S. (1987) *Le Mythe National. L'histoire de la France en Question*. Paris: Les Editions Ouvrières/Etudes et Documentation internationales.

Cole, A. (1994) *François Mitterrand. A Study in Political Leadership*. London: Routledge.

Conrad, P. (1996) A propos du voile islamique. In A. Laurent (ed) *Vivre avec l'Islam* (pp. 211-6). Versailles: Editions Saint-Paul.

Contact Bulletin. (Quarterly since 1983) *Contact Bulletin*. Dublin: The European Bureau for Lesser Used Languages.

Cooper, R. L. (1989) *Language Planning and Social Change*. Cambridge, Cambridge University Press.

Costa-Lascoux, J. (1994) L'immigration au gré des politiques. In G. Ferreol (ed) *Intégration et Exclusion dans la Société Française Contemporaine* (pp. 59-77). Lille: Presses Universitaires de Lille.

Cross, M. (1997) Feminism. In C. Flood and L. Bell (eds) *Political Ideologies in Contemporary France* (pp. 162-79). London: Cassell.

DGLF. (Annual from 1994) *Rapport au Parlement sur l'Application de la Loi du 4 août 1994 relative à l'Emploi de la Langue Française et des Dispositions des Conventions ou Traités Internationaux relatives au Statut de la Langue Française dans les Institutions Internationales*. Paris: Délégation Générale à la Langue française.

DGLF. Website. www.culture.fr/dglf.

Dossiers. (1996) *La Corse Démasquée*. Paris: Les Dossiers du Canard.

Druon, M. (1994) *Lettre aux Français sur leur Langue et leur Ame*. Paris: Julliard.

Durand-Prinborgne, C. 1994. (3rd ed) *L'Education Nationale: Une Culture, un Service, un Système*. Paris: Nathan Université

Eloy, J.-M. (1995) Postface. Les qualités de la langue. Une question à prendre au sérieux. In J-M. Eloy (ed) *La Qualité de la langue? Le Cas du Français* (pp. 387-422). Paris: Champion.

Eloy, J.-M. (ed) 1995. *La Qualité de la Langue? Le Cas du Français*. Paris: Champion.

Emploi. (1993) *L'emploi des Femmes. Actes de la Journée des Etudes du 4 mars 1993. Collection Document Travail et Emploi*. Paris: La Documentation Française.

Etat. (Annual from 1986) *Etat de la Francophonie dans le Monde: Rapport*. Paris: La Documentation Française.

Etat de la France. (Annual). Paris: La Découverte

Etiemble, R. (1964) *Parlez-vous franglais?* Paris: Gallimard.

Evans, H. (1987) The Government and linguistic change in France: the case of feminisation. *Association for the Study of Modern and Contemporary France Review* 31, 20-6.

Faure, M. (1986) La loi relative à l'emploi de la langue française. Histoire et limites. In C. Truchot and B. Wallis *Langue Française - Langue Anglaise. Actes du Deuxième Colloque du GEPE 23-24 mai 1986, Strasbourg* (pp. 161-70). Strasbourg: Université des Sciences Humaines.

Fenby, J. (1998) *On the Brink: The Trouble with France*. London: Little, Brown and Company

Ferney, F. (1992) *Eloge de la France Immobile*. Paris: François Burin

Ferreol, G. (ed) (1994) *Intégration et Exclusion dans la Société Française Contemporaine*. Lille: Presses Universitaires de Lille.

Ferrer, E. Blasco. (1990) Réflexions autour de l'identification: conscience linguistique = communauté minoritaire. In F. Pic (ed) *L'identité Occitane. Réflexions Théoriques et Expériences* (pp 7-19). Montpellier: Section française de l'Association Internationale d'Etudes Occitanes.

Fishman, J. A. (1991) *Reversing Language Shift*. Clevedon: Multilingual Matters.
Flaitz, J. (1988) *The Ideology of English. French Perceptions of English as a World Language*.Berlin: Mouton de Gruyter.
Flood, C. (1997) National populism. In C. Flood, and L. Bell (eds) *Political Ideologies in Contemporary France* (pp. 103-39). London: Cassell.
Flood, C. and Bell, L. (eds) (1997) *Political Ideologies in Contemporary France*. London: Cassell.
FM. (1996) *François Mitterrand au regard du Monde*. Paris: Le Monde Editions.
French Government. Website. www. pm. gouv.fr
Fugger, B. (1979) Les Français et les arrêtés ministériels. Etudes sur l'impact de la loi linguistique dans l'est de la France. *La Banque des Mots* 18, 157-70.
Fysh, P. (1997) Gaullism and Liberalism. In C. Flood and L. Bell (eds) *Political Ideologies in Contemporary France* (pp. 73-102). London: Cassell.
Gadet, F. (1992) *Le Français Populaire*. Paris: Presses Universitaires de France. (Que sais-je 1172).
Garvin, P.L. (1993) A conceptual framework for the study of language standardization. *International Journal of the Sociology of Language* 100/101, 37-54.
Gerbod, P. (1981) The baccalaureate and its role in the recruitment and formation of French elites in the nineteenth century. In J. Howorth and P. G. Cerny, P. G. *Elites in France* (pp. 46-56). London: Pinter.
Giordan, H. (1982) *Démocratie Culturelle et Droit à la Différence*. Paris: La Documentation Française.
Giordan, H. (1992) Les langues de France: de l'hégémonie républicaine à la démission de l'Etat. In H. Giordan (ed) *Les Minorités en Europe* (pp. 129-44). Editions Kimé.
Giordan, H. (ed) (1992) *Les Minorités en Europe*. Paris: Editions Kimé.
Girardet, R. (1983) *Le Nationalisme Français. Anthologie 1871-1914*. Paris: Seuil.
Girardet, R. (1986) *Mythes et Mythologies Politiques*. Paris: Seuil.
Glatigny, M. (1995) Purisme et insécurité linguistique dans la première partie du XIXe siècle. In J-M. Eloy (ed) *La Qualité de la Langue? Le Cas du Français* (pp. 133-47). Paris: Champion.
Gougenheim, G. (1958) *Dictionnaire Fondamental*. Paris: Didier
Grau, R. (1992) Le statut juridique des droits linguistiques en France. In H. Giordan (ed) *Les Minorités en Europe* (pp. 93-112). Paris: Editions Kimé.
Gueunier, N. (1985) La Crise du français en France. In J. Maurais (ed) *La Crise des Langues*. (pp. 3-38). Paris/Quebec: Le Robert.
Guilbert, L. (1975) *La Créativité Lexicale*. Paris: Larousse.
Hagège, C. (1987) *Le Français et les Siècles*. Paris: Seuil.
Hargreaves, A. G. (1995) *Immigration, 'Race' and Ethnicity in Contemporary France*. London: Routledge.
Hargreaves, A. (1997) Multiculturalism. In C. Flood and L. Bell (eds) *Political Ideologies in Contemporary France* (pp. 180-99). London: Cassell.
Hélias, P. J. (1975) *Le Cheval d'Orgueil*. Paris: Plon.
Héran, F. (1993) L'unification linguistique de la France. *Population et Sociétés*, 285, 1-4.
Houdebine, A. (1987) Le français au féminin. *La Linguistique* 23 (1), 13-34.
Howorth, J. and Cerny, P. G. (1981) *Elites in France*. London: Pinter.
Jenson, J. and Sineau, M. (1995) *Mitterrand et les Françaises. Un Rendez-vous Manqué*. Paris: Presses de la Fondation Nationale des Sciences Politiques.

Jospin, L. (1997) _Déclaration de Politique Générale. Discours du Premier Ministre, 19.6 1997._ French government website.

Journal Officiel. (Various dates) Paris: Journal Officiel de la République Française.

Judge, A. G. (1993) French: a planned language? In C. Sanders (ed) _French Today_ (pp. 7-26). Cambridge: Cambridge University Press.

Kepel, G. (1994) _A l'Ouest d'Allah._ Paris: Seuil.

Kloss, H. (1969) _Research Possibilities on Group Bilingualism: a Report._ Quebec: International Center for research on bilingualism.

Knapp, A. (1991) The cumul des mandats, local power and political parties in France. _West European Politics_ 14 (1), 18-40.

Kuisel, R. (1993) _Seducing the French. The Dilemma of Americanization._ Berkeley: University of California Press.

Labov, W. (1966) _The Social Stratification of English in New York City._ Washington: Center for Applied Linguistics,

Laurent, A. (ed) (1996) _Vivre avec l'Islam?_ Versailles: Editions Saint-Paul.

Le Figaro. (Daily) Paris: Le Figaro.

Le Figaro.Littéraire (Weekly) Paris: Le Figaro.

Legendre, J. (1994) _Rapport fait au nom de la Commission des Affaires Culturelles sur le Projet de Loi relatif à l'emploi de la Langue Française._ Sénat 309 (1993-4). Paris: Journal Officiel de la République Française.

Le Monde. (Daily). Paris: Le Monde.

Le Pen, J.-M. (1985) _La France est de Retour._ Paris: Carrère-Michel Lafon.

Lettre d'Information. (Bimonthly from March 1997) _Lettre d'Information._ Paris: Département de l'information et de la communication, Ministère de la Culture. ISSN 12556270

L'Express. (Weekly) Paris: L'Express

L'Humanité. (Daily) Paris: L'Humanité.

Libération. (Daily) Paris: Libération.

Lo Bianco, J. (1987) _National Policy on Languages._ Canberra: Department of Education.

Lodge, R. A. (1993) _French: from Dialect to Standard._ London: Routledge.

Martel, P. (1992) L'héritage révolutionnaire: de Coquebert de Montbret à Deixonne. In H. Giordan (ed) _Les Minorités en Europe_ (pp. 113-27). Paris: Editions Kimé.

Maurais, J. (ed) (1985) _La Crise des Langues._ Paris/Quebec: Le Robert.

McKesson, J. A. (1993) France and Africa: the evolving saga. _French Politics and Society_ 11 (2), 55-68.

Mitterrand, H. (1963 8th ed 1992) _Les Mots Français._ Paris: Presses Universitaires de France.

Molinié, G. (1991) _Le Français Moderne._ Paris: Presses Universitaires de France.

Mordrel, O. (1981) _Le Mythe de l'Hexagone._ Paris: Jean Picollec.

Muller, C. (1992) Données quantitatives et réforme. _Le Français Moderne_ 60 (20), 209-17.

Noguez, D. (1991) _La Colonisation Douce._ Paris: Editions du Rocher.

Note 97.24. 1997. _Note 97.24._ Paris: Ministère de l'Education Nationale.

Otman, G. (1995) La terminologie et la qualité de la connaissance. In J-M. Eloy (ed) _La Qualité de la Langue? Le Cas du Français_ (pp. 305-25).

Ozolins, U. (1993) _The Politics of Language in Australia._ Cambridge: Cambridge University Press.

Paugam, S. (1993) *La Société Française et ses Pauvres*. Paris: Presses Universitaires de France.

Pergnier, M. (1989) *Les Anglicismes*. Paris: Presses Universitaires de France.

Petit Larousse Illustré. (Annual) Paris: Larousse

Phillipson, R. (1992) *Linguistic Imperialism*. Oxford: Oxford University Press.

Pic, F. (1990) *L'identité Occitane. Réflexions Théoriques et Expériences*. Montpellier: Section française de l'Association Internationale d'Etudes Occitanes.

Poignant, B. (1998) *Langues et Cultures Régionales. Rapport au Premier Ministre*. Paris: La Documentation Française

Policar, A. (1994) Racisme et antiracisme: un réexamen. In G. Ferreol (ed) *Intégration et Exclusion dans la Société Française Contemporaine* (pp. 22-58). Lille: Presses Universitaires de Lille.

Politique. (1996) *Une Politique pour le Français*. Paris: Ministère des Affaires Etrangères.

Pope, M. K. (1934 2nd ed 1952) *From Latin to Modern French*. Manchester: Manchester University Press.

Posner, R. (1997) *Linguistic Change in French*. Oxford: Clarendon Press.

Quid. (Annual) Paris: Robert Laffont

Rickard, P. (1974 2nd ed 1989) *A History of the French Language*. London: Unwin Hyman

Riffault, H. (ed.). (1994) *Les Valeurs des Français*. Paris: Presses Universitaires de France.

Rivarol, A. (1784/1797/1991) *De l'Universalité de la Langue Française*. Paris: Obsidiane.

Rosenvallon, P. (1990) *L'Etat en France de 1789 à nos jours*. Paris: Seuil.

Sanders, C. (ed) (1993) *French Today*. Cambridge: Cambridge University Press.

Schiffman, H. E. (1996) *Linguistic Culture and Language Policy*. London: Routledge.

Schifres, A. (1990) *Les Parisiens*. Paris: J. C. Lattès

Silverman, M. (1992) *Deconstructing the Nation: Immigration, Racism and Citizenship in Modern France*. London: Routledge.

Silverman, M. (1996) State, nation and society in France. In D. Cesarinini and M. Fulbrook (eds) 1996. *Citizenship, Nationality and Migration in Europe* (pp. 146-59). London: Routledge.

SOFRES. (1994) *Les Français et la Défense de la Langue Française. Mars 1994*. Paris: Ministère de la Culture et de la Francophonie.

Stevens, A. (1996 2nd ed) *The Government and Politics of France*. London: Macmillan.

Szulmajster-Celnikier, A. (1996) Des serments de Strasbourg à la loi Toubon: le français comme affaire d'Etat. *Regards sur l'Actualité* mai 1996 (221), 39-54.

Taylor, J. (1996) *Sound Evidence: Speech Communities and Social Accents in Aix-en-Provence*. Berne: Peter Lang.

The Guardian. (Daily) London and Manchester: The Guardian.

The Observer. (Weekly) London: The Observer.

Thomas, G. (1991) *Linguistic Purism*. London: Longman.

Tolérances. (1997) *Les Tolérances Grammaticales et Orthographiques*. Paris: Ministère de l'Education Nationale.

Tollefson, J. W. (1991) *Planning Language, Planning Inequality*. London: Longman.

Trescases, P. (1982) *Le Franglais, Vingt Ans Après*. Montréal: Guérin.

Truchot, C. (1994) Introduction. In C. Truchot. (ed) *Le Plurilinguisme Européen* (pp. 21-33). Paris: Champion.

Truchot, C. (ed) (1994) *Le Plurilinguisme Européen*. Paris: Champion.

Truchot, C. and Wallis, B. (eds) (1986) *Langue Française - Langue Anglaise. Actes du Deuxième Colloque du GEPE 23-24 mai 1986, Strasbourg*. Strasbourg: Université des Sciences Humaines.

Trudgill, P. (1974) *The Social Differentiation of English in Norwich*. Cambridge: Cambridge University Press.

Van Deth, J.-P. (1995) *La Politique Linguistique de la France*. Lecture at Institut Français, London.

Varro, G. (1992) Les 'langues immigrées' face à l'école française. *Language Problems and Language Planning* 16 (2), 137-62.

Vassberg, L. M. (1993) *Alsatian Acts of Identity. Language Use and Language Attitudes in Alsace*. Clevedon: Multilingual Matters.

Walter, H. (1988) *Le Français dans Tous les Sens*. Paris: Robert Laffont.

Wievorka, M. (1992) *La France Raciste*. Paris: Seuil.

Wilks, C. and Bricks, N. (1997) Langue non-sexiste et politique éditoriale. *Modern and Contemporary France* 5 (3), 297-308.

Yaguello, M. (1978) *Les Mots et les Femmes*. Paris: Belfond.

Zeldin, T. (1983) *The French*. Glasgow: William Collins.

Index

Dates of principal Policy Documents